DEFLECTIVE WHITENESS

RACE AND MEDIATED CULTURES
Camilla Fojas and Mary Beltrán, Series Editors

DEFLECTIVE WHITENESS

CO-OPTING BLACK AND LATINX IDENTITY POLITICS

Hannah Noel

THE OHIO STATE UNIVERSITY PRESS
COLUMBUS

Copyright © 2022 by The Ohio State University.
All rights reserved.

Library of Congress Cataloging-in-Publication Data
Names: Noel, Hannah, 1986– author.
Title: Deflective Whiteness : co-opting Black and Latinx identity politics / Hannah Noel.
Other titles: Race and mediated cultures.
Description: Columbus : The Ohio State University Press, [2022] | Series: Race and mediated cultures | Includes bibliographical references and index. | Summary: "Provides a synthesis of critical Whiteness studies to date and uses a wide-ranging collection of cultural objects—memes, oration, music, advertisement, and news coverage—to show how the scripts of White deflection sustain and reproduce structures of inequality and injustice"—Provided by publisher.
Identifiers: LCCN 2022028746 | ISBN 9780814215180 (cloth) | ISBN 0814215181 (cloth) | ISBN 9780814282564 (ebook) | ISBN 0814282563 (ebook)
Subjects: LCSH: White nationalism. | White people—United States—Attitudes. | Racism—United States. | African Americans—Social conditions. | Hispanic Americans—Social conditions. | Social movements. | Social justice.
Classification: LCC HT1575 .N64 2022 | DDC 305.809/073—dc23/eng/20220818
LC record available at https://lccn.loc.gov/2022028746
Other identifiers: ISBN 9780814258545 (paper) | ISBN 0814258549 (paper)

Cover design by Caitlin Sacks and Laurence J. Nozik
Text design by Juliet Williams
Type set in Adobe Minion Pro

For Josh Haynes

CONTENTS

List of Illustrations ix

Acknowledgments xi

INTRODUCTION White Deflection: The Parasitic Nature of White Identity Politics 1

PART 1 OVERT WHITE DEFLECTION

CHAPTER 1 Of Memes, Militancy, and Masculinity: White Rhetoric and Racial Fabrication in Online Discourse 27

CHAPTER 2 Feminized Racial Pain: Cisgender Women, Whiteness, and Digital Masculine Rhetoric 63

CHAPTER 3 Trash Music: A Third-Wave Whiteness Approach to Bro-Country and Country-Rap 90

PART 2 INFERENTIAL DEFLECTIVE WHITENESS

CHAPTER 4 Brand Liberal: Ethical Consumption and Latina Representation under Racial Capitalism 123

CHAPTER 5 Framing Immigration: Legal Violence in NPR's Coverage of the Postville Raid 150

EPILOGUE Performative Allyship and the Future of Critical Whiteness Studies 187

Appendix 1	Blue Lives Matter "About Us"	195
Appendix 2	Letter to Dov Charney	197
Bibliography		199
Index		217

ILLUSTRATIONS

FIGURE 1	American Apparel, "Vertical Integration"	142
FIGURE 2	American Apparel, "American Apparel on Immigration"	144
FIGURE 3	American Apparel, "Legalize LA"	146
FIGURE 4	Chase CEO Jamie Dimon kneeling with workers	189

ACKNOWLEDGMENTS

I owe a tremendous amount of gratitude to the two anonymous reviewers from The Ohio State University Press whose guidance helped me strengthen my work. I would also like to thank the editor in chief of OSU Press, Kristin A. Elias Rowley, and her assistant editor, Robert Ramaswamy, for their assistance and continued correspondence throughout this entire process. I would also like to thank series editors Drs. Camilla Fojas and Mary Beltrán for seeing potential in this project, as well as the entire editorial board.

I would additionally like to extend extreme gratitude to Drs. Joshua Haynes and Cynthia Gwenn Yaudes who have read and given extensive commentary on this entire monograph. As a neurodiverse scholar, I am particularly indebted to Josh for reading every part of this manuscript, including the notes, for my characteristic transpositions. Thank you for taking the time to understand how my brain works and for helping me feel prepared for the inherent ableism of traditional academic conventions. I would like to thank Drs. Evelyn Alsultany, Brittany Aronson, Yamil Avivi, Lee Bebout, María Elena Cepeda, Esther Maria Claros Berlioz, Sarah Conrad Gothie, Maria Cotera, Kevin Escudero, George Lipsitz, Sarah Nilsen, Jennifer Sdunzik, and Sarah Turner for offering me invaluable commentary on individual chapters, conference papers, and other thought pieces that eventually became this book.

I owe additional gratitude to my teachers and mentors at Williams College, University of Michigan, and beyond for exposing me to new ideas and challenging my ways of thinking. Of note, Drs. Evelyn Alsultany, Amy Sarah Carrol, María Elena Cepeda, Gina Coleman, Maria Cotera, Mérida M. Rúa, Elizabeth Martinez, Anthony Mora, Sherrie Randolph, and Carmen T. Whalen each individually went out of their way to support me at some point in my academic career. I deeply thank you for believing in my aptitude. To my fellow union activists and mentors James Moriarty and Graziana D'Elia Brillante, I value your wisdom and our ability to disagree, debate, and remain strong allies. Thank you to Dr. Travis Beaver for his advice about readings on hegemonic masculinity. Finally, my writing group members read and offered comments on an early draft of what would become parts this book's introduction: Caren Beilin, Amber Engelson, Zack Finch, Vicky Papa, and Jenna Scuito.

I would like to thank my friends for pulling me into, and away from, my scholarship. Maria Flores is a beacon of wisdom. Maria, Fedel, Ezekial, and Gabby Flores are proof that miracles happen; Britney Danials, Yamil Avivi, Sarah Conrad Gothie, Sarah MacPherson, and Lusiana Tjandi Doyle are pillars of support; and Marissa Zelazo reminds me to take time to enjoy the natural beauty of life. Thank you to Ellen Janis and Terrie Pratt for keeping me on my toes.

I thank family, particularly my partner, for their support, encouragement, and inspiration. Thanks to my foundation—my parents James and Jane Noel—and also to my siblings Zach and Jennifer Knoel. My aunts are tremendously generous and make me feel so fortunate to be born into this matrilineal family: Nancy Lindabury, Bonnie Rogers Mathers, Debria Montalvo, and Sandra Greenlee—thank you for your unwavering love and radical hospitality. I am also fortunate to have supportive uncles—William, Gene, Tim, Jerry, and Al—thank you for watching out for us with Ruth and John.

Dr. Joshua Haynes offers me a lifetime of perspective, joy, laughter, support, love, and companionship. I dedicate the intellectual labor of this book to you, my dearest husband, on our paper wedding anniversary. Without our conversations, your encyclopedic knowledge of mundane to arcane epistemologies and Southern cultures, and your reassurances to stay focused, I likely would have moved on to my next project before finishing this one. Thank you for ensuring that our next adventures will happen and for forever keeping my list.

INTRODUCTION

White Deflection

The Parasitic Nature of White Identity Politics

> Blood and Soil!
> You will not replace us!
> Jews will not replace us!
> White Lives Matter!
> Our Blood, Our Soil!
> —Slogans chanted during "Unite the Right"
> rally in Charlottesville, Virginia, 2017

"Blut und Boden," or Blood and Soil, is an idiom symbolizing an ideology of nationalism and racial division. Used by the Third Reich to encourage Germans to nostalgically associate themselves with a rural agrarian past, Blood and Soil was a political slogan based in eugenic pseudoscience. The eugenic creed connected White[1] Arians (Blut) with pastoral geography (Boden) where a sedentary agricultural lifestyle supposedly led to Arian racial superiority. By World War II the strategic use of racialized environmentalism was already a tested political policy.[2] During both world wars, supporters of the Blut und

---

1. This book argues that the cultural politics of Whiteness operate, in part, through the co-optation and inversion of the identity politics of marginalized groups. In the process, the deflection and inversion of White identity politics goes unnoted by Whites as a colorblind form of protest against the identity politics of marginalized groups or commodified as a type of branding agenda. This colorblindness frequently works in tandem with overt racism. This is not to argue that Whites or full US citizens lack culture, as some Whites may believe (Cepeda, "Shakira," 214; Rosaldo, *Culture & Truth*, 198). But this deception is largely targeted at Whites and White-allied individuals who perpetuate systemic and institutionalized inequality. Rather, Whiteness is a carefully fabricated system. As a strategic identity designed to sustain unequal balances of power (Nakayama and Krizek, "Whiteness"), Whiteness attempts to remain invisible, yet is keenly apparent to marginalized communities. Given the White desire to render Whiteness as normative and quintessentially US American (Bebout, *Whiteness on the Border*), I follow other scholars (Cabrera, *White Guys of Campus*; Vega, *Latino Heartland*; Hill, *Everyday Language of White Racism*) in capitalizing White when I am discussing systems of power that attempt to oppress historically marginalized groups.

2. Weiner, "Demythologizing Environmentalism," 387–93.

Boden ideology were so enamored with the impact of rural environmentalism on Arian racial development that they sent their children to the German countryside.

Arian veneration for an agricultural heritage was a coded appeal to White supremacy. Articulating this ideology in 1930, Reich Minister of Food and Agriculture Richard Darré wrote the manuscript "A New Nobility Based on Blood and Soil," which identified Nazis as a "master race" and put rural farmworking people above their urban counterparts; urbanity and nomadism were associated with Judaism. Despite the anti-Semitic undercurrents, Darré avowed that his manuscript was primarily concerned with the protection of the German peasantry.[3] Darré deflected accusations of overt racism in this ideology by shifting discussion to the supposed victimhood of White Germans. This discourse conceals White supremacist function behind a rhetoric of paternalism, nostalgia, and rural environmentalism. Here discourse refers to all types of talk (song, spoken language, etc.) and text (images, advertisements, written language, etc.), whereas rhetoric refers directly to the art of persuasion.

I begin this introduction with an abbreviated history to foreground the intertextuality of White rhetoric. Fast-forward to the 2017 Unite the Right rally in Charlottesville, Virginia. While carrying tiki torches at night, groups largely comprised of male, US-based White supremacists rallied behind the same Nazi slogan, translated into English: "Blood and Soil!" or "Our Blood, Our Soil!" Marchers also chanted: "You will not replace us!," "Jews will not replace us!," and "White Lives Matter!" Across time and continents, these ideologically and rhetorically linked histories mark a crisis of White fraternity. Demonstrating the privileges of their Whiteness—marching and violently chanting demands without fear of consequence while co-opting the Black Lives Matter social movement frame—these individuals seem to mourn a perceived loss of White supremacy: they view themselves as victims—or so their rhetoric would lead one to believe.

This book is a study in White deflection. Contemporary White deflection is a predictable two-step dialectic: (1) calls of White victimhood, accompanied by (2) the appropriation of racial justice rhetoric. White deflection offers a script for how the emotion of victimization is mobilized by Whites to evoke the appropriation of social justice rhetoric, discursively conjuring a hegemonic White identity. An expression of White identity politics, White deflection works in the support of systemic inequality and injustice through using derivative language that claims Whiteness as *the* aggrieved social status.

---

3. Bramwell, *Blood and Soil.*

By understanding how, where, and why White deflection is used, scholars and social justice advocates can tag, deconstruct, and trace covert White supremacy at its rhetorical foundations.

Many of the characteristics of deflective Whiteness will not be new to scholars of critical race theory. Nevertheless, the concept has unique and distinct values for students, teachers, and scholars of rhetoric and media studies. First, it is a discursive pattern that deflects and willfully ignores the critiques of those who challenge White supremacy and White fragility. Second, this analysis extends David Roediger's (1999) elaboration of W. E. B. Du Bois's concept of the "wages of whiteness," as deflective Whiteness offers an affective benefit to those invested in White supremacy by deflecting critiques. When confronted with a challenge to White supremacy, deflective Whiteness reestablishes racial equilibrium and White racial comfort.[4] Third, my theorization of deflective Whiteness engages with the work of Drew Lopenzina (2012) on unwitnessing and Charles W. Mills (1997) on the epistemic impact of Whiteness, and applies it in cross-media spaces. Lopenzina describes the "absolute absence in the colonial archive" of Native viewpoints as a type of "cultural amnesia" that allows Whites to witness the impact of White supremacy on Native people yet also "unwitness" this experience in the dominant historical memory.[5] Deflective Whiteness often unwitnesses, or willfully misremembers, the systemic and institutional disenfranchisement of historically marginalized groups. Deflective Whiteness is similar to Mills's "racial contract"; it is a "conceptual bridge" designed to traverse the gap between hegemonic White histories and the experiences of people of color. Mills writes that Whiteness "is just taken for granted; it is the background against which other systems, which we *are* to see as political, are highlighted."[6] Although often unnamed, deflective Whiteness shows that the racial contract of Whiteness is still very much present, and it emerges in cross-media spaces with a seemingly contradictory dualism: overtly offensive or racist statements often accompany the deracialized rhetoric of colorblindness. Finally, deflective Whiteness is a representational strategy of White identity politics.[7] As such, it allows rhetors to deploy a deliberate process of White invisibility. I use the term White identity politics to stress its innate hypocrisy: in critiquing the identity politics of

---

4. DiAngelo, "White Fragility."
5. Lopenzina, *Red Ink*, 5.
6. Mills, *Racial Contract*, 2.
7. I invert this understanding of identity politics to conceptualize and contest how those with power and privilege co-opt marginalized identity politics to further their own economic, political, and social agendas, and to explain the often-unacknowledged ways that Whites and White-allied individuals maintain and advance White privilege.

historically marginalized groups, Whites maintain White supremacy, furthering their own identity-based political, social, and economic agendas. These agendas are deliberately constructed and seek to maintain the status quo or, in some instances, to turn society back to a time before the multicultural and Civil Rights movements.

White supremacy is not only an attribute of fringe White nationalists with tiki torches; it is a deliberate and carefully fabricated system of inequality that is pervasive across US culture, society, economic activity, media, and politics.[8] An organizing logic behind the often-visceral, defensive, and aggressive retort of deflective Whiteness is a tendency to view racism as an individual, not systemic, problem. Eduardo Bonilla-Silva (2014) writes that many people of color and Whites often cannot agree on racial matters because "whereas for most Whites racism is prejudice, for most people of color racism is systemic or institutionalized."[9] This tendency to individualize racism as a moral failing, rather than a systemic and institutionalized part of US society, is an embodiment of the neoliberal values of individual choice, meritocracy, and social responsibility.[10] A failure to recognize systemic racism is not exclusive to White subjects. Individuals of any national, racial, gendered, or sexual identity can recognize the intrinsic value of Whiteness and can uphold White supremacy.[11]

Deflective Whiteness augments Jane H. Hill's (2008) discussion of the folk theory of race. In the folk theory of race and racism, folk theorists are not trained in the skills of gathering contradictory evidence and critical analysis. Hill maintains, then, that when faced with contradictions—for example, that Blacks are significantly more likely than Whites to be victims of police violence—they are ignored through "erasure," a type of deliberate forgetting. With the addition of deflective rhetoric, my research demonstrates that this erasure can work aggressively in cross-media spaces both to deflect accusations that a speaker may be racist and to obscure the speaker's intrinsic investment in White supremacy. The myth of White victimhood—the notion that the United States is a meritocracy and Whiteness must be defended against unfair bias—is also a motivating factor behind deflective Whiteness. For instance, in folk understandings of race, Whiteness has long remained invisible.[12] Karyn McKinney (2005) studied the autobiographies of Whites and

---

8. Bebout, *Whiteness on the Border*, 41.
9. Bonilla-Silva, *Racism without Racists*, 4th ed., 8.
10. Winant, *New Politics of Race*; Harvey, *Brief History of Neoliberalism*; Noel, "Branding Guilt."
11. Haney-López, "Social Construction of Race"; Duggan, *Twilight of Equality?*; Feagin and Cobas, "Latinos/as and White Racial Frame," 40.
12. McIntosh, "White Privilege, Color, and Crime"; Dyer, *White*, 42–45; Bebout, *Whiteness on the Border*, 7.

found that that many did not perceive themselves as having a racial identity; of those who did, "most fail[ed] to recognize white privilege or take responsibility for dismantling racism."[13] When Whites did consider their racial identity, they represented their Whiteness as "empty, socially/culturally stigmatized, and economically disadvantaged—a *liability*."[14] Disregarding the history of and presently existing socioeconomic advantages of Whiteness, according to McKinney, left Whites feeling as "victims of racial disadvantages" that they associated with programs like affirmative action.[15] Rather than representing the rhetoric of a systematically victimized and stigmatized group, deflective Whiteness emerges as a reactionary manifestation of "white fright," or a defensive position taken when confronted with the statistic that US White racial groups will soon become demographic minorities.[16] In this way, deflective Whiteness works as a smokescreen that obscures an individual's investment in White supremacy through deriding historically marginalized groups as morally degenerate and anti-American, generally minimizing the experiences of people of color.[17] Far from being a liability, being born White gives individuals distinct social, economic, and political advantages. Roediger (1999) asserts that working-class Whites earn "psychological wages" from their allegiance to White supremacy,[18] and George Lipsitz (1998) meticulously details how Whites have a "possessive investment in whiteness" with political, economic, and social benefits.[19]

To highlight White deflection's omnipresence and ability to adapt to diverse mediated environments, I study this rhetoric across interdisciplinary sites including radio, social media, advertising, and music.[20] Discourse reflects and shapes our racial ideologies; engrained racist behaviors, like implicit bias, further shape our discourse communities.[21] Deflection is a strategic linguistic

---

13. McKinney, *Being White*, 220.
14. McKinney, 220.
15. McKinney, 211.
16. Myers, "White Fright," 129.
17. Bonilla-Silva, *Racism without Racists*, 4th ed., 77.
18. Roediger, *Wages of Whiteness*, 55.
19. Lipsitz, *Possessive Investment in Whiteness*.
20. I seek to make a largely theoretical contribution to the burgeoning study of White racial rhetoric within critical race theory. Critical race theory seeks to identify, explain, and deconstruct why structural and social inequality exists in a time when individuals almost universally position themselves as against racism (Delgado and Stefancic, *Introduction to Critical Race Theory*, 7; Hartmann and Bell, "Race-Based Critical Theory"; Bonilla-Silva, *Racism without Racists*, 4th ed.). Critical Whiteness studies' contributions to critical race theory include the recognition that Whiteness is an omnipresent socially constructed category and a "system of privilege" used to justify domination over people of color (Andersen, "Whitewashing Race," 24; Haney-López, "Social Construction of Race").
21. Hill, *Everyday Language of White Racism*, 32–33.

maneuver that hails others to espouse White supremacy as common sense.[22] Similar to the shared language used in Charlottesville and Nazi Germany, White rhetoric today endeavors to secure White supremacy for future generations yet uses a milieu of new and old media to accomplish this goal.

White Deflection

This book is about the rhetoric of race. There is nothing biological about race; it is an ideology given meaning and constituted through discourse.[23] Whiteness is a discursive construction strategically evoked by Whites and White-allied[24] individuals to sustain dominance through language and images. I use the term "White-allied" to refer to some Whites, but also to groups and individuals that may not be White yet support White supremacy.[25] Similarly, Cristina Beltrán (2021) terms non-Whites' support of White mob violence as "multiracial Whiteness" or an ideology, invested in White supremacy and settler colonialism, that "reflects an understanding of whiteness as a political color and not simply a racial identity—a discriminatory worldview in which feelings of freedom and belonging are produced through the persecution and dehumanization of others." My use of White-allied throughout this monograph recognizes the reality of multiracial Whiteness that Beltrán identifies wherein historically marginalized communities fall victim to "the politics of aggression, exclusion and domination" associated with Whiteness.[26]

Stuart Hall (2001) and Ella Shohat and Robert Stam (1994) remind us, however, that colonizing White race discourse works, in part, by linking marginalized groups with negative tropes including animalization, naturalization, and infantilization. Using Hall's terminology, animalization attempts to "fix difference" on non-Whites by associating them with primitive and carnal characteristics. Naturalization links cultural attributes with biology, performing the ideological work of connecting colonized and historically marginalized people with nature, and not the encephalon. Infantilization attempts to rationalize the stereotype that historically marginalized groups embody a rudimentary culture and a lower level of biological/intellectual development than Whites.[27]

---

22. Althusser, *Lenin and Philosophy.*
23. Flores, "Between Abundance and Marginalization."
24. I used the term "White-allied" to refer to Whites, but also to groups that may not be White yet support White Supremacy.
25. Feagin and Cobas, "Latinos/as and White Racial Frame."
26. Beltrán, "Opinion | to Understand Trump's Support."
27. These tropes justify colonialization and global White supremacy often by conflating biology, culture, and eugenic discourses. For more information on these tropes, please see Hall, "Spectacle of the 'Other,'" 336; Shohat and Stam, *Unthinking Eurocentrism,* 137–39.

Rhetorically embodying these tropes through slogans like "Blut and Boden," marginalized groups (Jews, homosexuals, immigrants, etc.) were associated with urbanity and uncleanliness (animalization), vice and the visceral (naturalization), and cultural degeneracy (infantilization). Arians, White Germans, were the antipode; connected with strength, intelligence, hard work, and rural (read: clean and wholesome) lifestyles. Germans blamed Jews, among others, for social problems, and the rural blood source of Arians made them supposedly exceptional—yet paradoxically in need of protection and implicitly weak.

Everyday modes of communication support systemic and institutionalized economic, social, and governmental policies—like those social policies and White political alliances championed under the mantra of "Blut und Boden"—that reinforce nativism and White supremacy.[28] Racialized ideologies impact our commonsense perceptions of all factors in society, including urban geography,[29] music,[30] consumption choices,[31] and beyond. The process of creating social "others," or historically marginalized groups, through discourse frequently involves the fabrication[32] of binary understandings of good versus bad (i.e., Black [bad] v. White [good]); patriotic Muslim v. Muslim terrorist; Dreamer v. criminal immigrant).[33] As the world has seen with disastrous consequences, ideologies of White supremacy rationalize and nationalize xenophobia, anti-Semitism, and racist policies through racial/ethnic scapegoating. This scapegoating often works contemporaneously with a nostalgic romanization of White, working-class, and rural lifestyles. Indeed, nostalgia, fear, and longing are powerful affects in shaping the "emotional politics of racism."[34] Shared affect, in this case of victimization, connects and mobilizes communities. While writing about the Aryan Nation's website, Sara Ahmed (2004) finds that "*it is the emotional reading of hate that works to bind the imagined white subject and nation together . . . together we hate, and this hate is what makes us together.*"[35] The feeling of shared victimization, regardless of merit, binds deflective White discourse, as does the co-optation of racial justice rhetoric. Undeniably, the will to appropriate is a colonizing rhetorical

---

28. Lipsitz, *Possessive Investment in Whiteness*; Mills, *Racial Contract*.
29. Rashad Shabazz, *Specializing Blackness*.
30. Mann, "Why Does Country Music Sound White?"; Fox, "'Alternative' to What?," 173; Bebout, *Whiteness on the Border*.
31. Guthman, "Fast Food/Organic Food"; Mukherjee and Banet-Weiser, "Introduction"; Noel, "Branding Guilt."
32. Haney-Lopez, "Social Construction of Race."
33. Hall, "Spectacle of the 'Other'"; Mamdani, *Good Muslim, Bad Muslim*; Gonzalez, *Reform without Justice*.
34. Ioanide, *Emotional Politics of Racism*.
35. Ahmed, "Affective Economies," 118.

move where White allies claim, by "right of discovery,"[36] all rhetoric, land, economies, humanity, and so on for Whiteness.[37]

"Our Blood, Our Soil!" only makes sense in the United States if we selectively misremember,[38] or unwitness,[39] the interrelated histories of indigenous genocide, slavery, and settler colonialism. The Charlottesville slogans all present US history from a White racial frame, or a collective set of stereotypes, histories, and frames of reference that position the past from a White-allied perspective.[40] Similarly, the use of Nazi slogans in Charlottesville is an example of Whiteness as a racial script used to link White supremacy across time and space.[41] Natalia Molina (2013) created the term "racial scripts to highlight the ways in which the lives of racialized groups are linked across time and space and thereby affect one another, even when they do not directly cross paths."[42] Evoking "Our Blood, Our Soil!" in the United States recalls patriotism, militarism, and veneration for the United States as a global superpower regardless of indigenous land claims and the genocidal history of White settler colonialism. Unite the Right's overtly racist slogans recycled Nazi rhetoric yet shifted the subjects of racial scripts blamed by White allies for White suffering toward US-based groups: Blacks, Latinxs, LGBTQIA+, and other historically marginalized communities.

White victimhood deflects critiques of systemic injustice through claiming Whiteness as the aggrieved social identity. I recounted earlier that Darré implied Blut und Boden was a dogma concerned primarily with rural Arian protection. Darré postured that the creed was a political strategy used to foster wider political alliances among Whites against "others" (Jews, homosexuals, etc.).[43] The notion that Arians need protection implies that they are victims of unfair persecution. This deflective rhetoric reveals a willful ignorance of privilege. For Whites, White suffering or victimhood becomes the rhetorical focus when, in reality, Whites in Nazi Germany were the dominant group who

---

36. I'm making an allusion here to the proclamation written by American Indian Movement activists announcing occupation of Alcatraz Island from 1969 to 1971. The rhetoric of this significant historical document inverts and plays with that of settler colonialists. For more information on this Civil Rights action, please see Casey Ryan Kelly, "Détournement, Decolonization, and the American Indian Occupation"; Milner, "By Right of Discovery."
37. Shohat and Stam, *Unthinking Eurocentrism*.
38. Hass, *Carried to the Wall*.
39. Lopenzina, *Red Ink*.
40. Joe Feagin, *White Racial Frame*.
41. Molina also discusses Whiteness as a racial script, highlighting the ways that White racialization, and racialized groups that compose "Whiteness," change over time. Please see Molina, *How Race Is Made in America*, 26.
42. Molina, 6.
43. Bramwell, *Blood and Soil*.

authorized and executed a holocaust. The focus on supposed White victimhood, despite bountiful evidence to the contrary in the form of White German supremacy (institutionalized state, economic, and social power), implicitly defines non-Whites as threatening, dangerous, and disruptive. Put differently, the ideology advanced marginalized groups as the cause of White suffering, thereby rationalizing, to some Whites, institutionalized discrimination and even genocide.

The Unite the Right slogans use a second type of deflection that relies on the parasitic appropriation and attempted inversion of the identity politics of those that suffer most from White supremacy. This second step of White deflection is rhetorical colonization. It occurs when Whites appropriate the identity politics of historically marginalized groups to further their own economic and social agendas. Examples include the co-optation of social movement frames or the linguistic appropriation and inversion of social movement messages (e.g., White Lives Matter, Blue Lives Matter, All Lives Matter, Unborn Lives Matter, etc.), as well as branding agendas that use social movements to sell products (e.g., Legalize LA [proimmigration reform apparel sold by American Apparel], ProjectRed [AIDS Awareness sold by Gap, Inc.], etc.). This rhetoric is parasitic because, rather than creating new social movement frames, deflection gains traction from attempts to take over countercultural movements in order to feed off their success and notoriety with the ultimate goal of destroying their "host" movement.

Parasitic manifestations of White race discourse maintain unequal power relations through the repurposing of social movement knowledge to benefit racial capitalism and, therefore, White supremacy. Cedric J. Robinson (2019) historicizes that race and capitalism, or racial capitalism, are inextricably linked and that "as the executors of an expansionist world system, capitalists require[ ] racism in order to police and rationalize the exploitation of workers"[44]; a White rationalization of the exploitation of historically marginalized people that Charles W. Mills terms the "racial contract" that Whites implicitly and explicitly subscribe to.[45] In a society that values diversity, racial capitalism explains the ways Whites, and historically White institutions, derive capital value from the identity of historically marginalized groups.[46] Similar to the Unite the Right protesters' embodiment of Nazi slogans, chanting "White Lives Matter" is an overt call for White supremacy that is derivative in origin as it parodies Black Lives Matter and repositions Whiteness as a liability; the slogan posits the marchers as the real victims.

44. Robinson, "Oliver Cromwell and the History of the West," 79.
45. Mills, *Racial Contract*.
46. Mills.

Deflection is a rhetorical strategy invested in sustaining the status quo and occasionally focuses on protests against White supremacy as a problem, rather than White supremacy itself. Whites and White-allied individuals practice deflection when they position historically marginalized groups as culpable for social unrest without considering, or truly hearing,[47] marginalized groups' critiques of White supremacy and systemic injustice. Jane H. Hill (2008) writes how White folk, or lay, understandings of race and racism frequently function through linguistic appropriation and the selective erasure of historical memory, and, rhetorically, "while White racist language has its subtle side, much of it is not subtle at all, and it is not underground. Instead, it is posed in the spotlight, wrapped in red, white, and blue."[48] As the dominant racial group, Whites have the luxury of not paying attention to the human rights demands of marginalized groups. As the most privileged group, Whites understand race and racism differently than marginalized groups.[49] Nolan L. Cabrera (2019) helps clarify that there is a "massive and pervasive misunderstanding about what constitutes racism," and this is particularly true among Whites.[50] As I discuss at length later in this book, the Black Lives Matter social movement critiques systemic and institutionalized racism. Echoing the previously mentioned work of Bonilla-Silva,[51] Cabrera finds that most White people view racism as an individual fault, *not* a systemic problem; that racism "requires meanness, hatred, or bitterness towards the outgroup"; and that every racial group can be racist.[52] Under White supremacy, racism includes prejudice, but also the privilege to act on hate through controlling institutions, governments, and economies.[53] In line with systemic racism theory, then, viewing historically marginalized groups as capable of racism is another type of White deflective discourse. Any racial group can be prejudiced, but under White supremacy only Whites can be racist because Whites have historically held the systemic power to shape hegemonic structures and institutions.

A study in historically White media, this book finds that the persistence of covert types of racism, across the political spectrum, set the discursive stage for a violent resurgence of overt, unabashed White supremacy supported by the US president in the late 2010s. This monograph seeks to define what White identity politics mean in our highly mediated age. No longer do we go to one, or even multiple, newspapers to better understand news and current

---

47. Ratcliff, *Rhetorical Listening*, 25.
48. Hill, *Everyday Language of White Racism*, 177.
49. Bonilla-Silva, Goar, and Embrick, "When Whites Flock Together."
50. Cabrera, *White Guys on Campus*, 3.
51. Bonilla-Silva, *Racism without Racists*.
52. Cabrera, *White Guys on Campus*, 7.
53. Feagin and Elias, "Rethinking Racial Formation Theory."

events. We digitally map, shape, and create our understandings of current events through reading online material, clicking on hyperlinks to get more context, scrolling through Instagram feeds to get yet more information. We might pick up a hard copy of a newspaper at a coffee shop, or even listen to a story on the TV news or radio. We share our opinions about these stories like never before, and develop our own cyber echo chambers, through social media groups, online posts, and shareable content. All this material shapes how we understand race and race relations, and decode social and political meaning. Today, we understand one media representation as a part of a larger transmedia story. As discussed more in the chapters that follow, this book is interested in mapping the transmedia story of how White identity politics manifests across media and the political, economic, and social spectrum. As a foundation, discussion of what is meant by "White identity politics" is a necessity.

White Identity Politics

White identity politics involve group-based social movements that perpetuate White supremacy. I started this book with two stories of White supremacy that most Whites are eager to chastise: German Nazis and US White supremacists. This is a comfortable narrative of racism for Whites that strategically overlooks the covert and institutionalized nature of racism; it names racism as a failing of particularly heinous individuals and does not focus on the ways that everyday behaviors enable and embolden state-sanctioned racism and violence. Most racism today is subtler and more covert than that preached during the Unite the Right protest.

Racism and White supremacy did not go away after the Civil Rights movements but was repackaged in more surreptitious discourse.[54] Overt racism works in concert with more covert racisms to normalize clandestine discriminatory behavior, even among those who may identify as liberally minded—discussing class when really speaking of race, for example. Stuart Hall (1981) terms more covert and subtle types of racism "inferential racism," or "those apparently naturalized representations of events and situations related to race, whether 'factual' or 'fictional,' which have racist premises and positions inscribed in them as a set of unquestioned assumptions."[55] In this book, I am particularly interested in the ways that inferential or covert racism works through co-opting the identity politics of historically marginalized groups.

---

54. Bonilla-Silva, Goar, and Embrick, "When Whites Flock Together"; Winant, *New Politics of Race*.
55. Hall, "Whites of Their Eyes."

If you are White, you may jump to the conclusion that my argument is that White people are all inherently "bad" because they have certain race-based privileges.[56] This is not my argument; I would like to emphasize the institutionalized nature of White supremacy—to (re)orient a focus on Whiteness as a system—an ideology with prescriptive, historically situated, rhetorical moves. We Whites need to move beyond a discourse of White privilege to one of White supremacy, as Zeus Leonardo (2004) writes, "White supremacy makes White privilege possible."[57] White domination has been forged through historical processes, and we Whites are responsible for our racist present, "despite the fact that White racial domination precedes us, Whites daily recreate it on both the individual and institutional level[s]"[58]—this includes well-meaning White liberals as well as the overt White nationalists in Charlottesville. Leonardo encourages us to understand the difference between dominance and domination; wherein "domination can be distinguished from dominance where the former connotes a process and the latter a state of being, the first a material precondition that makes possible the second as a social condition."[59]

Undeniably, White supremacy is often keenly visible to historically marginalized groups. When Whites acknowledge their race privilege they do so largely because of the readings, theories, and work of people of color. Critical Whiteness studies began in the work of Black radical thought; the writings of scholars like W. E. B. DuBois, James Baldwin, Derrick Bell, Charles Mills, Cedric Robinson, Audre Lorde, Kimberlé Crenshaw, among others, helped to shape the field. Indeed, since Whiteness often relies on its invisibility to other Whites, "oppression is best apprehended from the experiences or vantage point of the oppressed. . . . Critical analysis begins from the objective experiences of the oppressed in order to understand the dynamics of structural power relations."[60] While noting that "privilege is an expression and consequence of systems of inequality," Lee Bebout (2016) astutely defines the interdisciplinary academic field today as "a form of privilege studies, looking at how, without conscious recognition, race shapes the experience and imaginings of whites."[61] Writing about Whiteness studies with a "deep sense of ambivalence," Margaret L. Andersen (2003) cautions that "in shifting the subject of

---

56. DiAngelo, "White Fragility."
57. Leonardo, "Color of Supremacy," 137.
58. Leonardo, 139.
59. Leonardo, 140.
60. Leonardo, 141.
61. Bebout, Correspondence with Author, October 5, 2021. While reading a copy of this book, and in response to the partial quote from his book, Bebout commented: "I wish I had added the caveat that privilege is an expression and consequence of systems of inequality," and I added this additional context to more properly reflect his sentiments (Bebout, *Whiteness on the Border*, 7).

race from the experience of disadvantaged groups to white people, whiteness studies risks eclipsing the study of racial power, focusing solely on white identity, and analyzing 'whiteness' in the absence of the experience of people of color."[62] Recognizing this critique, I focus on the ways that the identity politics of historically marginalized groups are co-opted, decontextualized, and used by those invested in White supremacy to further their own racial project in seemingly benign, everyday cross-media discourse. Without acknowledging the speaker's own investment in White supremacy, such rhetoric emphasizes colorblind notions of common sense, democratic unity, patriotism, and law and order in efforts to disparage or discredit individuals linked with non-White identity-based social movements. Labeling and defining this social pattern can begin to make the ubiquitous influence of White racial rhetoric more discernible—particularly to Whites.

This book is a study of the racial project of Whiteness. Michael Omi and Howard Winant (2015) propose a theoretical model of "racial formation" to better understand the dominant historically situated way racial ideologies are created, embodied, and changed in what they term as "racial projects." For example, Steve Martinot (2010) studies the racial project of Whiteness, emphasizing that race is a construction designed by the European groups that became "White" to justify their supremacy over historically marginalized groups like Indigenous peoples, Blacks, and Latinxs. Whites created the system of racialization—to ascribe racial categorizations—to justify the colonial project, indigenous slavery, and African slavery. Martinot historicizes that the idea of a White identity was

> the resulting sense of unity and homogeneity [that] ... first emerged among the [US] colonists. That is, out of the reduction of Africans to other-than-human by the slave codes, the English transformed their own cultural identity from being European to being White. It was this sense of being White that was "biologized" in the eighteenth century by European naturalists to form the modern concept of "race."[63]

The racial project of Whiteness naturalizes racial difference and White racial superiority, ensuring historically White institutions and governments for future generations.

Engaging with Omi and Winant but in line with systemic racism theory, Joe Feagin and Sean Elias (2013) find that only two racial projects exist, "that of Whites who seek to maintain their exploitation, oppression and domina-

---

62. Andersen, "Whitewashing Race," 21.
63. Martinot, *Machinery of Whiteness*, 17.

tion of groups of colour, and that of people of colour who constantly battle uphill to overcome oppressive and systemic racism."[64] Similarly, to Martinot, being "White" cannot be divorced from White supremacy because the social construction of the White race is based on a racial hierarchy, justifying the rape, enslavement, and dehumanization of racial "others." As George Lipsitz (1998) reminds us, Whites have a long-standing economic investment in the social project of Whiteness.[65] Martinot concludes that racialization of "others" is always constructed as an antipode by Whites to secure White racial, social, economic, and political dominance. As such, he uses the term "machinery of Whiteness," to refer to those systemic and institutionalized mechanisms that produce systems of White supremacy that criminalize the behavior of racial others and legitimate the criminal behavior of Whites as benevolent. He uses the phrase "hegemonic mind" to explain the ways Whites can understand themselves as individuals (whereas Black people represent their own race) or where our race is never mentioned.[66]

Although perhaps not as overtly as in the Charlottesville protests, White indifference and racial ignorance are equally mechanisms of White supremacy in that they maintain the status quo. These more covert racist entitlements uphold and normalize racism, and extreme displays of overt racism similarly make covert racism seem more permissible by comparison. However, as I will argue throughout this book, both overt and covert types of White racisms rhetorically rely on one another. Through the existence of extreme White nationalists, race liberals can point to their alarmist rhetoric as the "truly racist" discourse rather than carefully examine how liberal consumption, rhetoric, and behaviors also perpetuate White supremacy.

Average White US Americans may not be entirely familiar with the discursive parentage of the rallying cries used by the US White nationalists at Charlottesville. Nevertheless, the Charlottesville protesters deliberately evoke connections, lineages, to a long-held White supremacist past while claiming White masculine victimhood. The myth of White victimhood was stoked long before Charlottesville. Scholars apply the terms White fright, White fragility, and White pain to make sense of some of the myriad ways that Whites respond to demographic change and diversity. Embodied by the liberally minded, "white pain" evokes the feelings that some Whites have when they are "forced to hear about or confront their racial past and present."[67] "White fright" refers to a fear that White supremacy may soon end due to changing

---

64. Feagin and Elias, "Rethinking Racial Formation Theory," 947.
65. Lipsitz, *Possessive Investment in Whiteness*.
66. Martinot, *Machinery of Whiteness*, 23.
67. Gresson, *America's Atonement*, 2.

demography.[68] Summarizing many theories, Robin DiAngelo proposes "white fragility" to describe a situation for Whites where "even a minimum amount of racial stress becomes intolerable, triggering a range of defensive moves . . . [and the] display of emotions such as anger, fear, and guilt, and behaviors such as argumentation, silence, and leaving the stress-inducing situation."[69] In the Unite the Right protest, and in everyday casual discourse, we see a multitude of these responses—particularly White fright (e.g., "Jews will not replace us!" and "White Lives Matter!"), and the entire protest was a demonstration of White fragility.

White race discourse defines what a White racial identity means through identifying groups that do not fit into the folk paradigm of "Whiteness," as Stuart Hall (2001) writes, attempting to naturalize and "fix difference" to "secure it forever."[70] Ian Haney-López (1994) emphasizes how notions of race and racial identity change over time; similarly, Hall maintains that "[racial] meaning floats."[71] Therefore, our understandings of race are historically situated. As Haney-López finds, "Race is neither an essence nor an illusion, but rather an ongoing, contradictory, self-reinforcing process subject to the macro forces of social and political struggle and the micro effects of daily decisions."[72] Here, White talk and text function as a pattern of communication that (re)enforces White identity as normative in both macro (television, radio, etc.) and micro (Twitter, Facebook, etc.) media spaces. These macro media representations support White identity fabrication in micro examples through creating a discourse that can be traced across various media genres, laws, policies, and institutions. This broad intertextuality, across genre and medium, creates a convergent media community that recycles White rhetoric as a "self-reinforcing process"[73] and forms a part of a racialized regime of representation.[74] Emphasizing this intertextuality, racial fabrication is a particularly apt term: it highlights that racial meanings change quickly and are constructed relationally.

As I have argued, for scholars of White racial discourse, deflective White rhetoric—one that jumps to the conclusion of White victimhood without hearing (or perhaps caring) about the issues of marginalized communities—marks a predictable discursive response. Whiteness, and therefore Whites,

---

68. Myers, "White Fright," 129.
69. DiAngelo, "White Fragility," 54.
70. Hall, "Spectacle of the 'Other,'" 336.
71. Hall, 335.
72. Haney-López, "Social Construction of Race," 7.
73. Haney-López, 7.
74. Hall, "Spectacle of the Other," 328.

historically maintain hegemonic power through creating Whiteness as the "normative" and sometimes invisible racial category for other Whites.[75] As seen in Nazi Germany and in Charlottesville, when Whites do recognize their racial identity, it is positioned as a *liability*[76] rather than an economic, historical, social, and political asset.[77] Supporting White supremacy, Donald Trump proclaimed that there were "good people on both sides" of the protests in Charlottesville: both for and against White supremacy. If you are White, I am speaking of the mechanisms of cultural and social supremacy that we Whites enjoy, and how they are maintained through everyday media and advertising, in ways we are not always consciously aware of. At the same time, we do— wittingly or unwittingly—reproduce exclusionary logics through defensive[78] strategic rhetoric[79] that, particularly for humanizing and liberally minded Whites, creates feelings of White pain and desires for racial atonement.[80] Yet, misplaced or spurious atonement can perpetuate systems of exclusion. For liberally minded Whites against racism and White supremacy, we can still reproduce systems of oppression through the co-optation of the identity politics of historically marginalized groups, naturalizing racial difference, using culturally based arguments to discuss race, and minimizing the impact of racism on marginalized groups.[81] Well-meaning Whites can reproduce these systems of inequity when we rush to judgement, fail to listen with investment, or assume our experiences as Whites in the United States are universal.[82] Hostility to the presumed identity politics of marginalized groups, complaints about alleged political correctness, and fears of being labeled as racist operate as triggers for Whites due to what Aaron David Gresson (2004) terms "white pain": the "pain many whites feel when forced to hear about or confront their racial past and present."[83] Gresson contends that White pain arises from "a special kind of vulnerability: a forced encounter with minorities' often painful images of whites in relation to themselves and their past and present relations."[84] Deflective White discourse upholds a recovery ideology of White supremacy, and,

---

75. McIntosh, "White Privilege, Color, and Crime"; Dyer, *White*, 42–45; Bebout, *Whiteness on the Border*, 7.

76. McKinney, *Being White*, 220.

77. Feagin and Elias, "Rethinking Racial Formation Theory"; Lipsitz, *Possessive Investment in Whiteness*.

78. DiAngelo, "White Fragility"; DiAngelo, "What Does It Mean to Be White in America?"

79. Nakayama and Krizek, "Whiteness."

80. Gresson, *America's Atonement*.

81. Bonilla-Silva, *Racism without Racists*, 4th ed., 56–57.

82. Lippi-Green, *English with an Accent*; Ratcliff, *Rhetorical Listening*; Hill, *Everyday Language of White Racism*.

83. Gresson, *America's Atonement*, 2.

84. Gresson, 2.

more broadly, some defensive moves suggest that many US Americans have moved past any desire for self-healing or atonement.

Deflective rhetoric can operate in a deracialized way, yet it evokes predictable and sometimes defensive responses from those aligned with White supremacy. While arguing for the importance of listening in rhetorical studies, Krista Ratcliff (2005) borrows from the work of Nikki Giovanni in her finding that racial bias promotes not listening. In a White supremacist society, it is easier for Whites to choose to not listen.[85] Whites can make this choice with few or no repercussions. Rosaria Lippi Green (1997) similarly argues that in the largely monolingual US the communicative burden of learning a different language is differentially levied on transmigrants and, more generally, marginalized communities.[86] Viewing "White racism as a cultural system" mediated through discourse, Jane H. Hill (2008) finds that the use of mock Spanish is a covert form of White racist discourse found in advertising and everyday talk. Although most White speakers of US English "vigorously reject" the pronouncement "that Mock Spanish presupposes and reproduces racist stereotypes," Hill argues that this everyday discourse of talk and text communicates the ideas that "to become 'American,' Spanish words must be transformed into light talk . . . or into jokes or insults."[87] These examples—of not listening or lacking investment in understanding—are mechanisms of excluding and policing Whiteness as normative. In addition to not truly hearing the realities of White supremacy, Whites have long actively listened to strategic silences, coded talk, and double entendre that carry racial meaning. Since the 1980s, the Republican Party has relied on racial appeals to impact electoral politics.[88] Without ever mentioning race, politicians and others make coded appeals to White voters. Ian Haney-López terms this dynamic "racial dog whistle politics" or "coded talk centered on race." Racial dog whistle politics manifest themselves in three ways: "A push that jabs race into the conversation through thinly veiled references to threatening nonwhites[,] . . . a parry that slaps away charges of racial pandering[,] . . . and finally, a kick that savages the critic for opportunistically alleging racial victimization."[89] Again, Whites often reject the notion that such dog whistles are racist.

Regardless of socioeconomic class, sitting with discomfort is not a skill well learned by the racially privileged.[90] Yet, not all Whites share the same privilege.

---

85. Ratcliff, *Rhetorical Listening*, 21.
86. Lippi Green, *English with an Accent*, 67.
87. Hill, *Everyday Language of White Racism*, 156–57.
88. Haney-López, *Dog Whistle Politics*, 3–4.
89. Haney-López, 4.
90. DiAngelo, "White Fragility."

Despite a shared benefit of White supremacy across classes and geography,[91] Whites are not all equal, and understanding the differences between Whites, in part, helps us understand rhetoric that attempts to scapegoat White racism onto those who are rural, White, working class or poor, and, more often than not, Southern. Whites are diverse and even discriminate against one another with terms like "White trash," "hillbilly," and "redneck," and scholars have suggested that these class and geographically based fissures in normative White identity suggest "one critical track to deconstruct whiteness" by "recognizing the complex and emotionally charged contests over belonging and difference that engage whites intraracially."[92] It is the very fissures within Whiteness—embodied in discriminatory terms like White trash, hillbilly, redneck—that help make Whiteness visible.[93] Shannon Sullivan (2014) notes the importance of class differences among Whites yet also emphasizes the difference between race and class:

> Class differences within the group of White people make a meaningful difference to their race, and this is a constitutive, not an additive difference. Class differences aren't lumped on top of homogenous Whiteness; they instead help constitute Whites differently for poor and middle-class White people. But the constitutive difference that class makes to race doesn't mean that race has been collapsed into class.[94]

In this book, I map discourse communities across sites that self-identify through branding as liberal and middle-class (National Public Radio [NPR], ethically branded goods), and conservative with a veneration for the working classes (bro-country music, social media) to highlight shared commonalities of White rhetoric across political ideologies. Middle-class suburban or urban Whites may not desire comparison to rural, working-class Whites, yet the rhetorical overlap of speech and text—though different—remains remarkably similar in intent. My research finds an appreciation of working-class ways of being by conservative media; however, these media producers are frequently not members of the working classes. Through highlighting the discursive disconnects between Whites, I endeavor to show, particularly to other Whites, the constructed nature of White identity.

---

91. Leonardo, "Color of Supremacy," 140.
92. Hartigan, "Who Are These White People?," 111.
93. DiAngelo, "My Class Didn't Trump My Race"; Hartigan, "Who Are These White People?"
94. Sullivan, *Good White People*, 39.

Approach and Chapter Overview—
Critical Racial Rhetorics

This book is a study in everyday White supremacy. Since Whites hold much institutionalized and political power, White identity politics are rarely called out as such unless they are connected with White nationalists, as in Charlottesville, yet White supremacist rhetoric is also "the domain of average, tolerant people, of lovers of diversity, and of believers in justice."[95] There is a "White investment" in White supremacy, and "in general, Whites recreate their own racial supremacy, despite good intentions."[96] Through analyzing a constellation of sites self-identified as both liberal and conservative, this intellectual project links White discourse across historically White media sites to better understand the shared rhetoric of trans-mediated White supremacy in our polarized political present.

I take a Third-Wave Whiteness approach that encourages scholars to nuance racial identities, including between Whites. Third-Wave Whiteness studies emphasizes the intersectionality of White identities across many politically motivated vectors including race, class, gender, sexual identification, and geography. Through highlighting the differences between Whites, including how Whites discriminate against one another (e.g., White trash, trailer trash, chauvinism, heterosexism), we can show the constructed nature of Whiteness. Third-Wave Whiteness applies research methodologies across genre and media like "internet sites, racial consciousness biographies, music, and photo-elicitation interviews,"[97] and I look toward many of these diverse sites in this book. Third-Wave Whiteness studies is purposely intersectional and interdisciplinary, but the research is distinguished "by an interest in the cultural practices and discursive strategies employed by whites as they struggle to recuperate, reconstitute and restore identities and the supremacy of whiteness in post-apartheid, post-industrial, post-imperial, post-Civil Rights" eras.[98] Scholars of Third-Wave Whiteness are also shifting focus away from the White racial formations of Europeans to those whose origins are in the Americas and other locations; this book follows this overture to the US.[99]

With this approach in mind, my research focuses on a constellation of deflective White rhetoric to highlight how our racial understandings are constructed relationally, across a variety of cultural sites. This interdisciplinarity

---

95. Leonardo, "Color of Supremacy," 143.
96. Leonardo, 144.
97. Twine and Gallagher, "Introduction: The Future of Whiteness," 12.
98. Twine and Gallagher, 13.
99. Twine and Gallagher, 13.

also allows me to highlight the omnipotence of this rhetoric of dominance—from a country song to NPR to social media, White deflection is all around us. Scholars of race often use the metaphor of "constellation" to describe the accumulation of diverse and interdisciplinary images, discourses, and ideologies that shape racial understanding. Lee Bebout (2016) uses the term to describe "Whiteness on the border," how Whites construct Whiteness, and Whiteness as Americanness, against a Mexican Other. Leo R. Chavez (2008) also uses the term to reference the Latino Threat Narrative, a set of alarmist discourses and representations that posit Latinxs as threatening, unassimilable, and hyperfertile. Joe Feagin (2009) uses constellation to refer to the ideologies, images, and discourses that contribute to the national "White racial frame" or the White-allied point of reference that perpetuates White supremacy.

Following Michael G. Lacy and Kent A. Ono (2011), I also find that "in today's discursive milieu," or what other scholars above have termed a discursive "constellation," "race and racism are often difficult to isolate, interpret, and explain." Therefore, this book is a study in the critical rhetoric of race, namely Whiteness, across media to make sense of how Whiteness adapts and changes across time, space, and media genre. Lacy and Ono write that critical rhetorical scholars should analyze representations of racist actions and racial discourse "because such images and stories form the basis of our knowledge and perspectives of race, which helps us to see how we perceive and define ourselves, others, and our material lives." The scholars note that

> when racialized discourse does not call attention to itself, responses to it become easily misunderstood or formulaic. We can overcome such misinterpretations and ideological scripts and being to understand different perspectives only if we question, challenge, interpret, and critical analyze cultural practice. While loud charges of race and racism have become media spectacles, we argue that mundane, everyday, and routine cultural practices perhaps have the greatest potential to service, work in tandem with overt racism, and affect us in their commonplace and taken-for-granted forms.[100]

I am particularly interested in how Whiteness mediates our environments in these "commonplace and taken-for-granted forms," and therefore I foreground the rhetorical moves of Whiteness through close readings of tweets, memes, discussions in online chat rooms, song lyrics, and advertising material that are joined by a shared use of rhetorical White deflection. Following Lacy and Ono, I have divided my book into sections based on *overt* deflec-

---

100. Ono and Lacy, *Critical Rhetorics of Race*, 2.

tive Whiteness and more *covert or inferential* deflective Whiteness. As the authors note, even within overt racist rhetoric there are insidious signatures of inferential rhetoric as well. This book seeks to make the overt and covert dimensions of deflective Whiteness—across social class, gender, and political identification—clearer.

This project is therefore invested in what Lisa A. Flores (2016) terms the "representational politics of race" across mediated, everyday representations.[101] Flores defines racial rhetorical criticism as work that is "reflective about and engages the persistence of racial oppression, logics, voices, and bodies and that theorizes the very production of race as rhetorical."[102] In so doing, I also argue that the "primary rhetorical function of representations of race is to legitimate racism while protecting the innocence of whiteness."[103] Distinctively, I focus on the comparative "points of convergence and divergence" between the ways that Whiteness co-opts the identity politics of both Blacks and Latinxs in furthering everyday White supremacy.[104]

Part 1—Overt White Deflection

The first three chapters in this book focus on overtly discriminatory White deflection that also shares some signatures of covert deflection. In so doing, I define and nuance the differences between White deflection in online and auditory environments. As a study in the critical rhetoric of race, I emphasize that rhetoric itself has many presentations across media—we hear rhetoric, but we also read online posts and interpret shared images. To fully understand the presentations of White deflection, we must consider what we hear and see, and the resulting affect.

Chapter 1, "Of Memes, Militancy, and Masculinity: White Rhetoric and Racial Fabrication in Online Discourse," takes a mixed-methods approach—using content analysis and critical discourse—to uncover how White rhetoric manifests in online communication frequently in opposition to the Black Lives Matter social movement. I study internet memes and a media corporation that each practice White deflection. Using content analysis, I code the social media presence of Blue Lives Matter media company (Blue Lives) for deflective rhetoric; Blue Lives is a corporation invested in producing news content empathetic to law enforcement officers, including Homeland Security

---

101. Flores, "Between Abundance and Marginalization," 13.
102. Flores, 5.
103. Flores, 13.
104. Flores, 16.

agents, police officers, and corrections officers. My research finds that Blue Lives uses a framing mechanism to shape its coverage that I term "militant victimhood"; this framework relies on White deflection to shape coverage by simultaneously claiming victimhood at the hands of historically marginalized groups, while also supporting at times extremist violence against individuals and social movements. Furthermore, throughout this chapter I find that rhetorical manifestations of toxic masculinity and Whiteness have overlapping investments in domination and are habitually codependent.

Chapter 2 further studies the masculine and White rhetoric behind deflection, but from feminized subjectivities. This chapter, "Feminized Racial Pain: Cisgender Women, Whiteness, and Digital Masculine Rhetoric," investigates how rhetorical attacks on critical race theory, feminism, multiculturalism, and religious minorities by cisgender women work to (re)secure patriarchy, compulsory heterosexuality, and Whiteness from the relative margins. This chapter furthers emergent conversations in the field of critical rhetoric on White cisgender women's unique role as the bedfellows and nurturers of White supremacy. In studying the connections between masculinity, White supremacy, power, and cisgender women orators, I argue that White women use masculinized rhetoric of fear, threat, and victimhood when confronting perceived provocations to their relative power as cisgender heteronormative White women. This rhetoric seeks to (re)secure cisgender heteronormative Whiteness as center, but from a feminized persona. This feminized subjectivity is imbued with vulnerability and paternalistic discourses, enabling, perpetuating, and linking hegemonic masculinity and White rhetoric. I also argue that the media framing mechanism identified in chapter 1, militant victimhood, changes based on the feminization of an orator/writer.

Chapter 3, "Trash Music: A Third-Wave Whiteness Approach to Bro-Country and Country-Rap," begins with an act that many music fans view as overtly racist: the removal of Lil Nas X's country-rap hit "Old Town Road" from the Billboard Top Country chart—right before it would have hit number 1 in the summer of 2019. Debate about Billboard's choice reverberated throughout the country music community, including in discussion on fan media pages and in song lyrics. Focusing on the interrelated country subgenres of bro-county and country-rap, this chapter analyzes the ways that song lyrics, music history, and internet discussion of the popular and profitable country subgenres strategically imagine mainstream country music as White despite bountiful evidence otherwise. This chapter uses a Third-Wave Whiteness approach to highlight representations of class between country music listeners, songs, and lyrics. Moreover, sound is racialized and, without images, allows a listener to pick up unique rhetorical cues that strategically construct images of race, class, and geography. Unlike the previous two chapters, the metaphoric nature of song lyrics contains a significant number of interferential examples of deflective White rhetoric, and therefore this chapter functions as a connecting one between the two parts of this book.

Part 2—Inferential Deflective Whiteness

Whites, particularly liberal Whites, often assume that racism and bigotry is the product of other Whites: conservatives, the poor and working classes, the uneducated, Southerners, rural people—as a White person studying White supremacy in the academy, I have heard many of these stereotypes, even among my highly educated peers. Following Eduardo Bonilla-Silva's canonical book *Racism without Racists*, I find that White liberal rhetoric is some of the most slippery and socially corrosive type of racism. Liberal White deflection is deeply invested in achieving an affect of altruism—despite, and often ignoring, the history, lived experience, and representations of historically marginalized groups. The second part of this book includes case studies of more covert types of White deflection, concluding with an epilogue suggesting future areas of study in this vein.

Chapter 4, "Brand Liberal: Ethical Consumption and Latina Representation under Racial Capitalism," focuses on branding strategies that appropriate the identity politics of historically marginalized groups to sell a product: clothing. This chapter studies ethical consumption under racial capitalism as a type of White deflection invested in consumer affect—feeling good about buying morally. However, the American Apparel corporate marketing campaign Legalize LA that I study sought to profit from the activism of its mostly Latinx workers. In the process, Latinx worker conditions at the company did not improve, and the corporate model was vehemently against worker unionization efforts. This case study in inferential White deflection explores the paradox of buying morally under racial capitalism. Strategic advertising campaigns appealed to middle-class consumers, who had liberal views on immigration reform, but who were not likely equally invested in the history of Latinx labor in Los Angeles or at the company they financially supported.

Similar to my discussions of overt framing mechanisms that shape media coverage in chapters 1 and 2, chapter 5 finds that liberal media outlets also use framing mechanisms that practice rhetorical White deflection—but these media frameworks are unique. "Framing Immigration: Strategic Whiteness and Legal Violence in NPR's Coverage of the Postville Raid," finds that NPR's coverage of the largest single immigration raid in US history relied on strategic erasures, discursive shifts, and episodic coverage that decontextualized and ignored the treatment, histories, and exploitation of apprehended transmigrants. After the raid, about four hundred largely Guatemalan workers were detained, tried in a makeshift courtroom assembled in a cattle exhibition field, and sentenced to about two years in federal prisons. My analysis focuses on the humanizing representation of the largely Latinx workforce in NPR's syndicated coverage, which nevertheless relies on exclusionary discourses that cast Latinxs outside of NPR's discourse community.

After summarizing the various manifestations of deflective White rhetoric mapped throughout this book, the final epilogue points to future trajectories of research. The epilogue, "Performative Allyship and the Future of Critical Whiteness Studies," revisits internet discourses, but focuses on the ways that performative allyship—where a person's political statements in support of marginalized communities garner a social or financial reward—manifested on social media in the summer of 2020 after the murder of George Floyd by Minnesota police.

It is easy to view rhetoric used during Unite the Right as exceptional, out of the ordinary, or beyond parallel. Tracking similar rhetorical defensive moves, in the remainder of this book I am concerned with the everyday mechanisms of White supremacy. In the next chapter, I will further explain how deflective rhetoric similar to that seen in Charlottesville manifests in everyday, online communication, easily shared through memes and intertextually linked through hashtags to a wider discourse community. Focusing on taken-for-granted forms of communication—social media posts, branding/marketing, radio, and music—I seek to map the ways that our daily consciousness receives an intertextual, often-unnoticed (particularly by Whites), onslaught of White supremacist rhetoric. Taken together as everyday modes of communication, these forms of discourse are more insidiously covert—and common—than exceptional displays of White nationalism.

PART 1

OVERT WHITE DEFLECTION

CHAPTER 1

Of Memes, Militancy, and Masculinity

White Rhetoric and Racial Fabrication in Online Discourse

In the summer of 2020, Black Minneapolis resident George Floyd was murdered by White police officer Derek Chauvin. Enraged by the frequent and senseless murders of unarmed Black men by US law enforcement officers, protesters took to the streets, first in the United States, and then throughout the world. By protesting police brutality, systemic racism, and institutional injustice, the independently organized demonstrations were in support of the global Black Lives Matter movement (BLM).

Seven years prior, in response to the acquittal of George Zimmerman for the murder of Trayvon Martin in the summer of 2013, Black Lives Matter began as a hashtag, the idea of Alicia Garza, Patrisse Cullors, and Opal Tometi, on Garza's Facebook page. Black social media use is quite complex and is frequently invested in social justice. For instance, scholars of Black Twitter like Andre Brock (2012) and Sarah Florini (2014) have borrowed from the work of Henry Louis Gates Jr. (1983)[1] on signifyin' and applied it to the study of Black Twitter. Signifyin' refers to the "genre of linguistic performance that allows for the communication of multiple levels of meaning simultaneously, most frequently involving wordplay and misdirection."[2] Propelled by online engagement, Black Lives Matter developed into a diverse social movement that does

---

1. Brock, "From the Blackhand Side"; Florini, "Tweets, Tweeps, and Signifyin' Communication"; Gates, "Blackness of Blackness."
2. Florini, "Tweets, Tweeps, and Signifyin' Communication."

not have a single leader or group of leaders. Instead, BLM activists share a political agenda and philosophical movement, operating in the heritage of Black intellectuals like Anna Julia Cooper, Audre Lorde, W. E. B. DuBois, and James Baldwin, that brings attention to the intersectional struggles of racial injustice.[3] Those who support Black Lives Matter mobilize in "condemning the state-sanctioned death of black women and girls, denoting the disproportionate incarceration of black men and women as well as boys and girls, calling for the end to violence against transgender women, and pounding the pavement against police brutality."[4] The ethics behind the BLM movement—that Black lives matter, too, as much as White lives—challenges the racial capitalist foundation of the US nation-state. The power of the Black Lives Matter movement to energize diverse people across racial, class, gendered, and ethnic difference all without a centralized leadership threatens those invested in White supremacy and its bedfellow, racial capitalism.

After Floyd's murder, the hashtags #AllLivesMatter and #BlueLivesMatter, two of many rallying cries used in opposition to the Black Lives Matter movement, appeared across social media with a renewed zeal.[5] Those allied with White supremacy became particularly agitated with the Black Lives Matter movement when US corporations, states, and local governments began to change corporate and government policies. Calls to defund the police were taken seriously in places like Minneapolis; NASCAR outlawed the use of the confederate flag; Aunt Jemimah and Uncle Ben were removed as racist corporate images; and the state of Mississippi introduced discussions in Jackson to remove the Confederate flag from its state flag.

This chapter studies the online reactionary rhetoric that pirates social movement frames, specifically those of BLM. Viewing Whiteness as a discursive construction that strategically (re)secures dominance,[6] the coded use of "All Lives Matter," similar to the Blue Lives Matter, is a benevolent type of racism that disengages with the wider critique of systemic and institutionalized racism brought about by BLM activists in favor of a fictitious egalitarianism.[7] The universality of the slogans deliberately and strategically disengages with the discussions of structural and institutional racism that differentially impact Black, Brown, and Indigenous communities; rendering the suffering of these

---

3. Lebron, *Making of Black Lives Matter*.
4. Biesecker, "From General History to Philosophy," 411.
5. Anderson, "Hermeneutical Impasses"; Biesecker, "From General History to Philosophy"; Bock and Figueroa, "Faith and Reason"; Carney, "All Lives Matter, but So Does Race"; Esposito and Romano, "Benevolent Racism"; Gallagher, "Divergent Discourse."
6. Hill, *Everyday Language of White Racism*; Nakayama and Krizek, "Whiteness."
7. Esposito and Romano, "Benevolent Racism."

communities under White supremacy ungrieveable. These structural inequities include, but are not limited to, police brutality, high rates of residential segregation, lower educational attainment, lower average wealth, higher incarceration rates, higher rates of infectious diseases like HIV/AIDS, and higher numbers of mental health issues when compared to Whites.[8]

From a vantage point of relative privilege, Whites have the luxury to not listen to the human rights demands of historically marginalized groups without the fear of physical, material, or mental distress.[9] Relying on data from social media, news reports, and police reports from 2015 to 2020, the *Washington Post* (2020) finds that nationwide Black Americans were murdered by law enforcement officers more than twice as often as White Americans. Police brutality differently impacts individuals in the prime of their adult lives, between the ages of twenty and forty. Many of those murdered by law enforcement likely have families, are wage earners, and have wider networks of family and friends reliant on their companionship and labor. Over 95 percent of these deadly encounters with law enforcement involve men. Despite their small relative population numbers as compared to Whites, Blacks and Latinxs are much more likely to be the victims of police brutality. Death rates at the hands of law enforcement officers reflect this; Blacks are killed at a rate of 31 per million people, Latinxs are killed at a rate of 23 per million people, and Whites are killed at a rate of 13 per million people. Protesters called to defund police departments, to overhaul the entire US law enforcement system by reallocating police funding to community-based organizations and programing. According to the most recent data by Pew Research (2020), the incarceration rates of Blacks from 2006 to 2018 have dropped by about one-third; however, "in 2018, black Americans represented 33 percent of the sentenced prison population, nearly triple their 12 percent share of the U.S. adult population. Whites accounted for 30 percent of prisoners, about half their 63 percent share of the adult population. Hispanics accounted for 23 percent of inmates, compared with 16 percent of the adult population."[10] Further illustrating the penetration of White supremacy throughout US institutions, Blacks and Latinxs also faced much higher death rates, in all age categories, from the

---

8. Delfi Mondragón, "No More 'Let Them Eat Admonitions'"; Mills, *Racial Contract*; Lipsitz, *Possessive Investment in Whiteness*; Uzzell, Pol, and Badenas, "Place Identification, Social Cohesion, and Environmental Sustainability"; Tatum, *Can We Talk about Race?*; Kirby and Kaneda, "Unhealthy and Uninsured"; DiAngelo, "White Fragility"; Shabazz, *Specializing Blackness*; Bebout, *Whiteness on the Border*.

9. Ratcliff, *Rhetorical Listening*, 21.

10. I changed the percent symbols in the original quotations to the word "percent" to follow The Ohio State University Press House Style Guide, Section 1.J.2. Gramlich, "Black Imprisonment in the US."

novel coronavirus pandemic.[11] After months of grieving, in quarantine, and serving as essential workers, protesters joined together in the streets demanding universal human rights and control over their own neighborhoods.

Using critical discourse and content analysis, I trace how those invested in White identity politics use social media in everyday and organized ways to police online environments. In so doing, this chapter extends Bonilla-Silva's theory of White habitus to mediated environments. Borrowing from Pierre Bourdieu (1984), "habitus" refers to the "socially acquired tendencies" that influence behavior, understanding, and recognition, reflecting "deep cultural conditioning that reproduces and legitimates social formations."[12] Bonilla-Silva (2006) defines White habitus as a "racialized, uninterrupted socialization process that conditions and creates whites' racial tastes, perceptions, feelings, and emotion and their views on racial matters."[13] Regarding interracial marriage or residential and social segregation, "white habitus promotes in-group solidarity and negative views about non-whites."[14] Since Whites experience more geographical and social segregation than other racial or ethnic groups, this "social and spatial isolation . . . leads to the development of group cohesion and identity formation."[15] Through framing mechanisms, I argue that this social segregation and development of group cohesion is also mediated, curating echo chambers of information, opinions, and shaping ideologies.

This chapter nuances the definition of deflective White rhetoric outlined in the introduction of this book through providing additional examples of White deflection in practice. It is divided into three sections. In "Framing Whiteness," I overview how Whiteness frames and co-opts social justice slogans in the service of White supremacy. I then study a tweet by the handle @ProudWarriorDad in "The Identity Politics of Deflective Whiteness" where I use critical discourse to further define the two-step process of White deflection; calls of victimhood followed by the appropriation of social justice frameworks. In "Blue Lives Matter Media Company," I use both critical discourse and content analysis to explain how a media company of the same name strategically curates news media coverage from a White racial frame.[16]

The various examples studied here emphasize a commitment to heteronormative masculinity, embodied in the US military and law enforcement,

---

11. Ford, Reber, and Reeves, "Up Front."
12. Bourdieu, *Distinction*; Bonilla-Silva, Goar, and Embrick, "When Whites Flock Together," 233.
13. Bonilla-Silva, Goar, and Embrick, 104.
14. Bonilla-Silva, Goar, and Embrick, 233.
15. Bonilla-Silva, Goar, and Embrick, 230.
16. Feagin, *White Racial Frame*.

and cast the identity politics of historically marginalized groups as superficial. There is an emphasis on White male pain—a crisis of hegemonic masculinity in an era of increasing transvisibility and discussions of systemic racism. Hegemonic masculinity is invested in maintaining male dominance and subjugating women. Masculine rhetoric is identified by presentations of anger, fear, self-centeredness, ressentiment, extreme competition, and violence. In studying how toxic masculinity negatively impacts mental health treatment for men, Terry Krupers (2005) defines the term as "constructed of those aspects of hegemonic masculinity that foster domination of others and are, thus, socially destructive." Attributes of toxic masculinity "include extreme competition and greed, insensitivity to or lack of consideration of the experiences and feelings of others, a strong need to dominate and control others, an incapacity to nurture, a dread of dependency, a readiness to resort to violence, and the stigmatization and subjugation of women, gays, and men who exhibit feminine characteristics."[17] A growing body of critical scholarship studies the strategic rhetorical mechanisms used by White men to maintain White supremacy while engaging with toxic hegemonic masculinity.[18] Casey Ryan Kelly (2020a) asserts that a "powerful script of white male victimization" was catalyzed by the 2016 election where White men were "aggrieved by feminism, multiculturalism, secularism, and demands for structural equality."[19] Such discourse indexes White men, and Whites more generally, as the casualties of the multicultural movement and identity politics. As a characteristic of presentations of deflective rhetoric, White masculine victimhood uses the threat historically marginalized groups pose to White hegemony to activate political and ideological formations.[20] In this chapter, these political and ideological formations link those responsible for enforcing hard power—the military, police, corrections officers, and so forth—with an oxymoronic affect of vulnerability and fragility. This deflects critiques of those with systemic and institutional power onto those fighting their historical exclusion.

---

17. Krupers, "Toxic Masculinity," 717.

18. For sources that discuss White male pain and its intersection with White supremacy, please see Cabrera, *White Guys on Campus*; Kelly, "Wounded Man"; Kelly, "Man-Apocalypse"; Kelly, "Donald J. Trump"; Kelly, *Apocalypse Man*; Kimmel, *Angry White Men*; Noel, "Deflective Whiteness," 322.

19. Kelly, *Apocalypse Man*, 2, 3.

20. Abrajano, Hajnal, and Hassell, "Media Framing and Partisan Identity"; Jardina, *White Identity Politics*.

Framing Whiteness

The reactionary [X] Lives Matter rhetoric used in opposition to Black Lives Matter is a classic example of parasitic White deflection that seeks to hijack a successful social movement for an ideologically divergent cause. Coupled with their derivative naming, "All Lives Matter," "Blue Lives Matter," and similar countermovement slogans represent the "frame co-optation" of the Black Lives Matter social movement. In their study of how the conservative right commandeered the queer agenda, Mary C. Burke and Mary Burnstein (2014) define "frame co-optation" as "a process where opponents adopt aspects of the content of a movement's discourse, while subverting its general intent."[21] When historically marginalized communities assert their human rights, it challenges White supremacy, and frame co-optation is a rhetorical attempt to colonize and reframe discourse threatening to the status quo in the service of hegemony. This reframing is a tool of mobilizing an already aggrieved White-allied base.

Frame co-optation, and media framing more generally, influence an audience's ability to think critically; at the same time, the White identity politics behind such deflection is rarely questioned.[22] Media framing occurs when an aspect of media coverage is emphasized over others. It refers to the process by which people understand or change their thinking about a topic due to this repetitive presentation. Framing has political and social consequences; for example, Stuart Hall (2001) terms a "racialized regime of representation" the repeated presentation of racial stereotypes over a given period of time that shifts ideology and influences discriminatory behavior.[23] While evaluating the impact of framing on White macropartisanship, Marisa Abrajano, Zoltan Hajnal, and Hans J. C. Hassell (2017) find that "by focusing repeatedly on a particular group, news coverage can lead to evaluations of issues based on attitudes towards the group in question rather than the issue at hand."[24] When

---

21. Burke and Bernstein, "How the Right Usurped the Queer Agenda."

22. "Identity politics," as I define the term, involves group-based social movements that represent and mobilize the interests of a particular group rather than the policy issues of society as a whole. Yet all politics is identity politics in some ways. The unifying strategies used by racial, ethnic, sexual, and other groups in their fight against systematic oppression present the experiences, aspirations, and analyses of individual groups as the starting point for a broader reconstruction of the entire society. This understanding of identity politics as the mobilization of marginalized people emphasizes its challenges to the social dimensions of neoliberal ideologies cloaked as personal responsibility and individual choice (Harvey, *Brief History of Neoliberalism*). Identity politics can, however, also work to uphold the prevailing social order, as in the case of White identity politics (Duggan, *Twilight of Equality?*).

23. Hall, "Spectacle of the 'Other.'"

24. Abrajano, Hajnal, and Hassell, "Media Framing and Partisan Identity," 7–8.

the liberal-leaning *New York Times* published negative stories about immigration, Whites shifted party identification in a corresponding magnitude to the Republican party while also championing restrictive anti-immigrant bills, laws, and initiatives.

Whether in the form of a hashtag, meme, or slogan, those who use All Lives Matter and Blue Lives Matter deflect attention away from racial capitalism and endemic injustice against historically marginalized groups in the United States. Attention is then redirected toward the supposed victims—Whites and the enforcers of hard power. This rhetoric grieves social and systemic power that Whites and historically White institutions have never lost. A tendency to not listen and shift rhetoric linked with the identity politics of marginalized groups to rhetoric focused on White identity politics is formulaic and indicative of a wider discursive and social pattern. This pattern of White discourse *deflects* the fear, discomfort, and aggression that those invested in White supremacy feel when confronted with challenges to systemic racism and inequity.[25] This fear and discomfort are *projected* on individuals linked with identity-based social movements who are then faulted for causing a social disruption. From the vantage point of deflective Whiteness, the framing of this disruption deliberately does not recognize the mission or goals of the social movement. Stylistically these verbal reprimands are retrospective, passive-aggressive, and often directed not at one individual but at a movement or ideology. Therefore, this type of online deflective Whiteness occurs in safe spaces where the individuals being reprimanded are not present or the event being critiqued has already occurred. These decontextualized chastisements are categorized as common sense; the original protest against White supremacy and structural racism are ignored and overshadowed by a colorblind critique disparaging those invested in the identity politics of marginalized groups as weak, unpatriotic, and naïve.

Individuals who engage in deflective Whiteness frequently lack knowledge or are complacent about how White supremacy operates and benefits those aligned with a White identity.[26] While there is a deliberate individualism inherent in the linguistic practice, deflective White rhetoric often sustains and maintains White supremacy by using deracialized, covert appeals. Rather than a truly universal ideology, All Lives Matter is a rallying cry for White inclusion, exhibiting a narcissistic need for Whites to be at the center of every discussion, hiding behind a façade of universalism. If all lives in the United

---

25. DiAngelo, "White Fragility," 58.
26. Mills, *Racial Contract*; McKinney, *Being White*; Lopenzina, *Red Ink*; Bebout, *Whiteness at the Border*.

States mattered and were treated equally, then the Black Lives Matter social movement would have no reason to exist.

The discursive shift central to online deflective Whiteness, that takes an event, image, and/or representation out of its original context, is not seamless and is often rife with logical fallacies. For example, consider a popular meme refashioned in numerous forms in support of the All Lives Matter ideology. This image frequently has a background of one or more crucifixes, an image of a White Jesus, or even a picture of a White Jesus on a crucifix. Despite Middle Eastern and North African origins of both Jesus and Christianity, the embodiment of a White Jesus, according to Richard Dyer (1997), "constitute[s] something of a thumbnail sketch of the white ideal" with the characteristics of "suffering, self-denial and self-control, and also material achievement, if it can be construed as the temporary and partial triumph of the mind over matter."[27] Put differently, by representing Jesus as a White man, White individuals are visually linked with Jesus, inherent piety, and morality. The text accompanying various iterations of these familiar Christian images reads: "2000 Years Ago Jesus Ended the Debate of Which Lives Matter He Died for All!" From a White racial frame, or the White-allied way of viewing and experiencing the world,[28] this colorblind meme implies that true Christians—who are inherently White—realize that all humans are created equal because Jesus gave his life for all mankind. An implicit statement here suggests that Black Lives Matter activists are not Christians, or at least not "good" Christians, and deliberately shifts the conversation about police brutality to one of Christian theology. The purportedly moralist argument is flawed. Similar to advocates of US monolingualism, the orator does not take the time to assume the communicative burden[29] to understand the message and mission of the BLM movement, or even the intent of the phrase "Black Lives Matter," which simply means that Black Lives Matter, too, in addition to White lives. BLM critiques persistent inequity in the US state; by turning this contemporary social movement into an affront to Christian values, these memes take significant direction from the Southern strategy and dog whistle politics that use coded talk about race.[30] Through this Christian meme, All Lives Matter supporters seek absolution from a reference to Jesus as evidence that "All Lives Matter"; yet, there is a deliberate miscommunication. This colorblind statement assumes that all people in US society have equal opportunity. Furthermore, in this line

---

27. Dyer, *White*, 17.
28. Feagin, *White Racial Frame*.
29. Lippi-Green, *English with an Accent*.
30. Haney-López, *Dog Whistle Politics*.

of thinking, Jesus would not feed the hungry first, before those with plenty of food, because all stomachs matter.

Practitioners of deflective Whiteness are invested in not listening; listening means implicating their own position in systems of inequity, and challenging White supremacy entails compromising an economic,[31] political and social,[32] and affective[33] investment in Whiteness. In addition to discussing the ways that White victimhood works in tandem with the appropriation of the identity politics of historically marginalized groups, this chapter focuses on masculine-coded rhetoric. This focus on masculinity allows me to introduce a trend seen throughout the forms of communication analyzed in this book; rhetorical performances of masculinity that are strategically used to reinforce White supremacy. This confrontational, in-your-face, and aggressive rhetoric is a defensive posturing designed to repel, through fear or threat of violence, those who may wish to challenge White supremacy. As I discuss in chapter 2, masculinity, or masculine Whiteness, should not be misunderstood as always connected to one's biological sex assigned at birth and is performed by cisgender White women as well as cisgender men.

When studying the emotional politics of racism, Paula Ioanide (2015) finds that "emotions attached to race and sexuality have their own unique logics of gain and loss" and that these emotions can encourage people to behave in ways that are sometimes against their best interests or that defy rational explanation.[34] In other words, people are often not aware of the ways that emotions impact racial understandings and communication. Research suggests that a lack of emotional intelligence is a key fixture in masculinity.[35] Similarly, Nolan L. Cabrera (2019) finds that "if emotional illiteracy . . . is a central facet of dominant forms of masculinity, this can become an important barrier to racial growth. Emotions are a form of cognition and are critically important to the maintenance of white supremacy."[36] Put differently, masculinity may impact one's willingness to perform the hard work of antiracism. Masculinity and White race discourse combine to create a distinct pattern of violent and confrontational rhetoric often present in deflective rhetoric.

---

31. Lipsitz, *Possessive Investment in Whiteness*.
32. Jardina, *White Identity Politics*.
33. Ioanide, *Emotional Politics of Racism*.
34. Ioanide, 2.
35. Kindlon and Thompson, *Raising Cain*; Krupers, "Toxic Masculinity."
36. Cabrera, *White Guys on Campus*, 109.

Methods

To contextualize deflective Whiteness as a tool of White supremacy, I consider everyday and corporate examples of White-allied media that attack the Black Lives Matter movement. This mixed-methods approach uses critical discourse analysis (CDA), content analysis, and Google Trends data to locate trending hashtags and terms across social media within a given time frame. By "everyday," I reference an individual's post not directly affiliated with a corporatized group. I choose to focus on individuals and corporations for two reasons: (1) to reflect on the overlap or divergence of ideologies between individual and corporate interests; (2) through studying a self-described media company, I use content analysis to uncover any framing mechanisms present in its curated media coverage shared on social media like Twitter. Furthermore, I am interested in the individual interpellation of ideologies under racial capitalism. Through critically reading an individual example, in this case by @ProudWarriorDad, in conversation with a media company, we can begin to extrapolate how racialized corporate media framing influences individualized discourse.

CDA is used in both sets of data analysis: analysis of a Twitter post and analysis of a media company's use of Twitter over a given period of time. CDA is a method and analytical framework that is useful to describe, interpret, and explain[37] how deflective Whiteness maintains and sustains Whiteness as a normative racial category.[38] CDA has the interrelated goals of *critiquing* discourse and *explaining* how discourse works in society as a basis for a future call to *action* to change the prevailing social order.[39] Given CDA's call to action and critique of structures of power, this method affords me the opportunity to describe this contemporary turn in discourse, media representation, White normativity,[40] and racial fabrication that has potentially dangerous consequences. These repercussions include casting marginalized groups as inherently untruthful and oversensitive, while normalizing points of view that are coded as White and male regardless of the speaker's actual embodied race or gender identity or identification. For the examples from corporate media, I use content analysis to code Twitter posts to identify framing mechanisms. Emphasized through its derivative naming, Blue Lives Matter media company

---

37. Van Dijk, "Critical Discourse Analysis"; Fairclough, *Language and Power*.
38. Mills, *Racial Contract*; Haney-López, *Dog Whistle Politics*; Bonilla-Silva, *Racism without Racists*, 4th ed.; DiAngelo, *White Fragility*; Bebout, *Whiteness on the Border*.
39. Fairclough, *Language and Power*, 6.
40. Hartmann and Bell, "Race-Based Critical Theory," 238–44.

(Blue Lives) is a social media company that derives its brand identity in direct opposition to the Black Lives Matter movement.[41]

Blue Lives' Twitter feed, analyzed later in this chapter, contains brief, free, and sharable content that, in each individual tweet, links to premium, pay-for-access features on the company's main webpage. Calling itself "America's largest law enforcement support community," Blue Lives is an internet-based media company headquartered in Ranson, West Virginia. Mapping a constellation of social media sites, including Twitter, YouTube, and Facebook, and providing pay-for-access materials on their main website,[42] Blue Lives offers both free and premium content. Since this Twitter page is a marketing tool of the media group, I choose to analyze it to better understand the ideologies and target audience of Blue Lives.

In examining rhetoric on Twitter, scholars have used a range of methodologies, such as surveying 100 tweets about a select event.[43] Using Twitter's enhanced-search function, other scholars select and examine 100 representative tweets out of an initial sample of 500 tweets from a five-day time period.[44] Sarah J. Jackson and Brooke Foucault Welles (2015) study how #myNYPD became hijacked as a tool of social media activism by networked counterpublics.[45] They focused on 13,631 tweets sent over a two-day period—10 percent of the tweets using #myNYPD sent during that time. Out of these tweets, Jackson and Foucault Welles identified the most-shared tweets, or 2,653 individual tweets.[46] In their comparative analysis of Black and Blue Lives Facebook pages, Mary Angela Bock and Ever Josue Figueroa (2018) analyze the top ten posts on each Facebook page, as well as the comments; this totaled

---

41. For example, the company's organizational history states that Blue Lives was founded in opposition to the mainstream media's coverage of the Black Lives Matter social movement. ("About Us History," Blue Lives Matter). Although the original website analyzed in this chapter is no longer live, at the time of this writing it was archived online. My research suggests that the platform was hosted in connection with WarriorMaven.com, formerly known as Scout Warrior, a digital media network that was "operated by long-time military reporter and former CNN Headline News anchor and military specialist Kris Osborn." The larger website "[wa]s devoted to coverage of cutting-edge weapons, technology and military strategy." According to Business Wire, a Berkshire Hathaway Company, since January of 2018 WarriorMaven.com has been publishing on the digital media network Maven (ticker symbol MVEN) as "dozens of award-winning journalists, best-selling authors, top analysts, important causes and foundations are bringing their organizations to Maven's coalition of elite content channels" ("Military Expert Kris Osborn," Bloomberg.com; "Military Expert Kris Osborn," Business Wire).

42. "Blue Lives Matter."
43. Cisneros and Nakayama, "New Media, Old Racisms," 123.
44. Carney, "All Lives Matter, but So Does Race."
45. Networked counter-publics refer to internet-based communities that activate behind marginalized ideologies, often uncovering historic injustice and hypocrisy.
46. Jackson and Welles, "Hijacking #myNYPD," 5–6.

140 posts.[47] Given the mixed-methods approach of this chapter, I surveyed 258 tweets from the Blue Lives official Twitter (@bluelivesmtr) profile over a thirty-one-day month during the summer of 2019. Following the work of other scholars, I selected the first 100 unique tweets from this time period.[48] Four of the first 100 tweets were retweets, or the same material tweeted a second time, but on a different day. Since each tweet had a double impression, I did not want to ignore their potential significance. Therefore, I choose to add 4 sequential tweets with unique messages to my data set. In total, I analyzed the first 104 tweets, with 100 discrete messages, for discernable trends.

Identity Politics of Deflective Whiteness

Context is essential when assessing whether a representation upholds the "linguistic order of racism."[49] An example of deflective Whiteness is easily found on social media by searching Twitter using the hashtag #snowflakes, a derogatory neologism for those perceived as overly invested in individual emotions, to find a meme. Since deflective Whiteness opposes identity politics, I searched Twitter using both #snowflakes and #BlackLivesMatter. A Google Trends worldwide data analysis indicates that shortly following peaks in the popularity of #BlackLivesMatter there is a corresponding, though smaller, peak in popularity of the term #snowflake. This pattern suggests that #snowflake may be a reactionary term used in digital spaces that responds to #BlackLivesMatter. Indicative of this trend, #BlackLivesMatter experienced a peak in popularity during the week of @ProudWarriorDad's selected tweet that I analyze below (January 22–28, 2017), and #snowflakes experienced a peak of equal magnitude the following week (January 29–February 4, 2017). After the Twitter search, I selected the first participatory internet meme that engaged in deflective Whiteness, a tweet by ProudWarriorDad (2017).

Memes, like race, have nothing to do with genetics but with learned cultural behavior. The choice of communicating deflective Whiteness with a meme has added cultural significance. The concept of the "meme" is derived from Richard Dawkins's book *The Selfish Gene* (1976), where he discusses human behavior as a combination of both genetics and culture. He argues that the fundamental unities of life are single genes, and that humans are not genetically inclined to act in altruistic ways. Genes determine human charac-

---

47. Bock and Figueroa, "Faith and Reason," 3101–2.
48. Cisneros and Nakayama, "New Media, Old Racisms"; Carney, "All Lives Matter, but So Does Race."
49. Hill, "Language, Race, and White Public Space," 686.

teristics, but what Dawkins terms "memes" determine culture and behavior through socialization. Therefore, memes shape White habitus. Lynn C. Lewis (2012) writes that individuals share and sometimes change internet memes to "reify identity and construct authorship within the same moment" and that they also "invite creativity, humor, and carefully constructed parodies."[50] Memes frequently function as jokes but do not always do so. Whether humorous or not, they can represent, shape, and reshape ideologies about race and national belonging, making them ideal to study rapidly shifting racial ideologies in convergent media. A participatory internet meme is a representation that is shared, and sometimes altered in the process, that often takes images or words out of their original contexts.[51] These images evoke nostalgia and reference other representations, ideas, or practices.[52] Here, I broaden the notion of the participatory internet meme by including interactive spreadable media, specifically tweets linked to other sources.[53] Similar to racial fabrication, the meaning of a meme shifts, and is understood relationally through linked images, hashtags, and social media handles.[54]

The selected meme posted by @ProudWarriorDad contains an appropriated picture of young, racially diverse, and perhaps gender-nonconforming individuals inlaid with a caption reading, "When the squad gettin ready to go out and be oppressed." Along with this image, ProudWarriorDad includes original commentary: "Jesus When Are The #snowflakes #BlackLivesMatter #LGBT #j20 #resist @DNC Gonna Get A Clue? You Lost GROW THE FUCK UP LMAO [Laughing My Ass Off]." The notion that one prepares to "go out and be oppressed" asserts that the oppression is not genuine but a deliberate performance. Through first listing the umbrella term #snowflakes, ProudWarriorDad connects the neologism to the individual group-based social movements that he then lists by name. The post refers to individuals concerned with identity politics as "clueless," suggesting that ProudWarriorDad does not value their political opinions. The hashtags form an easily traceable digital footprint, connecting the post to a wider White-allied community. Viewers can understand this tweet intertextually, in relation to and in conversation with these hashtags. This intertextuality validates the sentiments of the tweet as part of a larger, constantly evolving racial discourse, and it is

50. Lewis, "Participatory Meme Chronotope," 108.
51. Burgess, "All Your Chocolate Rain?"; Shifman, "Anatomy of a YouTube Meme"; Davison, "Language of Internet Memes."
52. Lewis, "Participatory Meme Chronotope."
53. "Spreadability" refers to the ability to share media content from mainstream, alternative, and social media formats to dominant as well as niche markets (Jenkins, Green, and Ford, *Spreadable Media*; Báez, "Spreadable Citizenship").
54. Haney-López, "Social Construction of Race."

possible to search for tweets expressing similar sentiments through searching the listed hashtags.

The statement "You Lost GROW THE FUCK UP LMAO" connects protests of the Trump administration's policies to tantrums caused by endorsing a losing candidate. Through being told to "grow up," Democrats, Blacks, and LGBT individuals are labeled emotionally immature. In the logic of the tweet, "growing up" is akin to accepting docility, passivity, and silence in the face of a political and social order that supports policies in conflict with, or overtly against, an individual's identity(ies). This silent docility is antithetical to democratic ideals. There is a visible struggle over representation: who gets to decide the intent of a protest concerned with the issues of marginalized groups?

The docility implicitly encouraged by the tweet stands in contrast to ProudWarriorDad's asserted identity as connected to warriors, masculinity, fatherhood, and the US military. This connection of Whiteness with Americanness is not idiosyncratic; rather, Whiteness is synonymous with Americanness.[55] Recent protests by activist groups following the election of President Trump, as well as those kneeling during the national anthem, overtly reject docility. The tweet posted at 12:05 p.m. on January 21, 2017 (J20), and, given the meaning of its various hashtags, was likely responding to protests of Trump's inauguration. For many social activists, J20 represented the day a racist, homophobic, xenophobic sexual predator was sworn into the highest office in the United States—the racial order colorblindness had ruptured and regressed to a moment where overt racism was accepted. By using the hashtags #j20 and #resist together, ProudWarriorDad alludes to the 214 protesters arrested and charged with felony rioting and other misdemeanors at Trump's inauguration the previous day. If convicted, these protestors face an unprecedented $25,000 fine and a ten-year prison term.[56] Even the prosecutors admitted they could not connect any of those charged with acts of violence, indicating that the prosecutions (which eventually were all dropped in response to court rulings unfavorable to the prosecution) were motivated by political rather than public safety concerns. Disrupt J20, a coalition of activist groups associated with the hashtag #j20, organized "mass protests to shut down the inauguration of Donald Trump"[57] because they shared the sentiment that "Communities under Attack Fight Back."[58] Identified by their black apparel, many of the protesters were also uniting under an anticapitalist and

---

55. Bebout, *Whiteness on the Border*, 34.
56. Lennard, "How the Government."
57. Weiner, "Protest Group Declares Victory."
58. Vargas, "Here's What We Know."

antifascist agenda—groups also targeted by the Trump administration during the summer 2020 protests mentioned in the introduction of this chapter. Acting like an occupying force, during the summer of 2020 in Portland, Oregon, federal government paramilitary officers were accused of disappearing, or kidnapping, protestors and ignored an order to withdraw from Oregon governor Kate Brown.[59] On Trump's first day in office as President of the United States he enacted radical policies that sidestepped legal precedents and foreshadowed his paramilitary crackdown on the Black Lives Matter and the so-called Antifa (antifascist) protesters.

Even while they organized at Trump's inauguration, each group maintained its distinct agenda. Disrupt J20 worked as an umbrella organization where diverse groups, each invested in their own identity politics, united to coordinate protest locations, for instance at inauguration ticket-check points. At each location, individual, smaller protests expressed the issues of particular groups, like LGBTQ rights and racial justice.[60] The references to political protests and social activism associated with the hashtags #j20, #resist, #snowflakes, #BlackLivesMatter, and #LGBT conflate these groups as the same, and, given the 214 arrests, potentially violent. However, the J20 protesters were overwhelmingly *not* violent. In an unprecedented move, when conflicts did occur at the march, law enforcement officers did not give the J20 protesters the opportunity to disperse. Instead, law enforcement charged everyone present, even those who were not violent, with felony offenses.[61] *Esquire* journalist Natasha Lennard writes: "No one—neither the police nor the government—suggest[s] that most or even many of the arrestees directly engaged in property destruction or violence."[62] Mara Verheyden-Hilliard, the director of Partnership for Civil Justice Fund, which fights for civil and human rights cases, contends that the arrests were not due to violent behavior but were "simply based on proximity or shared political views at a march." With these arrests and felony charges for nonviolent protestors as legal precedent, Verheyden-Hilliard warns that in future instances, "the entire demonstration can be subject to indiscriminate force and large groups of people can be suddenly arrested without notice or opportunity to disperse, and face life-altering charges."[63] Such a precedent would make protesting, and exercising First Amendment rights to free speech, more difficult. ProudWarriorDad, however, uses the meme and tweet to express his own right to free speech. In its calls

---

59. McGreal, "Federal Agents Show Stronger Force."
60. Vargas, "Here's What We Know."
61. Vargas; Lennard, "How the Government."
62. Lennard.
63. Qtd. in Lennard.

for individuals involved in identity-based social movements to "grow up" and not protest, the tweet expresses deflective Whiteness through a sentiment that supports silencing the free speech rights of those invested in identity-based social movements as well as denying their right to assembly. This hypocritical move exercises free speech while simultaneously expressing a desire to silence the right to free speech of those they perceive as engaged in identity politics. Trump and his supporters are framed as the victims of protesters—the protestors' concerns are deliberately overlooked. In these examples, the practitioner of deflective Whiteness engages in White identity politics and implicitly seeks to maintain White supremacy.

From the point of view of the practitioner, deflective Whiteness is a "counter-discourse" against a society overly invested in multiculturalism. Shared by a self-identified US Army father, the tweet assumes a patriarchal "white racial frame." This White racial frame refers to the historic pattern in US society to have "a positive orientation to whites and whiteness and a negative orientation to those racial 'others' who are exploited and oppressed."[64] Memes' lack of nuance constructs simplified representations; yet it is this very lack of complexity that makes their cultural and ideological work so impactful to large audiences. The tweet's White racial framing is distinctly heteronormative and capitalist as it minimizes and oversimplifies antifascist, anticapitalist, Black, and LGBTQ individuals as interchangeable while not acknowledging an unprecedented use of force by law enforcement. The tweet names and dismisses the identity politics of "others" as a performance; it does not recognize its own implicit investment in maintaining the United States as a male-dominated White nation.[65]

On the internet, deflective Whiteness often seeks out an argument and—to repel any possible accusations of racism—uses links to validate an opinion as widely supported and inherently nonracist. ProudWarriorDad's tweet relies on intertextuality and is aggressive in tone. Stylistically the example is formulaic in the way it upholds the new racism: it chastises identity-based social movements while not acknowledging an investment in White identity politics and White supremacy.[66] Another dualism occurs in some deployments of deflective Whiteness: while the tweet uses coded terms like "snowflake" to refer to historically marginalized groups,[67] it is also deliberately offensive, for instance using curse words. This argumentative and offensive tone, yet simultaneous

---

64. Feagin, *White Racial Frame*, 11.
65. Omi and Winant, *Racial Formation in the United States*, 75–79.
66. Lipsitz, *Possessive Investment in Whiteness*; Feagin, *White Racial Frame*; DiAngelo, *White Fragility*.
67. Bonilla-Silva, *Racism without Racists*, 4th ed.; Haney-López, *Dog Whistle Politics*.

reliance on coded colorblind terms, indicates an ostensibly contradictory dynamic. This tendency to provoke offense, but discuss race on colorblind terms, is characteristic of a new racism.

Those practicing deflective Whiteness often perform a masculine stance that faults marginalized groups for their "politically correct" and "oversensitive" behavior. ProudWarriorDad's chastisement of identity politics, and an adversarial discussion of politically correct rhetoric more generally, is indicative of the "crisis of multiculturalism" or the perceived failure of multiculturalism.[68] As an outgrowth of the Civil Rights movements, multiculturalism endeavored to create a more just and equitable society through policies like affirmative action and by increasing the institutional representation of diverse cultures and traditions. Those who ascribe to the belief that multiculturalism failed often seek to undo its influence by claiming, for instance, that putative politically correct behavior weakens US political, economic, and social structures. Stuart Hall (1994) notes that by labeling the discourse of others as politically correct—in a "confrontational, in-your-face mode of address" like that of ProudWarriorDad—a speaker actually defines what constitutes politically correct behavior.[69] Hall contends that the logic behind this argumentative stance—also a part of deflective Whiteness—is nominalism, or the apparent belief that if behaviors, such as an investment in identity politics, are highlighted they will end or disappear. In the process, the practitioner's investment in White supremacy and White invisibility is maintained. In the next section I use content analysis to further explicate how vulnerability is used as an affective tool of White rhetoric. While taking a mixed-methods approach, I find this type of militant victimhood pervasive throughout the Blue Lives Matter media company's Twitter feed, namely how it frames news stories for potential subscribers.

Blue Lives Matter Media Company

Using critical discourse and content analysis, this section evaluates the efficacy of the Blue Lives Matter media company's stated mission to properly represent law enforcement in the media and the corporation's embodiment of its core values of equality, justice, honesty/accuracy, and civil rights. I assess Blue Lives' mission, goals, and brand identity to gauge how these are, or are not, represented in its news coverage. Through close readings of material

---

68. Suhr and Johnson, "Re-visiting 'PC.'"
69. Hall, "Some 'Politically Incorrect' Pathways," 168.

taken from Blue Lives' network of media sites, I ground this qualitative data in critical discourse. I first perform a quantitative analysis of rhetorical trends on the company's official Twitter page. This investigation provides numerical and anecdotal evidence that contextualizes the ideologies reflected by the Blue Lives brand. Second, I conduct a critical analysis of the corporation's website, focusing on the "About Us—History" subsection, and the "Blue Lives Matter Media Kit," an audience demographic profile for potential advertisers. Although the rhetoric of Blue Lives' core mission and value statements promotes multiculturalism and gender diversity, the company's journalism uses framing mechanisms that maintain White habitus in transmediated spaces.

Blue Lives' dominant frame reflects a mix of White discourse and toxic masculinity that I term "militant victimhood." On their social media pages, Blue Lives represents police officers, ICE officers, and corrections officers as both victims of the liberal leftist media and as militant, Second Amendment–supporting heroes whose obituaries are highlighted in their "Hero Down" Facebook and Twitter posts. Adhering to color blindness, militant victimhood is a framing mechanism of White identity politics where Blue Lives simultaneously claims status as a victim, while asserting a militant and masculine sense of American patriotism. This rhetorical strategy deflects discussions of race while recycling racist stereotypes, particularly about Black men.

Deliberate media framing designed to sway opinion is a hallmark of unethical and poor journalism. In his essay "Objectivity, Impartiality, and Good Journalism," Michael Kieran (1998) debates media ethics and concludes: "A failure of impartiality in journalism is a failure to respect one of the methods required in order to fulfill the goal of journalism: getting at the truth of the matter."[70] Traditional journalistic ethics are tossed aside in Blue Lives' mission statement, which calls Blue Lives' journalists "Americans"—mentioned twice—"who believe in law and order and want to provide a counterbalance to the dangerous false narratives being propagated about law enforcement." Under this logic, to be a good US *American* citizen, one must support law enforcement officers. The "truth of the matter," for Blue Lives, is preordained: law enforcement officers are militant victims who need Blue Lives' protection.

While amassing profits from advertisers and subscribers, Blue Lives frames select media coverage deliberately to foreground White militant victimhood. This framing is not a surprise as rhetoric of threat is central to White political and ideological formations.[71] In her book *White Identity Politics,* Ashley E.

---

70. Kieran, "Objectivity, Impartiality and Good Journalism," 23.

71. Abrajano, Hajnal, and Hassell, "Media Framing and Partisan Identity"; Jardina, *White Identity Politics.*

Jardina (2019) finds that White identity is "a *mobilized* political identity" and "argue[s] that threat plays an important role in the acquisition and activation of group identities."[72] Although the rhetoric of threat—from immigrants, Black Lives Matter protestors, Muslims, and other historically marginalized groups—is often racialized, "whites have the luxury of not thinking about their racial group and its collective interests when their status at the top of the racial hierarchy is secure."[73] In other words, "whiteness quietly becomes second nature or habitual . . . whiteness constitutes normality and acceptance without stipulating that to be white is to be normal and right."[74] As the qualitative and quantitative data presented below suggests, militant victimhood champions an ideology linking Second Amendment rights; selfless acts of courage by law enforcement officers; random acts of violence toward law enforcement; the presumed hypocrisy and idiocy of liberal and left-leaning individuals; and a type of toxic masculinity that assumes the positionality of a White masculine viewership.

Militant Victimhood: Quantitative Twitter Analysis

Blue Lives (@bluelivesmtr) tweets directly link to stories on their webpage; although some content is free, this encourages viewers to pay for subscription-only access to specialized content. Blue Lives has a pattern of coding content based on keywords in all-caps: BREAKING, indicating a new news story that often involves a police officer being shot (6 tweets); JUST IN, also signifying a breaking news story (2 tweets); VIDEO, indexing tweets linked to video content (16 tweets); and HERO DOWN, that denotes the death of a police officer, corrections officer, or police canine (9 tweets). This coding also helps viewers find analogous content on the group's website.

Similar to other Twitter pages, Blue Lives uses hashtags and Twitter handles to link to other pages that support similar ideologies. Throughout the thirty-one-day month, Blue Lives pinned a tweet linking to its online store that it shares with the Warrior XII (@warrior_xii) page, indicating their ideological and commercial connection. In a different tweet, Blue Lives shared a meme taken from the Hollywood movie *The Matrix* with actor Keanu Reeves halting bullets mid-air. The meme contains the text "WHEN SOMEONE TRIES TO SHOOT YOU BUT THE GUN CONTROL LAWS KICK IN." It is flanked with the Warrior XII symbol; a gray-toned shield adorned with the US

---

72. Jardina, *White Identity Politics*, 40, 37.
73. Jardina, 40, 36.
74. Bonilla-Silva, Goar, and Embrick, "When Whites Flock Together," 231.

flag and the words Warrior XII written across it. Blue Lives adds the editorialized text, "Has anyone considered that if we just made murder illegal it would bring an end to mass shootings? Oh wait . . ." proceeded by "Follow @bluelivesmtr & @warrior_xii" and three hashtags that support law enforcement with the Second Amendment: #BlueLivesMatter, #BackTheBlue, and #2A. Blue Lives strategically recycles such memes that link to partner websites.

Blue Lives' tweets emphasize collective national tragedies, such as mass shootings, that imply the urgent need for law enforcement to protect citizens from an increasingly violent world of unsophisticated criminals. The tweets discuss current events, such as 2 tweets about the suicide of Jeffery Epstein and 8 tweets that critique those who question law enforcement's use of deadly force to detain suspects. In the unique tweets, the feed had 17 tweets about mass shootings or stabbings in Gilroy (3 tweets) and El Paso, Texas (3 tweets); Dayton, Ohio (4 tweets); Chicago, Illinois (2); New York City (1); as well as random shootings at unspecified locations (2 tweets) and 2 tweets about stabbing sprees. There were 4 tweets about the murders of young Black men by police: Michael Brown (1 tweet) and Alton Sterling (3 tweets). Tweets also ridicule criminals with chauvinistic side commentary. For example, the Twitter feed contained the mug shots of two different women who, after their arrest, were found to be hiding illegal drugs in their vaginas. Such mocking tweets of individuals are often accompanied with editorial commentary, including emojis.

Throughout the dataset is an association of images of Black people with negative tweets about crime, racism, and domestic violence. Indeed, the only individuals directly connected with actions of racial prejudice are Black men. There is an association of Donald J. Trump and images of a Blue Lives Matter US flag with the *false* accusation of racism. The term "racism" is mentioned only twice in the tweet sample: once in reference to a family flying a Blue Lives Matter flag ("Fallen Trooper's Family Forced to Remove Thin Blue Line Flag over 'Racism'") and once in reference to President Trump's purported antiracist stance coupled with his gun and immigration reform agenda ("Trump Condemns Racism, Calls to Expand Gun Background Checks, Immigration Reform"). There is a single tweet about an act of overt prejudice, or acts of violence motivated by racial hatred. This tweet is accompanied by an image of a young Black man with a gun standing next to a sedan with the text: "Man Shoots at Cars While Yelling, 'I Don't Like White People in My Hood.'" The wording of this tweet is rife with racist stereotypes of Black US Americans (loud voices, violent, the White parody of perceived Black English). Although this tweet is assigning racial hatred to a young Black male, it could just as easily be read as a tweet deeply engrained in White privilege.

Image, meme, and text must be read in conversation, particularly when the tweets contain images of Black individuals.[75] One tweet has the innocuous text reading "VIDEO: Police Chief Apologizes after Video of Mounted Arrest Goes Viral Showing Officers Using an Approved Tactic." The image accompanying this text is of a young Black man, with hands bound and a noose around his neck, being led by a White police officer on horseback. The image is horrific; the disgusting and racist imagery displays White terrorism and the still-present reality of state-sanctioned violence. The mock lynching is minimized and endorsed through lack of critique and the dissemination of a link to the "viral" video. Even representations of professional athletes can be read as contributing to a negative representation of Black individuals. There are 4 tweets about National Football League (NFL) athletes: 1 tweet about a White athlete supports law enforcement ("NFL's Baker Mayfield on Most Important Lesson in College: 'Don't Run from Cops'") and 3 tweets about Black NFL players associate them with violence or deviant behavior ("NFL Player LeSean McCoy Ordered to Pay Philly Cop He Hurt in Bar Brawl," "Man Claims Police Conspired to Cover For Cowboys' Ezekiel Elliott after Crash," and "NFL Suspends Player for 6 Games for Domestic Violence. Prosecutor Won't Charge").

In the increasingly violent world constructed through the tweets, law enforcement officers are routinely positioned as victims of overt violence (for example, being dragged by a car after a traffic stop) and acts of prejudice (such as unjust employment termination). Over one-third of the unique tweets contain messages that imply that law enforcement officers were the overt victims of violence or injustice, and that, in many of these cases, the law they enforced did not protect them. I coded 35 tweets referring to law enforcement officers (specifically, corrections officers, police officers, and Immigration Control and Enforcement officers) as victims of direct physical violence (shootings, stabbings, an officer being beaten, being dragged behind a moving vehicle, a police officer's horse being hit while on duty, reports of a police officer's murder), indirect overt violence (unjust firing, being refused hospitality services because of being a police officer), and/or injustice because of an asserted identity as a law enforcement officer (being questioned for using a firearm to shoot a suspect, accusations of racism for flying a Blue Lives Matter flag). Nine tweets, in addition to these 35 tweets, were labeled "Hero Down," and detailed the unfortunate and untimely deaths of nine law enforcement personnel and one law enforcement canine. Counting the "Hero Down" Tweets in the tally of tweets that discuss cops as overt victims means that about half of Blue Lives' tweets—or 44 individual tweets—in the selected month overtly

---

75. Hall, "Some 'Politically Incorrect' Pathways through PC."

cast police officers as victims of physical violence, bias, and death at the hands of the citizenry or a greater law enforcement structure that did not support them.

Nineteen tweets contained openly partisan content referencing particular politicians (Pete Buttigieg, Alexandria Ocasio Cortez, Mario Cuomo, Donald Trump) or political affiliations (left, socialists). This partisan content supports Republican over Democratic politicians; 12 of the tweets overtly reference leftists, socialists, or Democrats, and 7 directly referenced a single Republican: Donald Trump. These seven references to Trump were laudatory, twice noting his perceived antiracism (such as "Trump Condemns Racism, Calls to Expand Gun Background Checks, Immigration Reform"); twice critiquing the *New York Times* coverage of Trump (for example, "After the newspaper accidentally posted an accurate headline about President Trump, they immediately took corrective action. // New York Times Backtracks after Posting Accurate Headline about President Trump"); twice noting his support for military personnel and cops (such as "President Trump Recognizes 6 Dayton Officers Who Took Out Mass Killer"); providing support for Trump's tweets about Baltimore, Maryland, as "a rodent-infested mess" (for example, "Rep. Cummings' Home Burglarized Hours before Trump Tweeted about Baltimore"); and also asserting Trump's unfair persecution (for example, "Man with Brain Injury Attacks 13-Year-Old Boy. Attorney Blames President Trump").

Trump's positive representation stands in sharp contrast to the views of those associated with the ideological left. The 12 tweets referencing leftists denote them as violent (such as "Man Who Asked for Gun to Kill 200 People Says He's Not a Killer, Just a Leftist"); subjects of ridicule (for example, "VIDEO: Their [sic] Fighting over who can one-up everybody else by acting the most woke is both hilarious AND horrifying. // Socialists Convention Erupts over Gendered Pronoun Use, Excessive Whispering"); bigoted and violent (for example, "Freshman US Representative encourages people to riot, then spouts more antisemitic [sic] ignorance. @RepAOC // @AOC Says Marginalized Communities Have 'No Choice but to Riot'"); and as anti–law enforcement (for example, "He sold out his officers for political points, but now he's seeing the consequences. // South Bend Police Facing 'Mass Exodus' after Mayor Attacks Cops during Debate").

It is worth noting that the Blue Lives Twitter feed does, at times, critique law enforcement officers. The 100 unique tweets contain seven instances of cops being charged with acting poorly in their positions (see table 1). However, under closer scrutiny, Black individuals are the only officers officially condemned for their actions with additional editorial commentary blaming these

Black individuals for victimizing law enforcement. Since race is not overtly mentioned in these tweets, it is essential to read the text with the image. One tweet accompanied by a picture of a middle-aged Black couple reads: "After her agency saw her post, she tried to excuse it away, but they weren't about to law [sic] something this extreme go. // NYC Correction Officer Suspended for Social Media Post Encouraging Cop Killers." Another tweet features an image of Michael Brown's father, along with a small portrait of his son in the upper left-hand corner, and reads: "Years after the shooting was repeatedly ruled justified, he's about to demand another investigation. // Michael Brown's Father Calls for Case to Be Reopened 5 Years after Shooting." The tweets attempting to shame the officers who have behaved wrongly contain only images of Black individuals. Another example shows an image of the mug shot of a Black man in the upper left-hand corner, and a Black man talking at a press conference with a White man behind him. This tweet reads: "Cop Arrested after Faking Attack on Himself, Accused of Stolen Valor." The placement of the press conference led by a Black man could defray accusations of racism; however, other strategic framing is more overt. Take, for instance, the objectively racist tweet reading "VIDEO: Police Chief Apologizes after Video of Mounted Arrest Goes Viral Showing Officers Using an Approved Tactic," mentioned earlier, that is accompanied by a White officer on horseback holding a rope connected to a shackled Black man who is following behind him. A second example shows two White police officers forcibly holding down a Black man on the ground. The text reads: "Officer Criminally Charged for Winning Fight in Viral Video." This stands in contrast to an image of two White men involved in a physical altercation near a gas pump: "VIDEO: Police Officer Arrested for Punching Fire Chief in Viral Video." This tweet about two White men offers no similar editorial commentary or overt judgement.

The Blue Lives Twitter feed positions law enforcement officers as heroes who willingly sacrifice their lives to protect citizens from an increasingly violent world. At the same time, in nearly half of the tweets these heroes are also portrayed as the victims of prejudice and physical violence. The tweets use a frame of militant victimhood to position law enforcement officers as defiant victims of corrupt institutions. This framing of militant victimhood maintains White habitus through overt and covert racist content that follows the signatures of colorblind rhetoric. Tweets including images of Black men often contain racist imagery or blame Black individuals for acts of racism. This rhetoric of heroism, threat, and victimhood must be read in conversation with Blue Lives' main website that discusses its organizational history, mission, values, and the demographic profile for potential advertisers.

TABLE 1. Selling and profiting from militant victimhood: qualitative analysis of the "About Us—History" and "Blue Lives Media Kit" webpages

TWEET NUMBER	EXACT TEXT	IMAGE DESCRIPTION
15	After her agency saw her post, she tried to excuse it away, but they weren't about to law [sic] something this extreme go. // NYC Correction Officer Suspended for Social Media Post Encouraging Cop Killers	Middle-aged Black man and woman smiling
38	5 Cops Now Facing Discipline for Arresting Stormy Daniels at Strip Club	Image of White woman, Ms. Daniels at press conference
42	Years after the shooting was repeatedly ruled justified, he's about to demand another investigation. // Michael Brown's Father Calls for Case to Be Reopened 5 Years after Shooting	Michael Brown's father with Michael Brown's image in the upper left corner
80	Officer Criminally Charged for Winning Fight in Viral Video	Two White officers holding Black man on ground
81	VIDEO: Police Officer Arrested for Punching Fire Chief in Viral Video	White man punching another White man at gas pump
83	VIDEO: Police Chief Apologizes after Video of Mounted Arrest Goes Viral Showing Officers Using an Approved Tactic	White male officer on horse holding a rope attached to shackled Black man walking behind
95	Cop Arrested after Faking Attack on Himself, Accused of Stolen Valor	Black man and White man at press conference (Black man talking); mug shot of Black man in upper left corner

On August 9, 2014, eighteen-year-old Michael Brown, a Black man, was shot and killed by White police officer Darren Wilson in Ferguson, Missouri. According to the media company's History page, on this same day a group of law enforcement officers and their families founded the Blue Lives Matter company in response to the negative mainstream media coverage about Wilson.[76] As mentioned in the Twitter analysis above, new critiques of Mr. Brown and his family are posted on the group's social media sites. In its website's organizational history subsection, Blue Lives further clarifies their origin story as a reactionary movement:

---

76. "About Us—History," Blue Lives Matter.

The media catered to movements such as Black Lives Matter, whose goal was the vilification of law enforcement. Criminals who rioted and victimized innocent citizens were further given legitimacy by the media as "protestors."[77]

This allegiance to law enforcement—no matter what—conflicts with the ideal of impartial, ethical, or objective journalism. "News" is "associated with professionally produced information that is accurate, timely, relevant, clearly communicated, and fair."[78] Blue Lives deliberately frames law enforcement officers as always already victims "seen as easy targets" by "the news media, celebrities and politicians . . . and are consequently bullied by slander, illegitimate complaints, frivolous law suits [sic], and physical attacks."

Blue Lives' frame co-optation of Black Lives Matter deliberately draws on a distrust in mainstream media that is increasingly common in an era of "fake news." Rasmus Kleis Nielsen and Lucas Graves (2017) found that audiences view fake news as "much more about a wider discontent with the information landscape" and that the separation between "fake news and news as one of degree rather than a clear distinction." Fake news is an old concept that has become a "politicized buzzword" and can refer to "fake news [disinformation]" that respondents in their study "identify [as] poor journalism, propaganda (including both lying politicians and hyperpartisan content), and some kinds of advertising more frequently than false information designed to masquerade as news reports."[79] Although Blue Lives purports to be more truthful than other sources of media, their use of poor journalism (framing mechanisms and bias), partisan content, sensationalism, and advertising (both subscriptions and the Blue Lives apparel store) are all hallmarks of colloquial understandings of "fake news."

Blue Lives cannot be simply dismissed as fake news, poor journalism, or partisan politics. The media outlet serves as a radicalizing echo chamber for millions of like-minded individuals. It produces and spreads free content, which is a teaser for pay-for-view, with nearly 3.5 million subscribers, that publicizes, condones, and reifies violent, state-sanctioned expressions of White masculine pain toward historically marginalized people. When speaking of the cisgender male-led Minuteman Project's online media presence, Michelle Holling borrows from Aaron Gresson's notion of "white pain" in her theorization of "white masculine pain." Holling explains that "the nuances of White masculine pain derive from a national sense of victimhood stemming

---

77. "About Us—History," Blue Lives Matter.
78. Nielsen and Graves, "'News You Don't Believe,'" 3.
79. Nielsen and Graves, 1, 3, 1.

from acts of terror and from fear of other's colonization of the United States." On its Twitter feed, Blue Lives expresses concern about domestic terrorism, the activism of undocumented immigrants and their supporters, and the persecution of law enforcement. However, the cumulative effect of the framing of Black lives in the Twitter feed is to "express fears of becoming a numerical minority, being displaced from one's employment, home, geographic locale and nation, and being a potential victim of crimes committed by immigrants" and other historically marginalized groups.[80] Yet, these expressions of militant toxic masculinity are also supported by cisgender women. In its Media Toolkit, Blue Lives has two women listed as content producers—specifically as a managing editor and a writer—and lists nearly 40 percent of its target market demographic as female.

Another important "truth of the matter" is that social media websites are not mass communications businesses; they sell consumer data for profit. Blue Lives sells its audience, supporters of Blue Lives Matter, to advertisers. Consequently, its stance as a news agency that speaks to and for an echo chamber celebratory of law enforcement warrants critical attention from public relations and brand marketing perspectives. The company uses its main website as a digital hub where—for a fee of $5.00 per month—like-minded individuals can access stories posted by journalists identified as either former law enforcement officers or their immediate families. Visitors can affirm their membership in the imagined Blue Lives Matter community through replying to members-only comment feeds on stories as well as buying t-shirts, hats, bumper stickers, and other products on Blue Lives' online store.[81] The digital store, along with the online subscription fee, is reminiscent of the "buy American" movement that grew in popularity after the terrorist attacks of September 11, 2001. Such consumer products promote an ethos of ethical capitalism through the purchase of patriotic goods that ostensibly support US civil servants and their families.[82]

Despite the interactivity encouraged through its main platform, Blue Lives does not self-identify as a social media hub, but as a legitimate news media outlet. In explaining "Who We Are," Blue Lives critiques what it perceives as the "common practice in the news media to report grossly inaccurate information about law enforcement." In contrast, the media group attests that "our [Blue Lives] goal is to report news without these inaccuracies in order to reach people before they are misinformed." Blue Lives is clear about its audi-

---

80. Holling, "5. Patrolling National Identity," 112.

81. Throughout the research conducted for this chapter, a link to this store was the pinned Tweet at the top of the Blue Lives' official Twitter feed.

82. Gobé, *Citizen Brand*, xxix; Noel, "Branding Guilt."

ence, and asks others to "Advertise with Us" by providing a "Blue Lives Matter Media Kit" on their website. The media company has about 3,587,000 unique users per month, and this "audience is made up primarily of Americans who support law enforcement, including law enforcement officers and their families." Refining this statistic, about 65 percent are over forty-five years of age, and the gender of their audience is mostly male (62 percent), although many women (38 percent) also are content producers and consumers. The majority of users access their content on mobile devices (49 percent), followed by desktop computers (29 percent) and tablets (22 percent).[83]

For potential sponsors, the media company elaborates on its values of equality, justice, honesty/accuracy, and civil rights:

> Equality—All people are created equal, no matter their race, religion, ethnicity, disability, skin color, gender, or sexual orientation. Blue Lives are made up of all lives—Law enforcement officers come from all manner of backgrounds and beliefs and they all deserve our respect. Law enforcement is very diverse, and we believe that diversity is a strength.
>
> Justice—The world is full of injustice and we will ensure that it is brought to light.
>
> Honesty/Accuracy—We strive to make our content honest and accurate so that people can be exposed to the truth.
>
> Civil Rights—Thanks to the Constitution, all people within the United States of America are afforded civil rights which much [sic] be acknowledged and respected.[84]

Standing in contrast to the overt dismissal of the Black Lives Matter movement, Blue Lives promotes a colorblind, postracial, and egalitarian ethos based on justice, honesty, accuracy, and the US Constitution. Implicitly, these core values of the organization are also the core values of its imagined audience. As an alternate source of media, the organization implies that these core values are not present in more mainstream media outlets. Although the exact names of the mainstream media outlets critiqued are unmentioned, the Blue Lives Twitter feed does overtly censure both Democratic politicians and the *New York Times*.

In the corporate sector,[85] including telecommunications industries,[86] companies incorporate citizenship initiatives (like environmental awareness, fun-

---

83. "Advertising," Blue Lives Matter.
84. "Advertising," Blue Lives Matter.
85. Gobé, *Citizen Brand*; Willmott, "Citizen Brands."
86. Oullette, "Citizen Brand."

draising for charities, etc.) as a part of a highly successful branding agenda.[87] Blue Lives' mission "to support law enforcement is accomplished through our supporters, the world's largest community of Americans who support law enforcement" can be viewed as a type of public relations campaign termed Citizen Brand. Citizen Brand "plac[es] corporations and consumer culture at the center of governing and citizenship."[88] In his book *Citizen Brand*, Marc Gobé (2002) writes that in a consumer democracy "people today are keenly interested in buying an *emotional experience*." This emotional experience, Gobé contends, is more than a new type of brand; it is "an entire *philosophy* and a *motivational tool* that reaches beyond mere observations to inspire *creative solutions*."[89] As a philosophy that motivates both employees and consumers, Citizen Brand—in the case of Blue Lives—provides an ideological and affective experience that works to build brand loyalty, particularly in receptive publics.

Michael Willmott (2003) suggests that, under Citizen Brand, companies support initiatives and branding agendas "precisely for their environmental or social impact but which also result in tangible commercial benefits."[90] Blue Lives journalist and former police officer Christopher Berg (@OfficerBlue) introduces the media company's mission to potential advertisers and subscribers as dedicated to the mission of supporting law enforcement:

> Due to the nature of the profession, law enforcement personnel are seen as easy targets and are consequently bullied by slander, illegitimate complaints, frivolous law suits [sic], and physical attacks.
>
> Unjust attacks from the new media, celebrities and politicians have damaged community relations and endanger the lives and safety of law enforcement officers.
>
> We are supported by Americans who believe in law and order and want to provide a counterbalance to the dangerous false narratives being propagated about law enforcement.
>
> Our mission to support law enforcement is accomplished through our supporters, the world's largest community of Americans who support law enforcement.[91]

---

87. To secure lower prices and better-quality services for consumers, the Telecommunications Act of 1996 made encouraged media cross ownership through the deregulation broadcast and telecommunications industries "entrust[ing] the free market to oversee its contribution to civil society and political democracy" (Ouellette, 58).
88. Ouellette, 62.
89. Gobé, xv.
90. Willmott, "Citizen Brands," 363.
91. "About Blue Lives Matter," Warrior Maven.

The Blue Lives Citizen Brand public relations campaign sells an audience of conservative, pro–law enforcement consumers to advertisers. In turn, this consumer audience is offered a feel-good media product and the satisfaction of belonging to an imagined community of law enforcement officers and supporters. A subscriber also may feel good knowing that, through their membership dollars and online purchases, they are supporting a staff comprising only former law enforcement personnel and their families. This satisfying brand expresses a particular American civic virtue (support of law enforcement) while also making a profit. This fosters brand loyalty emboldened by feelings of membership and patriotism.

Across its media sites, Blue Lives misrepresents the Black Lives Matter social movement as a violent, riotous group of criminals. The Blue Lives "About Us—History"[92] emphasizes that the company was "founded based on the need of law enforcement," first on Facebook and then on its own website. This history is vague in its references to ambiguous media outlets that vilify law enforcement and in its claims of "an unprecedented number of ambush attacks on law enforcement officers" in 2016. The history indexes the killing of Michael Brown by Officer Darren Wilson, who was charged with aggravated assault, as a touchstone moment for the media movement. The group directly blames nebulous "political leaders" and Black Lives Matter activists for the negative portrayal of law enforcement in the media:

> The media catered to movements such as Black Lives Matter, whose goal was the vilification of law enforcement. Criminals who rioted and victimized innocent citizens were further given legitimacy by the media as "protesters."
>
> America watched as criminals destroyed property, and assaulted and murdered innocent people, and they labeled these criminals as victims.
>
> Personal responsibility for one's actions went away, replaced by accusations of racism and an unjust government.[93]

Following the killings of New York Police Department officers Ravel Ramos and Wenjian Liu on December 20, 2014, Blue Lives found that "even the largest law enforcement media companies, who purport to be all for the police, helped spread misinformation through re-posting articles written with an anti-police bias." What specific corporations "law enforcement media companies" refers to is unclear. However, Blue Lives reflects that, after their perceived victimization even by supportive press, the corporation "began to

---

92. Given Blue Lives' attempt to reframe historical narratives and the inherent malleability of online content, the entirety of this history is available in appendix 1.

93. "About Us—History," Blue Lives Matter.

provide law enforcement officers with life-saving [sic] equipment, at no cost to them"; this "equipment" is their empathetic news coverage.

I emphasize this organizational history because the ideologies articulated here—a vilification of Black Lives Matter and resurgent discussions of those, like Michael Brown, murdered by law enforcement officers; an assertion that the neoliberal virtue of personal responsibility has been lost by those who do not support law enforcement; a fundamental distrust in the mainstream media; and a perception that law enforcement officers are under "an unprecedented number of ambush attacks"—are all used as framing mechanisms that reoccur as motifs in the news coverage highlighted on the Blue Lives Twitter page, website, and in its store. In other words, this organizational history presents a frame co-optation of Black Lives Matter that then influences the types of stories covered by Blue Lives on their other forms of internet media. The reality behind Black Lives Matter's goals and ideologies is far more complex than suggested by Blue Lives; Black Lives Matter is a diverse and defuse social movement with a political and philosophical agenda that operates in the heritage of Black struggles for racial justice[94] and mobilizes to fight violence against Black men and women, Black boys and girls, and Black transpeople and gender-queer people.[95]

The Blue Lives "About Us—History" section is not alone in its misrepresentation of Black Lives Matter as solely a response to police brutality. Barbara A. Biesecker (2017) writes that the view of Black Lives Matter as only about police brutality is a "media effect."[96] The media's role in framing Black Lives Matter as a single issue has led to All Lives Matter and Blue Lives Matter:

> Without a doubt, it is in part because mainstream as well as other media outlets reductively reframed BLM [Black Lives Matter] as an unruly, even confrontational and violent, single-issue movement protesting the lack of accountability for police who use excessive force against Black boys and men that the signifying chain extending from "white lives matter" to "all lives matter" is made to count, at best, as an ethical response to or, at worst, as a vitriolic dismissal of BLM [Black Lives Matter].[97]

Similar to All Lives Matter, Blue Lives Matter is a colorblind response to Black Lives Matter—a misunderstanding of the implied meaning of the social movement that Black Lives Matter, *too*. Or, as Biko Agozio (2018) puts

---

94. Lebron, *Making of Black Lives Matter*.
95. Biesecker, "From General History to Philosophy."
96. Biesecker, 413.
97. Biesecker, 411.

it, "since All Lives Matter, it follows that Black Lives Matter too and if by any logic Black Lives do not Matter, then All Lives do not Matter."[98]

Discussion

While plotting the social terrain of discursive misunderstanding, Luvell Anderson (2017) defines such encounters as hermeneutical impasses or "various obstacles that leave us without understanding" that can arise from a "lack of cultural familiarity."[99] These exchanges happen within the structures of discourse,[100] and it is important to pay attention to the positionality of the speaker, the process of information transfer, as well as structures of power. In the case of the individual tweet by @ProudWarriorDad, the intentionality of an individual as hermeneutical impasse is anecdotal; however, Blue Lives is a corporation that sells news and is ostensibly more critical and thoughtful with media postings than an individual social media user. Focusing on Blue Lives Matter as a media corporation that sells ideologies, apparel, and member subscriptions, the question of intentional audience manipulation is more pertinent and proven through deliberate framing mechanisms like militant victimhood. This dynamic of power—that of state-sanctioned violence supported by racial capitalism—is significant in discussions of the transmedia postings of the group. Blue Lives is a media group sustained by hermeneutical impasses—whether media successfully influences its audience or not—and receives direct financial support by perpetuating separatism and misunderstanding in an audience that serves as an already receptive echo chamber. Through studying hermeneutical impasses, Anderson says we can better understand the problems of mutual understanding and how "power relations constrain our discursive practices."[101] Elaborating on the concept, Anderson notes:

> Hermeneutical impasses are instances in which agents engaged in communicative exchange are unable to achieve understanding due to a gap in shared hermeneutical resources. Hermeneutical resources are roughly sets consisting of *cognitive tools* used for sense-making (e.g., concepts and conceptions) and *expressive tools* used for communicating experiences to others (e.g., locations and manners of speaking).[102]

---

98. Agozio, "Black Lives Matter Otherwise All Lives Do Not Matter," i.
99. Anderson, "Hermeneutical Impasses," 1, 4.
100. Anderson, 13.
101. Anderson, 1.
102. Anderson, 3.

Hermeneutical impasses can be unwilful, when a genuine lack of understanding exists, or willful. Blue Lives' strategic use of multiculturalism on its main webpage contrasts with the racialized representations of Black men on its Twitter feed that strategically fail to mention racial identity in words, but do so through pictures. This patterned behavior suggests willful hermeneutical impasses. Willful impasses, like those discussed in the final chapter of this book, can include "refusal[s] to engage with sources or situations" that are unfamiliar as well as matters of deliberate obfuscation, for instance in the songs enslaved people used to communicate messages slave owners could not understand.[103]

From social movement literature, Luigi Esposito and Victor Romano (2016) focus on frame co-optation and how social media is used to structure events, make assertions about those events, and as a tool for mobilization.[104] Specifically, they are interested in how benevolent racism is a motivating factor behind the frame co-optation of the Black Lives Matter movement. @ProudWarriorDad's tweet displays an informal and unsophisticated relationship to frame co-optation; it is not overt and the meme is more about ridiculing queer people. Such a frame co-optation is apparent in Blue Lives' derivative naming and its calls for equity, justice, honesty, civil rights, and statements that "diversity is a strength" in its "Blue Lives Matter Media Kit." Despite the racial significations pervasive across its Twitter feed, this media kit is blatantly colorblind. Esposito and Romano define benevolent racism as a subtle type of new, frequently termed colorblind, racism:

> Benevolent racism acknowledges the plight of Black Americans and ostensibly condemns the devaluation of Black lives. However, it does so in ways that further reinforce attitudes and practices that perpetuate racial inequity and Black disenfranchisement. It is therefore important to expose and recognize this type of "benevolent" racist discourse if those who are interested in racial justice want to prevent the transformative potential of BLMM [Black Lives Matter Movement] from being appropriated by reactionary segments of US society that support—either deliberately or inadvertently—the prevailing racial status quo.[105]

In making this argument, they point to supporters of the "Ferguson effect," or the notion that it has been harder for law enforcement officers to fight

---

103. Anderson, 5–6.
104. Esposito and Romano, "Benevolent Racism."
105. Esposito and Romano, 162.

crime after Black Lives Matter.[106] The Ferguson effect—in this case the mainstream media coverage of Brown's murder—is the origin story for Blue Lives. Esposito and Romano point to opponents of Black Lives Matter who move focus away from systemic inequities in law enforcement and instead focus on Black-on-Black crime—as if a focus on intergroup violence and systemic inequity were mutually exclusive.[107] This focus on Black-on-Black crime is also seen in the Blue Lives Twitter feed when the group mourns the loss of two Black women in Chicago who were killed by gun violence ("A tragedy out of Chicago. // 2 Members of Chicago Anti-Violence Group Murdered in Drive By"). A tougher focus on Black-on-Black crime calls for more intensive policing, while not addressing the systemic problems within law enforcement's disproportionate targeting of Black men. Tangentially, benevolent racism—similar to other neoliberal ideologies—emphasizes personal responsibility.[108] The authors note how opponents of Black Lives Matter at times "abandon colorblindness," and this is also seen in the racialized framing of Black men.[109] Following Bonilla-Silva, Esposito and Romano find that the most significant challenge to fighting racism today is not overt acts, but more covert types of racism—like benevolent racism. A first stop toward combating benevolent racism is making visible how it sustains White supremacy, as through the strategic rhetoric of Blue Lives.

In their comparative study of the Blue Matters (not affiliated with Blue Lives) and the Black Lives Matter Facebook pages, Mary Angela Bock and Ever Josue Figueroa (2018) claim that a focus on "blue lives" works to "cultivate a belief that the ruling system of power is moral."[110] @ProudWarriorDad also focuses on the US Army as a moral group, and Blue Lives focuses on law enforcement generally, including ICE, corrections, and police officers. The authors maintain that the rhetorical patterns between the two Facebook pages represent an ideological conflict between faith and reason in their respective uses of color, hashtags, memes, values, slurs, and video, concluding, "The most striking characteristic of the whole corpus, however, is the overlapping values of Christianity, patriarchy, and White supremacy expressed on the Blue Matters page."[111] Although it may not be surprising that Blue Matters would support the police, the page also notably encouraged "authoritarian, patriarchal,

---

106. Esposito and Romano, 166.
107. Esposito and Romano, 167.
108. Esposito and Romano, 168.
109. Esposito and Romano, 169.
110. Bock and Figueroa, "Faith and Reason," 3099.
111. Bock and Figueroa, 3109.

religious discipline" and overtly connected Blacks with criminality.[112] The Blue Matters Facebook page was polemical and "adhere(d) to hierarchical, authoritarian principles and the binary of good and evil"[113]; as discussed in the first section of this chapter, similar codes are present in the Blue Lives Twitter feed. This is significant and suggests a wider social movement beyond the Blue Lives media sites that espouse similar ideologies.

The hashtags #AllLivesMatter and #BlueLivesMatter each evoke color-blind, benevolent racism that seeks to support the prevailing social order centered on White normativity and authoritarian control. Using a statistical analysis of tweets, Gallagher et al. found that the hashtag #AllLivesMatter also has a positive connection with law enforcement and users tend to demonstrate a more conservative ideology. In their comparative survey of the hashtags #AllLivesMatter and #BlueLivesMatter, Gallagher et al. did "not find evidence of significant discussion of 'all lives' within #AllLivesMatter"; rather, discussion focused on the lives of law enforcement officers during periods when individuals were protesting Black deaths at the hands of law enforcement officers. Blue Lives similarly used overtly offensive and racist content while perpetuating the racist stereotypes that Black men are prone to violence and that police officers are mostly benevolent victims.

Mediating Militant Victimhood

Debates on social media platforms like Twitter symbolize a larger struggle for power over discourse and representation.[114] Based on interactivity and connectivity, social media creates a type of public where practitioners both consume discourse and shape it.[115] Nikita Carney (2016) argues that "social media serves as both a weak public in which people formulate opinions and a 'strong' public that puts pressure on the state to reform its practices by raising awareness and organizing protests."[116] For example, those who use the hashtag #AllLivesMatter in opposition to the hashtag #BlackLivesMatter "tend to oversimplify the discourse, engaging in color-blind racism."[117] This is clearly seen in the tweet by @ProudWarriorDad. Given the Blue Lives organizational history, the group was found in direct opposition to Black Lives Matter. The

---

112. Bock and Figueroa, 3110.
113. Bock and Figueroa, 3113.
114. Carney, "All Lives Matter, but So Does Race," 181.
115. Carney, 183; Dahlgren, *Television and the Public Sphere*.
116. Carney, "All Lives Matter, but So Does Race," 184.
117. Carney, 185.

hashtag #BlueLivesMatter also oversimplifies the Black Lives Matter campaign as being solely against all law enforcement officers. Carney finds that "while the claim that all human life is valuable is not "wrong," it intentionally erases the complexities of race, class, gender, and sexuality in the lives of people who suffer from systematic police brutality."[118] Blue Lives takes Carney's argument further and fundamentally refutes the existence of systemic police brutality. This is achieved, in part, through an emphasis on personal responsibility and multiculturalism reflected in its organizational history and tweets. As Carney suggests, social media can also function as a strong site of public debate that can disrupt White habitus. A possible first step in this disruption of White habitus on the internet is an analysis of how White rhetoric works and to what effect. Though painfully visible to non-Whites, such rhetoric uses frames like militant victimhood as diversions.

Branding itself a news outlet, the Blue Lives Matter company produces media that, despite its stated goals, gives law enforcement officers a bad reputation. Blue Lives insists that the government is not working, the media is not working, and that any ideological focus away from Whiteness as normative and central is not working *for White lives*. Edward S. Herman and Noam Chomsky (1998) argue that "the media serve, and propagandize on behalf of, the powerful societal interests that control and finance them."[119] The creation of alternative digital media outlets like Blue Lives presents a unique set of issues from the vast corporate entities that Herman and Chomsky condemn. Yet, the connection between profit and corporate support remains intact as Blue Lives actively seeks financial support through selling merchandise, subscription fees, and advertising that builds on their Citizen Brand. The Blue Lives Matter media company gains support through Trumpist rhetoric that dismisses mainstream media's critical coverage of events as "fake news" or biased news. However, critical analysis of alternative media sites like Blue Lives also offers the opportunity to disrupt White habitus through showing how White habitus works. This media coverage defies norms of journalistic integrity and ethnics, using militant victimhood as a framing mechanism for its news stories. This militant victimhood links policing, the Second Amendment, and vigilantism with a brand of US patriotism and racial capitalism emboldened by the rhetoric of fear, crisis, and implicit White saviorism.

Blue Lives and @ProudWarriorDad emphasize a commitment to heteronormative masculinity and the US military, and cast the identity politics of historically marginalized groups as superficial. It would be incorrect, how-

---

118. Carney, 185.
119. Herman and Chomsky, *Manufacturing Consent*, 1.

ever, to presume that this masculine rhetoric is embodied, performed, and espoused only by White men; such notions reinforce hegemonic masculinity and falsely link masculinity to only cisgender men. In the next chapter I explore rhetorical presentations of White masculinity outside of a cisgender-male body. In so doing, I highlight the constructed natures of both masculinity and whiteness.

CHAPTER 2

Feminized Racial Pain

Cisgender Women, Whiteness, and Digital Masculine Rhetoric

Scholars have well noted the connection between White supremacy, White men, and White male pain.[1] I further nuance such connections throughout this monograph. The "Unite the Right" protests in Charlottesville were largely led by White men. The militant rhetoric analyzed in the previous chapter self-identified with fatherhood, the military, and law enforcement; all of which were gendered as masculine. Given these connections between masculinity and Whiteness, I would be remiss not to overtly note that the performance of hegemonic masculinity frequently accompanies rhetorical deflection. Hegemonic masculine rhetoric includes "presentations of anger, fear, self-centeredness, ressentiment, extreme competition, and violence."[2] Rhetorical manifestations of Whiteness and hegemonic masculinity both maintain dominance and normativity, and exclude "othered" historically marginalized groups.[3]

To Jack Halberstam (1998), dominant masculinity is a "naturalized relation between maleness and power" that "becomes legible as masculinity where and

---

1. For sources that discuss White male pain and its intersection with White supremacy, please see Cabrera, *White Guys on Campus*; Kelly, "Wounded Man"; Casey Ryan Kelly, "Man-Apocalypse"; Kelly, "Donald J. Trump"; Kelly, *Apocalypse Man*; Kimmel, *Angry White Men*; Noel, "Deflective Whiteness."
2. Noel, "White Female Pain."
3. Connell and Messerschmidt, "Hegemonic Masculinity," 832.

when it leaves the white male middle-class body."[4] Accompanying White male pain, a White female rhetoric of pain, victimhood, and masculinity simultaneously emphasizes the constructed and performative nature of Whiteness, as well as masculinity.[5] White female pain refers to an affect embodied by feminized subjects that shapes rhetorical posturing, presentation, and ideas about race.[6] White male and female pain are mutually sustaining and reinforcing, but following Halberstam, by locating rhetorical White masculinity outside of its assumed cisgender-male subject position, we can better understand how hegemonic masculinity works to sustain White supremacy. Building on these arguments in this chapter, I refine my discussion of the gendered dynamics of White deflection by focusing on the ways that hegemonic gender roles work in tandem with White rhetoric to uphold repressive systems. I contend that rhetorical manifestations of masculinity and Whiteness share an individualized and self-centered focus on power at the expense of historically marginalized groups. In the case studies I examine, I find that masculinity, similar to Whiteness, is a rhetorical construction that can be—and is—embodied by individuals of any identity. Further, Whiteness and hegemonic masculinity are codependent; they rely on and borrow from one another to legitimize White male dominance as the natural order of things.

Masculinity and femininity characterize a spectrum of learned behaviors and discourses. Distinctively, "hegemonic masculinity . . . is the pattern of practice (i.e., things done, not just a set of role expectations or an identity) . . . [that] allow[s] men's dominance over women to continue."[7] Hegemonic masculinity is achieved through force and consent, frequently operating as common sense. Cisgender women also consent to and reinforce hegemonic masculinity as "hegemony d[oes] not mean violence, although it could be supported by force; it means ascendancy."[8] My analysis of hegemonic mascu-

---

4. Halberstam, *Female Masculinity*, 2.
5. I have written about White female masculinity elsewhere, and this book focuses on masculine presentation from largely White males. However, in addition to my forthcoming work, there is an extensive literature that explores these topics further. For discussions of hegemonic masculinity, please see Halberstam, *Female Masculinity*; Connell and Messerschmidt, "Hegemonic Masculinity," 848; Noel, "White Female Pain." For rhetorical discussions of White, please see Moon and Holling, "'White Supremacy in Heels'"; Moon, "White Enculturation and Bourgeois Ideology." For literature on how cis women and girls engage in masculine acts and discourse, please see Pascoe, *Dude, You're a Fag*; Kazyak, "Midwest or Lesbian?"; Pilgeram, "'Ass-Kicking' Women"; Halberstam, *Female Masculinity*. Finally, for some examples on cis women's enactments of masculinity that are not accepted by social norms, resulting in stigma, please see Halberstam, *Female Masculinity*; Mimi Schippers, "Recovering the Feminine Other."
6. Noel, "White Female Pain."
7. Connell and Messerschmidt, "Hegemonic Masculinity," 832.
8. Connell and Messerschmidt, 832.

linity recognizes that women, and in some cases representations of children, play a significant role in upholding repressive gender roles[9] and women can situationally adopt signatures of hegemonic masculinity through discourse.[10] That is, through the rhetorical performance of female masculinity in mediated spaces, cisgender women orators are particularly apt in persuading others that toxic hegemonic masculinity is not only normal, but a coveted and patriotic rhetoric.

By rhetorically linking representations of masculinity, White supremacy, power, and cisgender women orators, this chapter maps a constellation of what Michelle A. Holling (2019) terms discursive violence or rhetoric that involves "masking or effacing other forms of violence and/or productive of negative valence, that colludes with other manifestations of violence."[11] This discursive violence emboldens White supremacy, heteropatriarchy, and authoritarianism through a gendered rhetoric that upholds hegemonic masculinity and, congruently, hegemonic notions of femininity that maintain the status quo while claiming victimhood when faced with a discursive or material challenge. As a performance of discursive violence, deflective Whiteness is particularly effective at claiming victimhood, and empathy, outside of White, cisgender-male presentations.

Through plotting discursive violence committed by and in the name of cisgender women, we are better able to uncover the performative nature of White masculine rhetoric, rendering it as *inherently performative* rather than naturalized. In a racialized regime of representation, Stuart Hall (2001) defines a naturalized discourse as one that advances learned cultural behavior as natural and consequently unchangeable. Yet, language and discourse are embodied and resist fixed meaning(s). Hall locates that "naturalization is . . . a representational strategy designed to *fix* 'difference,' and thus *secure it forever.*"[12] As I discuss in the pages that follow, the naturalization of masculinity by cisgender women functions as a representational strategy to maintain the status quo by "fixing" the meaning of masculinity and its relationship to Whiteness.

Through implicating cisgender women as upholding both hegemonic masculinity and Whiteness as structures of oppression, this chapter functions as a tactic to disrupt White supremacy, heteropatriarchy, and, more generally, relations of power. In his study of how ordinary individuals can use space, time, and discourse to disrupt systems of power, Michel de Certeau (1984) defines

---

9. Connell and Messerschmitt, 848.
10. Connell and Messerschmitt, 841.
11. Holling, "Rhetorical Contours of Violent Frames," 250.
12. Hall, "Spectacle of the 'Other,'" 336.

the crucial differences between strategies and tactics. Defining strategy as "the calculation (or manipulation) of power relationships that becomes possible as soon as a subject with will and power (a business, an army, a city, a scientific institution) can be isolated."[13] Once those in power are isolated, they claim and map out space—in de Certeau's words, "the place of its own power and will."[14] Conversely, "a tactic is an art of the weak" and "the space of the other" that operates within the territorial boundaries of those in power yet has the benefit of time and mobility. De Certeau writes that a tactic operates "in isolated actions blow by blow. . . . It takes advantage of 'opportunities' and depends on them, being without any base where it could stockpile its winnings, build its own position, and plan raid. . . . This nowhere gives a tactic mobility."[15] Borrowing from this work, Thomas K. Nakayama and Robert L. Krizek find "whiteness as a rhetorical construction" that, as I argue in this chapter, supports systems of inequity through a strategic use of masculine rhetoric. The rhetoricians call on others to "seek an understanding of the ways that this rhetorical construction [Whiteness] makes itself visible and invisible, eluding analysis yet exerting influence over everyday life."[16] Similar to the previous chapter, this chapter also extends such discussions of everyday life to include online discourse.

Viewing "whiteness as a multiplicity of identities that are historically grounded, class specific, politically manipulated, and gendered," France Winddance Twine and Charles Gallagher (2008) invite "empirical accounts of how whiteness is deployed, and the discursive strategies used to maintain and destabilize white identity and privilege."[17] Respectively, this chapter utilizes critical theory to analyze empirical accounts of cisgender women's rhetoric—social media posts and linked content within the posts—while also paying attention to the frequency of corresponding hashtags across the internet as a gauge for assessing the popularity, and social impact, of the trending data. In charting rhetoric on social media, scholars have used Google Trends data to access the popularity of terms, as well as content analysis of select tweets about an event in a given period of time.[18]

---

13. De Certeau, *Practice of Everyday Life*, 35–36.
14. De Certeau, 36.
15. De Certeau, 37.
16. Nakayama and Krizek, "Whiteness," 293.
17. Twine and Gallagher, "Future of Whiteness," 12–13.
18. For examples of other work that uses similar methods, see Noel, "Deflective Whiteness," 322; Cisneros and Nakayama, "New Media, Old Racisms"; Carney, "All Lives Matter, but So Does Race."

Deflective Whiteness is an adaptable and at times ostensibly contradictory rhetoric. This chapter accomplishes two interrelated goals. Deflective Whiteness begins by claiming victimhood followed by attempts to subvert social justice claims. In my next section, I outline the theoretical underpinning of my argument. In the following section, I study empirical examples of social media posts and their online audience reception. This section focuses on rhetoric surrounding Ashli Babbitt—a White cisgender woman, US veteran, and private citizen—as well as Gina Carano—a well-known White cisgender woman, actor, model, and athlete. The last section of this chapter studies feminizing social media posts that reshare posts from conservative news media and that adhere to the media frame identified in chapter 2, militant victimhood. Militant victimhood is a framing mechanism of news media that shapes coverage in a combative or bombastic way that claims Whites are the aggrieved racial status. Here, I discuss how women from historically marginalized communities are used to frame the debates around critical race theory on conservative media outlets whose content they share on their personal social media pages. I study the social media posts of Ambassador Nikki Haley, an Indian American cisgender woman, and Candace Owens, a Black cisgender woman political commentator, against critical race theory. As my analysis suggests, Haley and Owens engage in what Cristina Beltrán (2021) terms multiracial Whiteness, or "a discriminatory worldview in which feelings of freedom and belonging are produced through the persecution and dehumanization of others."[19]

Women and White Victimhood

Following other authors who utilize critical theory to deconstruct popular mediated messages,[20] I study the rhetoric and reception of cisgender women who also use the masculine language of victimhood and pain. I argue that White-allied women use a masculinized rhetoric of fear, threat, and victimhood in/when confronting perceived threats to their relative power as cisgender, heteronormative, White women. This rhetoric (re)secures cisgender heteronormative Whiteness as the center, but from a feminized persona. This feminized subjectivity is further linked with vulnerability and paternalistic discourses often resulting in symbolic, or literal, martyrdom for the White-

---

19. Beltrán, "Opinion | to Understand Trump's Support."
20. For further research on the application of critical theory to analyze race and Whiteness using a similar empirical approach that focuses on transmedia case studies, please see the following sources: Doane and Bonilla-Silva, *White Out*; Doane, "Shades of Colorblindness"; Noel, "Deflective Whiteness," 322.

allied cause when racist acts and discourse meets retribution. Viewing Whiteness as a rhetorical manifestation of asymmetrical power relationships, I use White-allied here to refer to rhetorical presentations that support the cause of White supremacy and Whiteness more generally.

In a study of the rhetoric of Donald Trump, Casey Ryan Kelly also finds a pattern of "ressentiment (re-sentiment)," or "a condition in which a subject is addled by rage and envy yet remains impotent, subjugated and unable to act on or adequately express frustration" influencing his political and other rhetoric. Through affective expressions of ressentiment and anger, Kelly "suggest[s] that ressentiment accounts for the unique intersection where powerful sentiments and self-serving morality are coupled with feelings of powerlessness and ruminations on past injuries."[21] White women, however, are often on the sidelines of this discourse and—although they do support and sustain it—are not the primary focus of a significant body of literature. Ressentiment, feelings of perceived wrongdoing that an orator feels they cannot control, is common throughout the White cisgender women's rhetoric, as will be seen in my analysis of Babbitt and Carano's tweets.

This chapter contributes to a still-emerging body of literature on White women's views of race, as well as work on cisgender women's presentations of masculinity. "Race shapes white women's lives," and yet Ruth Frankenberg (1993) found nearly thirty years ago that, even when White women acknowledged how they benefited from Whiteness, they did not take action to end racism.[22] Although scholars have considered how White women perform what Dreama G. Moon (1999) termed a "good (white) girl" identity, White women nevertheless position themselves as victims of White male hegemony rather than recognizing their own intersectional culpability in maintaining White supremacy.[23] A scholarly opening remains around how White cisgender women also evoke masculine rhetoric while supporting White supremacy. Regardless of gender identity, any subject can perform masculinity. Specifically, sociological scholars find that women and girls engage in masculine behavior, practices, and rhetoric.[24] Although some scholars find this behavior as transgressive of gender roles and socially unsettling,[25] others find that,

---

21. Kelly, "Donald J. Trump," 2.
22. Frankenburg, *White Women, Race Matters*, 236, 241.
23. For more context about the representation of White womanhood, please see Moon and Holling, "'White Supremacy in Heels'"; Moon, "White Enculturation and Bourgeois Ideology."
24. For a discussion of how cis women and girls engage in masculine acts and discourse, please see Pascoe, *Dude, You're a Fag*; Kazyak, "Midwest or Lesbian?"; Pilgram, "'Ass-Kicking' Women"; Halberstam, *Female Masculinity*.
25. For examples of how cisgender women's enactments of masculinity are not accepted by social norms, resulting in stigma, please see Halberstam, *Female Masculinity*; Schippers, "Recovering the Feminine Other."

depending on context or geography, some expressions of female masculinity—like masculine dress, stereotypically cisgender-male activities/professions, and aggressive behavior—are not only socially accepted, but can *situationally* increase an individual's popularity and social status.[26]

White female pain can be more carcinogenic and socially corrosive than White male pain as it relies on the interpellation of heteropatriarchy to obfuscate White racialization and to naturalize feminized White fragility as normative.[27] Dreama G. Moon and Michelle A Holling (2020) similarly find that, in attempts to gain footing within a White power structure, White feminism

> ideologically grounds itself in a gendered victimology that masks its participation and functionality in white supremacy . . . by erasing women of color, positioning women as victims of white male hegemony, and failing to hold white women accountable for the production and reproduction of (white) feminism [that] manifests its allegiance to whiteness and in doing so commits "discursive violence."[28]

Gendered discursive violence is used to maintain White hegemony in an ostensibly covert way—through cisgender women orators who are simultaneously presented as aggressive yet still *socially recognized as vulnerable, feminized, and therefore, as potential victims*. Operating within heteronormative patriarchal notions of femininity, this vulnerability does not mandate stigma but rather social support.

In the next section I focus on the case studies of Carano and Babbitt, cisgender White women orators whose social media discourse ascended to national prominence after they were caught in the backlash against their White supremacist politics—Babbitt was shot while trying to occupy the US Capitol, and Carano was fired from her job with Disney and Lucasfilm due to her anti-Semitic social media posts. Both women used masculine, aggressive, and violent imagery, rhetoric, and gender presentation in their social media posts and, when they faced respective backlash, were widely seen by their empathetic audiences as vulnerable victims. Rather than permanently hurting their representations, this situational feminized victimhood elevated their respective social capital within like-minded communities.

---

26. For examples where cisgender women's enactment of masculinity is regionally accepted, please see Kazak, "Midwest or Lesbian?," 828; Pilgeram, "'Ass-Kicking' Women," 120.

27. DiAngelo, *White Fragility*.

28. Moon and Holling, "'White Supremacy in Heels,'" 1–2.

White Female Pain

On April 14, 2021, the United States Department of Justice exonerated the US Capitol police officer who shot and killed US Air Force Veteran Ashli Babbitt, a White San Diego resident, QAnon conspiracy theorist, anti-immigration advocate, and ardent Donald Trump supporter who breached the US Capitol building on January 6, 2021. In response, right-wing social media erupted in a predictable way. Similar to the social movement frame co-optation of Black Lives Matter seen in the monikers Blue Lives Matter, All Lives Matter, and Unborn Lives Matter, individuals appropriated the hashtag #SayHerName in reference to Babbitt.[29] #SayHerName is a popular hashtag first used by members of the Black Lives Matter social movement to memorialize Black women who were murdered by police such as Sandra Bland, Alberta Spruill, Rekia Boyd, Shantel Davis, Shelly Frey, Kayla Moore, Breonna Taylor, Kyam Livingston, Miriam Carey, Michelle Cusseaux, and Tanisha Anderson among too many others. Mary C. Burke and Mary Bernstein (2014) find that the conservative right also hijacked aspects of the queer agenda through what they term "frame co-optation" or the appropriation of a social movement's rhetoric to serve an ideologically detergent cause.[30] A similar type of frame co-optation is clearly used in the case of Babbitt and the #SayHerName hashtag. Unlike Babbitt, a White cisgender woman who decided to disregard the law and died from a single gunshot wound sustained while breaking into a window in the Speaker's Lobby of the US Capitol, #SayHerName calls for the remembrance of victims of systemic and state-sanctioned violence. Babbitt was shot in the act of treason, an attempt to literally overthrow the US government, while also vandalizing federal property.

Any analysis of the hashtag must preface the original intent of #SayHerName. When studying racial power, specifically the "mechanisms and sites of racial domination and subordination," Margaret L. Anderson (2003) cautions scholars not to "analyz[e] whiteness" while forgetting the "experience of people of color."[31] Founded in December 2014, #SayHerName refers to a campaign:

> Launched . . . by the African American Policy Forum (AAPF) and Center for Intersectionality and Social Policy Studies (CISPS), the #SayHerName campaign brings awareness to the often-invisible names and stories of Black

---

29. Later in this chapter I study Twitter discourse related to the #SayHerName hashtag and Babbitt.
30. Burke and Bernstein, "How the Right Usurped the Queer Agenda," 184.
31. Anderson, "Whitewashing Race," 28, 21.

women and girls who have been victimized by racist police violence, and provides support to their families.[32]

Kimberlé Crenshaw, cofounder and executive director of the African American Policy Forum, told National Public Radio (NPR) that the #SayHerName campaign is a part of the broader Black Lives Matter movement and raises awareness regarding the systemic and state-sanctioned violence against women, girls, and femme-presenting individuals:

> Black women have been killed in many of the same circumstances as their brothers, fathers and sons. They've been killed driving while Black, being in their homes while Black, having mental crises while Black and their losses just haven't registered in the same way. So Say Her Name is trying to raise awareness by insisting that we say their names because if we can say their names we can know more about their stories.[33]

Babbitt was a trained solider—specifically trained to stop violence against the US Capitol.[34] Other than her death by a police officer and her gender identity, Babbitt does not share any similarities with the victims commemorated by the #SayHerName campaign. Babbitt's story is one of presumed entitlement that enabled her to break the law and commit acts of violence against the state without the fear of retribution—White privilege. White privilege includes the ways that White-passing individuals benefit from structural and systemic inequalities because of their socially assigned racial identity.[35] In this example, the presumption that one can violate federal law without a fear of reciprocal police violence is a luxury of a White way of viewing and living in the world, what Joe Feagin terms a "white racial frame," that is diametrically opposed to the lived experiences of many Black and Brown individuals.

On the day before her death, Babbitt tweeted: "Nothing will stop us. . . . They can try and try and try but the storm is here and it is descending upon DC in less than 24 hours . . . dark to light."[36] Babbitt's tweet, reminiscent of calls for a military assault on a foreign nation, referred to protests surrounding the certification of Joseph Biden's presidential win against Donald Trump on January 6, 2021. At this time, Babbitt's social media presence was

---

32. "SAY HER NAME."
33. Kelly and Glenn, "Say Her Name."
34. Barry, Bogel-Burroughs, and Philipps, "Woman Killed in Capitol."
35. For a further discussion about the differences between asserted and assigned racial and ethnic identities, please see Cornell and Hartmann, *Ethnicity and Race*.
36. Eustachewich, "Ashli Babbitt, Killed in Capitol."

peppered with hopeful messages about the outcome of the January 6, 2021, protests along with admonishments of several Californian Democratic politicians like Maxine Watters.[37] Responding to a tweet that read, "When do we start winning," Babbitt replied, "Jan 6, 2021."[38] Throughout her social media posts she included numerous videos where she yelled into her cell phone and bemoaned politicians who, in her view, put immigrants first above Americans. On social media, Babbitt made clear she was eager to enter violent combat for her beliefs.[39] Joining those who violently broke past US Capitol police and barricades, Babbitt forced herself into the Capitol building.[40] Like some of the other Americans who committed treason against the United States on that day, Babbitt was a US Air Force veteran who served fourteen years in the military, was a combat veteran in both Afghanistan and Iraq, and served in the Air Force Reserves and the Air National Guard. While a member of the Guard, she served near Washington, DC, as a "Capitol Guardian" whose "primary mission . . . is defending the city. Security forces in the squadron regularly train with riot shields and clubs for what the Air Force calls 'civil disturbance missions'"; Babbitt was trained to stop the very violence against the US government that she now supported and actively engaged in. Although she grew up apolitical, Babbitt wore a Trump flag wrapped around her neck like a cape[41] as she was lifted by two men through a broken window into the Speaker's Lobby in the Chamber of the House of Representatives. As Babbitt attempted to enter the broken window, she was struck on the left shoulder,[42] or upper neck,[43] by a single bullet fired by a Capitol police officer. Babbitt later died of her gunshot wound at Washington Hospital Center. The United States Department of Justice investigated Babbitt's death; specifically, "the focus of the criminal investigation was to determine whether federal prosecutors could prove that the officer violated any federal laws, concentrating on the possible application of 18 U.S.C. § 242, a federal criminal civil rights statute." In a press release dated April 14, 2021, "the investigation revealed no evidence to establish that . . . the officer did not reasonably believe that it was necessary to do so in self-defense or in defense of the Members of Congress and oth-

---

37. Eustachewich. Babbitt's social media posts often criticize Gov. Jerry Brown, Gov. Gavin Newsom, Rep. Maxine Waters, Sen. Kamala Harris, and former Rep. Duncan Hunter. Hunter is the only Republican in this list; he was convicted of stealing campaign funds but was pardoned by President Trump.
38. Barry, Bogel-Burroughs, and Philipps, "Woman Killed in Capitol."
39. Eustachewich, "Ashli Babbitt, Killed in Capitol."
40. "Department of Justice Closes Investigation."
41. Barry, Bogel-Burroughs, and Philipps, "Woman Killed in Capitol."
42. Jones, "Officer Cleared."
43. Swain et al., "Video Shows Fatal Shooting."

ers evacuating the House Chamber,"[44] thereby exonerating the officer, whose name was never officially released, of any accountability in Babbitt's death.[45]

Echoing her own fervent social media posts supporting far-right causes like QAnon, anti-immigrant platforms, and pro-Trump conspiracy theories, social media erupted following the Department of Justice press release so much so that, even two weeks after the ruling, individuals online were still tweeting, sharing, and posting about the verdict. These tweets are arguably more impactful to public discourse than her earlier social media posts as they follow her posthumous rise as a public figure and martyr for the far-right causes noted earlier that she embraced in life. On April 28, 2021, a Twitter search of the #AshliBabbitt hashtag found a social media debate overwhelmingly in support of Babbitt—tweeters called for justice or fairness for the dead veteran in the form of holding the US Capitol officer accountable for her death or claimed that she was simply murdered. Of the 63 tweets that appeared as the result of the search, only a single tweet accused Babbitt of any wrongdoing, specifically "treason"—and this tweet was in reply to another tweet in support of Babbitt's cause. Rather than being a figure of both conservative and liberal debates, #AshliBabbitt appeared relevant on Twitter only to those who subscribed to similar ideologies that Babbitt held when she was alive, allowing her death to become a rallying cry behind which similarly aligned individuals could claim victimization at the hands of the so-called liberal media and state.

Of the surveyed tweets, 6 were by news organizations reporting updates on the story, and 4 posts were retweets of news organizations with no editorial commentary; it should be noted that the only news outlet that shared original posts about Babbitt was a right-leaning outlet, and the retweets of stories were often from mainstream media outlets like MSNBC. Although the #SayHerName hashtag was popular immediately following Babbitt's death, a total of 3 tweets were accompanied by #SayHerName two weeks after the Department of Justice verdict. Ten tweets rhetorically asked "who killed her?" thereby demanding the name of the US Capitol officer. Seventeen tweets demanded fairness or justice for Babbitt—often citing a civil lawsuit Babbitt's family took out against the officer who shot her—and/or calls to remember Babbitt as a patriot. Eighteen tweets claimed that Babbitt was murdered, executed, or "killed" after being "peaceful" or "unarmed"; some of these tweets also asked, rhetorically, who had killed Babbitt. Seven of the aforementioned tweets—in addition to calls for someone to face charges for the death of Babbitt—also claimed that Babbitt was killed by a Black officer, implying that race was the

---

44. "Department of Justice Closes Investigation."
45. Babbitt's family is currently suing the US Capital Police in civil court for her death.

reason the officer was acquitted and their name not released to the general public. This significant framing overtly highlights a perceived White victimhood at the hands of Black Americans.[46] Ironically, however, these predictable racist calls of Black criminality by White-allied communities similarly show a *lack of support* for law enforcement—only when the police officer is supposedly not White.

The co-optation of the hashtag say his, her, or their, name is a popular tactic to direct discussions away from issues of social justice and toward individual acts of horrendous violence. Of note, the co-optation of this hashtag is used to emphasize the victimhood of individuals who often cannot protect themselves. All deaths, particularly those of children, are tragic, yet events can be taken out of context and used in a wider deflective claim. This can be seen in the strategic use of the innocence and victimhood of White children to misdirect discussions of systemic racism toward an individual act of violence that happened to be committed by a person of color. This is a common rhetorical tool of White deflection that emphasizes the feminization of childhood/child rearing. For instance, on Sunday, August 9, 2020, a five-year-old boy named Cannon Hinnant was playing with his sisters, aged seven and eight, in their yard in North Carolina. At around 5:30 p.m., Hinnant was senselessly shot in the head at point blank range by his twenty-five-year-old neighbor Darius Sessoms. Sessoms, a Black man, was immediately arrested and charged with first-degree murder. Hinnant died later that day in the hospital. Although this story did receive national media attention on outlets like the *Washington Post,* the *New York Post,* NBC's Today Show, Yahoo, and CNN, among others, conservatives responded with backlash, memes critiquing the supposed lack of national coverage, and with the hashtag #sayhisname as a critique of a lack of liberal media coverage. The *Daily Wire,* which defines itself as "one of America's fastest-growing conservative media companies and counter-cultural outlets for news, opinion, and entertainment," posted an editorial about Hinnant's murder. The content of Matt Walsh's editorial was summed up succinctly it its title "National Media Refuse to Cover Murder of 5-Year-Old Because It Doesn't Fit Their Racial Narrative"—the supposedly truthful racial narrative being that all Black men can be prone to unforeseen violence, like that of Sessoms. Memes also populated social media commenting on the supposed lack of public outrage. One included a black-and-white picture of a twenty-something White man with his hands over his mouth and read: "White on Brown Crimes = Hate Crimes / Brown on White Crimes = Hush Crimes." Another popular meme included the images of Officer Derek Chauvin next to

---

46. Three tweets surveyed were unrelated to the controversy.

an image of George Floyd at the top and photographs of Hinnant and Sessoms at the bottom; the two White individuals, Hinnant and Chauvin, were on the left of the meme, and Floyd and Sessoms were on the right of the meme. On May 25, 2020, Minneapolis Police Officer Chauvin kneeled on Floyd's neck for eight minutes, killing him. These photographs were overlaid with the large white wording, in capital letters, reading "National Attention" over the images of Chauvin and Floyd. The word "VS" was put in the middle of all four images, with the text "Not Gonna Mention What Happened Media? You Suddenly Got So Quiet" written over the images of the young Hinnant and Sessoms.

Again, the life of George Floyd and others who died at the hands of police are positioned by the editorial and memes as ungrieveable. These two murders are also taken out of context; they simply are not similar situations. Chauvin was not immediately arrested or charged with the murder of Floyd, whereas Sessoms was immediately arrested and incarcerated. Floyd was murdered by a representative of the state who was supposed to protect innocent people, like Floyd. Hinnant was murdered by a neighbor in a horrific act of violence. The innocence of a young child and horrific nature of Hinnant's murder, as well as a misrepresentation of national media coverage of it, is used to support a racist, White-allied argument that Black men are inherently violent and that Black Lives Matter supporters are somehow hypocrites. In fact, this is yet another example of a lack of communicative understanding; it assumes Black Lives Matter activists are concerned, primarily, with individual assailants outside of the law, rather than those supported by the law. It is a racist dog whistle appealing to White-allied communities that use a fear of Black men to justify White supremacy. It is a rhetorical deflection that deliberately confuses state-sanctioned murder without immediate consequences with an individual, tragic act of violence. In the case of Babbitt, her acts of violence against the US capitol are ignored. Whites are positioned as victims, and those engaged in Black identity politics are faulted. Emphasis is placed on the vulnerability of Whiteness, as well as the neoliberal move to humanize and individualize manifestations of hard power—the military, corrections officers, the police.

Similar to the social media response to Babbitt's death, Gina Carano's career and social media use became a popular touchpoint for White-allied conservative communities who claim victimization. Carano is an actor known for her roles in action films like *Deadpool* and *Fast and Furious 6*, as well as her previous professional careers as a fitness model and mixed-martial artist. The actor is also an outspoken conservative whose social media posts include provocative pronouncements such as posts mocking individuals wearing masks during the Covid-19 pandemic, sharing a meme with the hidden message "Jeffery Epstein didn't kill himself," and promoting the discredited claim that the 2020 presidential election was rigged by election fraud.[47] These provocative social media posts gained the ire of those who resented a popular celebrity's endorsement of false conspiracy theories that legitimated the siege on the US Capitol and harmful antiscientific statements that berated mask-wearing in the middle of a global pandemic.

According to Google Trends, the hashtag #FireGinaCarano reached peak popularity across social media at three times from late 2020 to early 2021, each trend reflecting a separate media controversy spurred by the actor's social media presence. In September 2020, Carano used the words "beep/bop/boop" in her Twitter biography in lieu of gender pronouns; a gesture that many viewed as openly ridiculing the trans community and blatantly homophobic. Responding to this negative media attention, and further igniting the controversy, the actor posted the following unapologetic tweet on September 14:

> Beep/bop/boop has zero to do with mocking trans people ♡ & 💯 to do with exposing the bullying mentality of the mob that has taken over the voices of many genuine causes. I want people to know you can take hate with a smile. So BOOP you for misunderstanding. 😊 #AllLoveNoHate.[48]

Carano eventually deleted the derivative pronouns—but also asserted that she would not share her own pronouns in her profile—after a conversation with her former Disney costar, Pedro Pascal, whose sister, Lux, is a Chilean-American transgender activist.[49] After this controversy met widespread media attention November 15–22, 2020, #FireGinaCarano reached a peak trend in popularity across the internet.

Spurred by yet more controversial social media posts and in the immediate wake of the riot at the US Capitol, #FireGinaCarano remained a top trending hashtag across social media January 10–30, 2021. The hashtag reached its zenith in popularity February 7–13, 2021, when Lucasfilm, the production company that employed Carano, was compelled to act. On February 10, 2021, Disney fired Carano from her role as Cara Dune on the show "The Mandalorian" after a sequence of anti-Semitic Instagram and social media posts.[50] Carano posted an image of a woman in undergarments apparently fleeing children as she ran down a street covered in rubble, perhaps from a bombing, with the accompanied text: "Jews were beaten in the streets, not by Nazi soldiers but by their neighbors . . . even by children, 'Because history is edited,

---

47. Moreau, "'Mandalorian' Star Gina Carano under Fire."
48. Carano, "Beep/Bop/Boop."
49. Langmann, "Gina Carano's 'The Mandalorian' Controversy."
50. "Mandalorian Star Gina Carano."

most people today don't realize that to get to the point where Nazi soldiers could easily round up thousands of Jews, the government first made their own neighbors hate them simply for being Jews.'" This tweet was followed by one reading "Meanwhile in California . . ." with the image of a person wearing a mask.[51] The succession of these tweets, along with their tandem deletion by Carano, horrifically linked being a conservative in the United States today to being a persecuted Jew during the Holocaust. Waving a flag of victimization, these abhorrent Instagram posts likened *critiques of positions* she holds, namely antimasking, with the *genocide* of Jews by the Nazis during World War II. Such a callous analogy supports both White supremacy and its strategy of Holocaust denial through obscene minimization. Lucasfilm, the producer of the hit streaming series "The Mandalorian" for Disney+, released a statement attributing Carano's firing to her social media posts:

> Gina Carano is not currently employed by Lucasfilm and there are no plans for her to be in the future. Nevertheless, her social media posts denigrating people based on their cultural and religious identities are abhorrent and unacceptable.

Shortly after Carano was fired from Lucasfilm, she was similarly let go by her talent agency UTA.[52] In response to the fallout from her social media post, Carano wrote on Instagram that her post was

> inspired by the gentle spirit of the Jewish people going through that time. . . . When I posted that it wasn't something that I felt was controversial. It was something that I thought, well, maybe all of us need to ask ourselves how that happened. I've got every single big publication saying she's comparing conservatives and Republicans to this and that's not really what I was doing. . . . I have love for everyone. I'm not a hateful person.[53]

Many individuals empathized and believed Carano's claims that her post was not anti-Semitic and was misunderstood by the mainstream media.

What is perhaps the most telling of national sentiment is the response on social media that erupted after the firing. Following this controversy, Carano's fans shared notes of support with the hashtags #CancelDisney, #WeLoveGinaCarano, #IStandwithGinaCarano, and #WeLoveCaraDune; during the week of April 19, 2021, #WeLoveGinaCarano was a trending hashtag under the

---

51. Langmann, "Gina Carano's 'The Mandalorian' Controversy."
52. "Mandalorian Star Gina Carano."
53. Bisset, "Disney Includes Gina Carano."

politics section on Twitter. In fact, Carano saw a partisan boost to her career, announcing within days of her termination that she would star in a film backed by conservative political commentator, practicing Orthodox Jew, and editor emeritus of the *Daily Wire* Ben Shapiro.[54] The actor released a statement about the project to the *Daily Wire*—part of the company's future entertainment ventures is to partner with Dallas Sonnier and his production company, Bonfire Legend, to help Carano develop and produce her own film. Refusing politically correct language, Carano told the conservative media company,

> The *Daily Wire* is helping make one of my dreams—to develop and produce my own film—come true. I cried out and my prayer was answered. . . . I am sending out a direct message of hope to everyone living in fear of cancellation by the totalitarian mob. I have only just begun using my voice which is now freer than ever before, and I hope it inspires others to do the same. They can't cancel us if we don't let them.[55]

This film will be available only to members of the *Daily Wire,* and the article announcing the venture offered new members a 25 percent discount on membership with the promotional code "Gina." Reflecting on the collaboration, Shapiro did not engage with accusations of Carano's anti-Jewish racism. Rather, Shapiro celebrated:

> We could not be more excited to be working with Gina Carano, an incredible talent dumped by Disney and Lucasfilm for offending the authoritarian Hollywood Left. This is what Daily Wire exists to do: provide an alternative not just for consumers, but for creators who refuse to bow to the mob. . . . We're eager to bring Gina's talent to Americans who love her, and we're just as eager to show Hollywood that if they want to keep cancelling those who think differently, they'll just be helping us build the X-wing to take down their Death Star. . . . Social movements have consequences, and we are now in the middle of a mass social movement to expel half of the American population from the body politic.[56]

In attempts to defy so-called "cancel culture" and social movements that strive for gender and racial equity, Carano received support from social media and the *Daily Wire* that allowed her to harness her so-called victimhood, or can-

---

54. Pearce, "Gina Carano to Produce and Star."
55. Pearce.
56. Pearce.

celled status, and turn herself into a transmedia celebrity for conservative causes.

The true extent of Carano's banishment from a career in mainstream Hollywood, and from Disney specifically, is evolving and a point of serious debate. Despite Lucasfilm supposedly parting ways with Carano, it included the actor on its Emmy Awards "for your consideration" list for the best supporting actress category for "The Mandalorian."[57] After the corporation decided to part ways with the star, Disney ostensibly went back on its word deciding to air an episode of "Running Wild with Bear Grylls" featuring Carano on the National Geographic Channel (owned by Disney) on Monday, May 10, 2021.[58] At the time of this writing, Carano's future partnerships with Disney are unclear; however, it does not appear that Disney, and their subsidiary Lucasfilm, cut all ties with the actor.

This analysis highlights the performative nature of hegemonic masculinity through mapping its presentation outside of the cisgender-male body. Carano and Babbitt embody the masculine subjectivities of warriors who lack adherence to politically correct discourse. The social media posts of both of these women decry topics that include democratic agendas, immigration, science, and trans rights, and do so through embodying a dominant rhetorical hegemonic masculinity that seeks to manipulate others through curt and offensive posts. Although the ends Carano and Babbitt met are different, audiences utilized their respective downfalls in rhetorically similar ways. Babbitt's death and Carano's termination as Cara Dune by Lucasfilm were both used as symbolic—and literal—examples of martyrdom for the conservative cause. In the case of Carano and the apparent backtracking of Disney and Lucasfilm on their pronouncements to part ways with the actor, it seems that—in life—the controversy may have actually boosted her notoriety and career. At the time of this writing Carano's future career prospects are still officially unresolved, yet it appears that Carano's social media may have helped—rather than hurt—her acting career. This suggests a conservative audience that has significant financial sway over ostensibly liberal-leaning Hollywood. Although their public personas reinforced hegemonic masculinity and toxic tropes of femininity, their representation as literal and figurative victims of the ideological left allowed each woman to become a martyr for far-right agendas—a suitable feminized victim of so-called cancel culture. The next section explores how the performance of feminized militant victimhood is used as a framing mechanism to shape discussions surrounding critical race theory. In chapter 1

---

57. Bisset, "Disney Includes Gina Carano."
58. Cooper, "What TV to Watch."

of this book, I found that militant victimhood was a common framing mechanism of the Blue Lives Matter movement and media company. As a framing mechanism of White discourse, the next section explores how this framework can be femininized.

Feminized Militant Victimhood

Media framing refers to a repeated emphasis within media coverage that influences an audience's opinions and critical thinking skills. Media framing has an influence on White macropartisanship,[59] or political identifications, as well as stereotypes about historically marginalized communities.[60] Using a mixed-methods approach including content analysis and critical discourse analysis, in chapter 1 I found the Blue Lives Matter media company used the frame of militant victimhood to curate its online media coverage, particularly its use of social media like Twitter. Militant victimhood is a colorblind frame of White identity politics where an aggrieved status is stressed, while asserting a militant and masculine sense of defiance. In the previous chapter, I studied rhetoric focusing on masculine personas who claimed allegiance to the US armed forces, as well as a media company founded to represent the interests of law enforcement officers including ICE agents, the police, and corrections officers.

Frequently within Whiteness studies literature, there is a focus on White male pain or victimhood; this focus is significant and important. Indeed, I add to these discussions in this book, but masculine rhetoric also is supported and maintained by cisgender women. I'm interested in how cisgender women embody similar rhetoric, but their feminized subjectivity, from a heterosexist standpoint, makes them simultaneously in need of White patriarchal support. This creates a recursive structure of victimhood that reinforces hegemonic gender roles, heterosexism, and White rhetoric while the aggrieved status is transferred to a feminized orator. This section also follows Jack Halberstam's call to study masculinity outside of the White male body.[61] In so doing, I'm interested in how news media organizations shape coverage of racially charged topics using the framing mechanism of militant victimhood, but delivered from a feminized subjectivity. As my examples below show, these feminized orators commit acts of discursive violence when claiming victimhood not for themselves, but for their own or the nation's children. I'm concerned with how

---

59. Abrajano, Hajnal, and Hassel, "Media Framing and Partisan Identity," 7–8.
60. Hall, "Spectacle of the 'Other'"; Shohat and Stam, *Unthinking Eurocentrism*.
61. Halberstam, *Female Masculinity*.

cisgender women's voices are elevated in media coverage of these topics, and to what ends.

This section uses critical discourse to evaluate examples of a *feminized* militant victimhood frame observed in media coverage filtered through social media. To locate examples, I searched Twitter for official pages with blue check marks of media personalities sharing content they created with larger media outlets. I then chose to analyze examples that fit the framework I identified in chapter 1, but from a feminized subjectivity. Feminization refers to individuals embodying characteristics that are largely stereotyped as female.[62] Scholars write that feminized rhetoric often means a focus on female perspectives and ways of knowing; such writings challenge narratives of history that are male dominated,[63] or male-centric, in a way that centers women's voices.[64] Heteronormative understandings of feminization focus on biological cisgender women and their "natural" reproductive and child-rearing abilities. Adhering to this traditional trope of a female character, in the field of education, a feminized pedagogy of rhetoric can be considered youth centered, participatory, and nurturing.[65] The personal essay and personal writing in general has been thought of as women's genres[66] as they emphasize emotion, personal experience, and the view that the personal is political. Whether from the right or left, a rhetoric that is feminized is sometimes dismissed as overly emotional and lacking clarity of opinion. The use of personal experience as a means to feminize discourse is particularly compelling as, in the case of my previous discussion of the militant victimhood frame, male-coded orators focus on objectivity and impartiality as keys to journalism—a focus on the science of good journalism, while serendipitously framing media content in a formulaic way. As I will explore, the use of first-person experience and childhood is a common strategy used to feminize militant victimhood. This process of feminization elevates the victimization inherent in the militant victimhood frame to a position outside of the individual, to our collective future—children. This ostensible selflessness makes feminized applications of the militant victimhood framework particularly persuasive.

Similar to feminized, the terms of "militant and masculine" should be understood rhetorically. Race and gender are learned cultural behaviors and, as such, individuals of any racial or gendered identity can engage in gendered discourse seemingly opposed to their subject position. As discussed in the

---

62. Fondas, "Feminization Unveiled," 258.
63. Biesecker, "Negotiating with Our Tradition," 238.
64. Fondas, "Feminization Unveiled," 257.
65. Lauer, "Feminization of Rhetoric and Composition Studies?"
66. Bordelon, "Contradicting and Complicating Feminization," 103.

previous chapter, "emotional illiteracy" is a characterization of both White supremacist and masculine discourses.[67] Masculine discourse includes performances of anger, egotism, fear, competition, and violence.[68] As a rhetorical presentation, militant victimhood can—and frequently is—feminized through a connection to female orators, or through discourse about child-rearing. This feminization of the masculine victimhood frame upholds hegemonic notions of femininity, masculinity, and heterosexism, and, in effect, seeks to make the masculine victimhood frame *authentic and beyond challenge* through gendered, racialized, and age-specific tokenism. As a study of framing mechanisms, I am less concerned with the individual intent of orators than in the ways that news corporations elevate these feminized and racialized voices to shape national debates.

Since the 1980s, the so-called culture wars have shaped political discourses and macropartisanship identifications. Contemporary cultural debates include whether critical race theory—or a systemic view of race and racism—should be taught in elementary schools. Founded in law schools in the late 1970s and 1980s by intellectuals like Derrick Bell, Kimberlé Crenshaw, and Richard Delgado, this academic field helps to explain existing structural inequities between historically marginalized communities and Whites. Critical race theory is a type of academic scholarship, often taught at the postsecondary level, that evaluates the historic impact of systemic racism on communities today. Based on the examples found for this chapter, news coverage of this current episode in the culture wars rarely defines *how* a postgraduate law school curriculum directly translates to elementary school pedagogy. Indeed, there appears to be a disconnect between liberal and conservative understanding of what critical race theory really means.

At its core, critical race theory focuses on the social construction of race—that is, how institutions systemically reproduce inequality. Conservative opponents emphasize a very neoliberal, individualistic understanding of the field—focusing on how terms like "oppressive" or "systemic racism" can be (mis)understood by children as implicating them as perpetually marginalized or as an oppressor of others. A focus on individualism is central to colorblindness, or the belief that race is no longer a useful category of analysis and that to see race then makes one racist. Frequently, proponents of colorblindness will point toward exceptional individuals who have accomplished extraordinary feats as a way to prove that systemic inequality is simply liberal jargon. From this point of view, everyone begins life from the same relative

---

67. Cabrera, *White Guys on Campus*, 109.
68. Noel, "White Female Pain."

starting position, and through hard work and personal responsibility, anyone can be exceptional. From the standpoint of a critical race theorist, a focus on individualism works to obscure the systematic exclusion of historically marginalized communities under racial capitalism. In this rationale, focusing on exceptional individuals as the rule, rather than the exception, is a tool of oppression, as it overlooks the structural impediments that impact other marginalized communities and casts their lack of similar success as individual faults and failings. Simply put, from the standpoint of critical race theory, due to region, race, class, gender, and other factors, not everyone starts out in life at the same relative starting position—economic and career success is easier for some to attain over others. As long as debates revolve around individualistic versus collectivist arguments, the right and left will never agree on what critical race theory represents.

Candace Owens and Ambassador Nikki Haley, two well-known conservative Republican politicians and women of color, are outspoken critics of critical race theory. Conservative media outlets like the *Daily Wire* and *Fox News* have elevated the voices of Owens and Haylee; both commenters have since retweeted their statements to news outlets about critical race theory on their official Twitter accounts. These conservative media outlets' reliance on the expertise of women of color to frame the debate around critical race theory is clearly not a colorblind approach. This strategy of dominant discourse is common, as Lisa A. Flores (2016) finds:

> In their attention to dominant cultural, legal, and political texts, racial rhetorical scholars have centered the public figurations of race, noting how racially marked bodies are consistently made to do the cultural and political work of racism. In other words, dominant discourse typically and easily invokes race through figurations of raced bodies.[69]

In doing the "cultural and political work of racism," Owens and Haley are each making race-neutral arguments about public school education, serving as the race experts for conservative, largely White, audiences. The posts suggest that if children are knowledgeable about race and racism, they will internalize these ideas as self-implicating—that they are oppressors and bad people—and it will impact their emotional and psychosocial development. White discourse endeavors to maintain status. Similar to masculine rhetoric, White rhetoric is also interested in rhetorical domination but on racial, rather than gendered,

---

69. Flores, "Between Abundance and Marginalization," 13.

terms. Therefore, as a rhetorical construction, anyone—regardless of subjectivity—can contribute to the discourse of dominance.

In my analysis, I am focusing on information shared in tweets by Owens and Haley respectively, and the corporate content that they directly link to within their posts. This content is curated, with provocative language and key soundbites emphasized, and is easily accessed without a paywall. Candace Owens identifies as a Black author and a cisgender woman who has a show on the conservative media outlet the *Daily Wire,* called "Candace." Owens is well known as the founder of the Blexit movement, or the Black exit from the Democratic party to the Republican party. The *Daily Wire* dominates social media engagement, particularly Facebook, making posts reshared by this media outlet particularly impactful. In fact, using sensational rhetoric meant to "outrage" is a strategy for conservative news outlets that frequently use provocative titles to drum up social media followings, particularly on Facebook. NPR's Miles Parks (2021) reported that, based on data analysis by NPR of data gathered by the media intelligence company NewsWhip, "In May [2021], the *Daily Wire* generated more Facebook engagement on its articles than the *New York Times,* the *Washington Post,* NBC News and CNN combined." Parks finds that the *Daily Wire,* along with other conservative media platforms, domination of Facebook "may also undermine conservatives' oft-repeated claims that the social media network has an anti-conservative bias."[70]

On July 10, 2021, the Twitter page for Owens's show, @thecandaceshow, released a short thirty-two-second video montage advertising episode 16, "Our Children Are Under Attack," of her talk show podcast. The text accompanying the advertising video reads "Need something to watch this weekend? We got you covered! Don't miss Episode 16 where @realcandaceo reminds us that WE are the parents, not the government! Watch over at @realDailyWire!" Also on July 10, 2021, Owens (@RealCandaceO) retweeted the post adding the additional text: "Use my code "Trust the science" to get 20% of [*sic*] your new membership at dailywire.com/subscribe." Despite the discount code advertising a belief in science, the video included within the tweet focuses on attacking critical race theory and liberal ideological beliefs. The video begins with Owens in a tan suit looking into the camera as she warns: "The public school system is not free. It is costing you your child's mind." The words "THEN EDUCATION OR INDOCTRINATION?" in all capital letters comes over screen, then the image returns to Owens who cautions her audience, "They're teaching critical race theory, which is really just teaching your children how to be racist. They're teaching equitable math, which is teaching your children

---

70. Parks, "Outrage as a Business Model."

how to be stupid. Kids these days are apparently being read stories about abortion." At this point the video transitions to Owens's guest Rogan O'Handley, a White man who is identified as a lawyer and conservative activist who offers a carnivorous analogy of what it is like for a child to read a story about an abortion: "To me it's like writing a book for a turkey and telling them why Thanksgiving is a good thing. I mean it's evil, down to its core." The video ends, returning to Owens, who summarizes: "The government is not the parent. WE ARE."

On the *Daily Wire*'s website advertising this linked episode,[71] the webpage includes a montage advertisement with a large close-up picture of Owens pointing her finger at a Black male Black Lives Matter activist with his fist raised with a "BLM" flag behind him. The montage also includes a White woman with a cricket bat in her hand with the letters "CRT," or critical race theory, on it, as well as a blackboard behind her with the wording "Porn Literacy 101." The text accompanying the image does not actually mention critical race theory, but does relate back to the discount code referencing science. The paragraph explaining the content of the episode makes the connection to science, specifically of vaccinations, clearer:

> Host Candace Owens is joined by Spencer Klaven, Rogan O'Handley and Brandon Tatum to discuss vaccine propaganda, the Free Britney movement, and an anti-violence guide released by an American university. Plus, Candace sits down with the founder of Operation Underground Railroad, Tim Ballard, to discuss how he's changing the world by rescuing children from sex slavery and sexual exploitation.

With an introductory video focused on protecting future generations of young conservatives from liberal ideologies, the information presented in Owens's posts and on the *Daily Wire* conflates sexual violence toward children, pornography, and children's books about abortion with critical race theory. The media is marketed toward an echo chamber invested in distrusting critical race theory, and linking it with violence towards children, notably sexual violence, is an easy way to accomplish this task.

From an uninformed perspective, there is no clear definition of what critical race theory actually is in Owens's post. There is no clear definition of what many topics mean—like equitable math—and this seems to be a rhetorical strategy; the repeated use of buzz words to garner a militant affect without

---

71. For a link to this episode, please see https://www.dailywire.com/episode/episode-16-our-children-are-under-attack.

greater context. From abortion, to education, to gun reform, to vaccine science, to pornography in schools, to child sex trafficking, to Britney Spears's conservatorship, Owens's podcast seems to mention nearly every conservative rallying cry. Through framing these disparate topics together—all topics that conservatives decry—there is an insinuation that critical race theory, somehow, is an ideology that connects all of these topics. The brief video and accompanying links present the militant victimhood frame; it is a conservative call to action to change the future of US public education based on a fear of what liberal ideologies, like critical race theory, might do to US children. This frame is feminized through its focus on childhood, defending White women like Britney Spears, and, from a colorblind standpoint, the delivery by Owens affirms that the content cannot be racist as her understanding of race is based on personal experience. Moreover, her nurturing feminized subjectivity is direct and confrontational, similar to other militant rhetorical framing discussed in chapter 1.

Owens's post and its accompanying links are not alone in advertising a distain for critical race theory. On July 7, 2021, former UN Ambassador Nikki Haley (@NikkiHaley) also tweeted her thoughts on critical race theory. In her tweet, Haley shared her opinion based on her parents' advice and her experience:

> Critical race theory is going to hold back generations of young people. My parents always taught us to focus on what brings us together not sets us apart.
>
> America should be united around shared values, not divided by different shades of color.

Haley's post is declarative and strong in its chastisement of critical race theory, yet it foregoes much of the bombastic presentation of random, seemingly unrelated information, that Owens's advertises for her listeners. Instead, Haley assumes a personal and empathetic stance where she relies on family values and inherited ideas about belonging to inform her opinions. Following this tweet, on July 13, 2021, Haley tweeted again about the topic saying: "Every governor in the country should ban funding for critical race theory. Period." Accompanying the text was a link to a Fox News interview where Haley explains her position. The edited interview segment details Haley's exchange with the Fox show "America Reports." In it, Haley comments that critical race theory does not need to be taught to elementary students in the same way that it is taught to college-level students; she calls on "every governor in the country" to ban critical race theory because of its "long-lasting effects on children." The idea that an academic curriculum could be interchangeably taught at the elementary and college level is ridiculous. Without clearly defining what critical race theory at the elementary level versus college level would look like, Haley explains her rationale: "Think about a 5-year-old that starts kindergarten and they don't know anything about color. If she's White, you're telling her she's bad. If she's Brown or Black, you're telling her she will never be enough and she's always a victim. That's harmful for the well-being of our children." Similar to Owens, critical race theory is being used out of context and in an individualized way. As a woman of color growing up in rural South Carolina, Haley reflects on her own experience as a testament to why teaching children about systemic racial bias is wrong: "I remember getting teased when I was younger in rural South Carolina and my mom would say, 'Your job is to show them how you're similar and not how you're different.'" She suggests that it is the work of those individuals who are the victims of prejudice to take it upon themselves to educate racists about how "similar" they are to Whites. This assimilationist mindset clearly supports the status quo while leveraging personal experience from a position of a highly successful and exceptional women.

Haley then explains a course of action for stopping the instruction of critical race theory in elementary schools:

> Every governor in the country needs to ban funding for critical race theory. Governors can decide this. They decide what money they take from the Department of Education. Don't take this money.... They don't need to be told what label they are when they walk in the school. We need to treat kids as the opportunities they're going to be to fix America, not break them before they start.[72]

Relying on personal narrative and discussions of nurturing children, Haley takes a firm yet femininized position on critical race theory. Similar to Owens's advertisement, this interview with Fox News is brief and includes Haley's opinions. Neither Haley nor Owens take the time to explain what critical race theory is, nor how and why it might be taught at the elementary level. Indeed, critical race theory is often misused by media outlets like Fox News, by activists, and by parents. According to a survey done by NBC News of about 165 local and national groups aimed at stopping critical race theory being taught at the K–12 level,

---

72. Nelson, "America to Ban Funding."

Virtually all school districts [in the United States] insist they are not teaching critical race theory, but many activists and parents have begun using it as a catch-all term to refer to what schools often call equity programs, teaching about racism or LGBTQ-inclusive policies.[73]

Each presentation of critical race theory relies on buzz words and a misunderstanding of the field; it is used to foreground conservative victimhood in liberal excesses in education and to incite outrage. The repetition of the misuse of critical race theory has become a rallying cry for conservative causes; yet, there is no clear engagement with the intent or ideologies put forth by the diverse academic field. If, according to NBC News, critical race theory is just a catch-all term for education that teaches the inclusion of diverse groups, the attack on critical race theory tells us much more about conserve tactics than it does about the application of critical race theory at the elementary and high school levels. By delivering opposition to critical race theory using women of color, the *Daily Wire* and Fox News show the illusion of inclusion of historically marginalized communities as experts. Yet, as the cases of the posts by Owens and Haley show, membership in historically marginalized communities does not automatically guarantee an understanding of a complex and extensive academic field. People of color are often pointed to by Whites as experts in race *because they have experienced it,* as if Whites are not also racialized.[74] Such presentation gives a façade of inclusion to racial tokenism.

Performing a Rhetoric of Dominance

White rhetoric is strategically invested in dominance. Through mapping discursive violence, we can better understand how White rhetoric and hegemonic masculinity and femininity rely on one another in the service of maintaining dominance. A naturalized view of hegemonic gender roles assumes unequal power dynamics and male dominance. Within these gendered dynamics, a naturalized presupposition that Whiteness is the normative, privileged, and entitled racial classification allows for White male ascendency as natural. Through studying Whiteness and masculinity outside of White male subjectivities, the constructed nature of such discourse is clear.

White women play a key role in the normalization of White rhetoric and hegemonic gender roles. Sociologists find that White women situationally

---

73. Kingkade, Zadrozny, and Collins, "Critical Race Theory Battle."
74. Bonilla-Silva, *Racism without Racists,* 4th ed.

experience an increase in popularity and social status when they embody masculine characteristics,[75] and this is also true when it comes to discourse. Babbitt's and Carrano's tweets help us to understand how White cisgender women use media—and are used by media—to further narratives intended to sow racial strife. Babbitt experienced a posthumous rise in popularity that elevated her extensive social media engagement to national stage in a way that never occurred when she was alive. Carrano's work at Lucasfilm may be over, but with the help of the *Daily Wire* she is directing her own dream project. Owens and Haley use techniques of feminizing discourse—a focus on nurturing themes, child-rearing, and personal narrative—while attacking a false controversy and garnering media attention. Also working for the *Daily Wire*, Candace Owens reshares content from her podcast that shares similarities with the militant victimhood frame studied in the previous chapter. These posts advertise her talk show using provocative and bombastic language to reach an echo chamber of like-minded fans. On Fox News, former UN Ambassador Nikki Haley remains in the news through her commentary on identity politics and critical race theory, and she reshares edited segments of her followers' comments on Twitter. Through studying of social media posts that adhere to the signatures of the militant victimhood frame from these feminized personas, we also see how feminization of militant rhetoric can work in the service of White supremacy.

---

75. For examples where cisgender women's enactment of masculinity is regionally accepted, please see Kazak, "Midwest or Lesbian?," 828; Pilgeram, "'Ass-Kicking' Women," 120.

CHAPTER 3

Trash Music

A Third-Wave Whiteness Approach to Bro-Country and Country-Rap

Using the video sharing app TikTok, Lil Nas X created a short viral video out of his song "Old Town Road" ("Road") that helped catapult it to three of *Billboard*'s charts: Hot Country, Hot R&B/Hip-Hop, and Hot 100, where a remix of the song with country music veteran Billy Ray Cyrus remained number 1 for seventeen weeks.[1] "Road" tells the story of a financially successful and philandering young man. In the lyrics, Lil Nas X intermeshes cowboy and country tropes—like horse riding, Wrangler jeans, and black cowboy boots—with rap bravado—bragging of cheating on a partner, wearing designer clothing, and enjoying a life of affluence similar a movie star.[2] Columbia Music signed the young artist from Atlanta and marketed the song as a "country-inspired rap track." "Old Town Road" became a viral hit; over 67 million videos on social media reference it.[3] Despite success, *Billboard* removed the song from

---

1. The remix of "Old Town Road" with Billy Ray Cyrus won this honor, and "Road" is the first song to earn this honor in the chart's nearly sixty-year history (Abshire, "Lil Nas X Lassos the Record").

2. Writers: Trent Reznor, Atticus Ross, Kiowa Roukema; Performer: Lil Nas X.

3. These posts reference the song while using the hashtag #yeehaw. Also popular in summer 2019 but beyond the arguments in this chapter was the hashtag #yeehawagenda or #TheYeehawAgenda. The YeeHaw Agenda was coined and trademarked by digital archivist and Black cultural critic Bri Malandro, who reflected that the Yeehaw Agenda was "literally just about the aesthetic" of attractive young Black people wearing Western clothes. As she shows on her Instagram account, Malandro told *Jezebel* that there was nothing new about young,

its Hot Country chart in the summer of 2019, saying that its original placement was a mistake.[4] *Billboard* finds that "while Old Town Road incorporates references to country and cowboy imagery, it does not embrace enough elements of today's country music to chart in its current version."[5] Scholars define "elements of today's country music" as singer-and-lyric centric, featuring songs about ordinary people,[6] nostalgia,[7] abjection and alienation,[8] and with a "softer twang" as compared to "heavy metal or rap."[9] Lil Nas X's version of country music belongs to the country-rap subgenre. The hybridization of country and rap traditions is not new and has been termed "country-rap," "country-trap," "redneck hip-hop," "hick-hop," "redneck rap," or "country hip-hop." Country-rap blends the narrative themes and twang of country with the more fast-paced vocal stylings of hip-hop.[10] As a common theme in contemporary lyrics, a discussion of the term *country* references a musical genre, racialized geography, and way of life. The "Old Town Road" controversy is indicative of a wider debate within the genre: *what* is "country" and *who* gets to define it?

Country stars joined the "Old Town Road" *Billboard* debate. Blake Shelton criticized "Road" in his 2019 song "Hell Right," singing: "Then the girl *from* the small town took *off* the '*Old Town*,' *put* on a little *Hank Jr.* (Thank God)."[11] Shelton romanticizes rural life and references Hank Williams Jr., a country star whose comparison in 2011 of Barak Obama to Adolf Hitler led ESPN to terminate his contract for singing *Monday Night Football*'s opening anthem

---

attractive Black people wearing Western garb, and she references that Mary J. Blige, Beyoncé, and others were wearing similar outfits in the 2000s, and "it's not subversive at all." Like any fashion trend, Malandro reflects in her interview, the popularity of Western apparel will come and go (Reese, "What Everyone Is Getting Wrong").

4. Chow, "Lil Nas X Talks 'Old Town Road.'"
5. Adjei-Kontoh, "Lil Nas' Song Was Removed."
6. Sanjek, "Blue Moon of Kentucky Rising," 27, 24, 38.
7. Mann, "Why Does Country Music Sound White?"
8. Fox, "White Trash Alchemies," 54.
9. Although "difficult to describe," a twang "refers paradigmatically to the short sustain and dynamic resonance of instruments like banjo, mandolin or dobro, the sounds of which are distinguished by an abrupt, relatively sharp initiation when plucked, which is followed by quick, usually slightly ascending, muting." Vocals contribute to country's twang as "the music is almost always sung with the diction and inflect of the southern US, whether or not the performer is a southerner" by "gliding a single vowel sound to give [a word] two audibly distinct segments." A musical twang and a Southern inflection "are so constantly paired as to give the impression that twang is the direct musical expression of a white southern accent" (Mann, "Why Does Country Music Sound White?," 79).
10. I choose the term country-rap as it makes the hybridity of the genres clear.
11. Italics indicate words emphasized by the singer.

"All My Rowdy Friends Are Here on Monday Night."[12] On vocals, Shelton is joined by country legend Trace Adkins, whose music is discussed later in this chapter. In the official music video, Shelton and Adkins sing near a rural bonfire surrounded by pickup trucks and a crowd of White partygoers. HARDY, a bro-country singer/songwriter who helped write "Hell Right" and who is also analyzed later, makes an appearance in the video as the male protagonist who gains a young brunette woman's attention. In light of such critiques, Lil Nas X's supporters fired back against the historically White-dominated country establishment, countering that his identity as an urban, Black, and gay artist marked him as not "country." In contrast to the video for "Hell Right," the music video of Lil Nas X's "Old Town Road" remix with Cyrus takes place in urban and suburban locations, led by a Black protagonist (Lil Nas X) with a group of racially mixed actors.

Despite perception that Lil Nas X's sound and stylings were avant garde, this is rhetorical White deflection because country music has long been indebted to Black artists and musical traditions. As early as the 1940s, King Records, founded by Syd Natan, requested that Black US songwriter Henry Glover "produce versions of the same songs by both White country and Black rhythm and blues artists; indeed, even the bands on a number of these recordings were racially mixed."[13] Historically, Charley Pride, Aaron Neville, Cowboy Troy, Tina Turner, Petrella Ann Bonner, and other Black performers left indelible impacts on country music.[14] Lil Nas X is also not the only popular Black country artist today; Darius Rucker, Kane Brown, Cowboy Troy, and Jimmie Allen are all frequently played on nationally syndicated country countdowns and feature as top artists on Apple Music, Spotify, and other streaming channels. The Black roots of country music are adopted, frequently without attribution, by White performers. Elvis Presley, Trace Adkins, Big Smo, Kid Rock, and other White country artists received criticism from musical fans and scholars for their appropriation of Black cultural traditions.[15] Although Lil Nas X has grown as a performer since the release of "Old Town Road," he has not forgotten his country roots. Reaffirming his connections to country in 2021, Lil Nas X even released a successful cover of Dolly Parton's hit song "Jolene."

While noting this history and the multiplicities of genres and subgenres that influence contemporary country music (including rhythm and blues, folk, alt-country, etc.), my analysis is focused on two interrelated subgenres of country music often deemed "low culture" that, in my opinion, remain

---

12. Johnson, "Monday Night Football: Brand Identity," 28.
13. Sanjek, "Blue Moon of Kentucky Rising," 33.
14. Gussow, "Playing Chicken with the Train."
15. Gussow, "Playing Chicken with the Train"; Morris, "Hick-Hop Hooray?"; Fox, "White Trash Alchemies," 48; Caramanica, "History of Hick-Hop."

understudied by academics due to their low-class appeal: country-rap and bro-country. The types of White deflection in this chapter are multiple and nuanced. Overt types of White racism, such as a White artist wearing blackface makeup, are excused; critiques are deflected as people being "over sensitive"; and superficial apologies are offered. More covert types of deflection include the appropriation of Black musical stylings that are co-opted by White artists, depoliticized, and racialized as White music. As author of a book examining critical rhetorics of race, I am primarily interested in rhetoric; therefore, my analysis is lyric-centered and narrative-centered. As other scholars have noted, country musicians have long been preoccupied with defining "country" through their lyrics.[16] I am attentive to the racialized, coded, and strategic use of the word country and other terms, like redneck, in the song lyrics that mark differences in class and race. For the sake of simplicity, popular themes in the overlapping subgenres of bro-country and country-rap include nostalgia,[17] abjection,[18] attractive and objectified women,[19] relaxing/partying while drinking alcohol, and pickup trucks/tractors/heavy machinery. Beyond the thematic narrative overlap, for fans, the connection between bro-country and country-rap may seem rather obvious: popular Nashville bro-country frequently samples country-rap. The borrowings between these two popular subgenres warrant comparison. What makes this case study in White deflection unique is that my analysis uncovers the ways that upper-class White singers and songwriters construct a classed and at times politically divisive and masculine Whiteness, deflecting even the insinuation of racialized discourse through monikers of crass "country" credibility (read: working class, rural, and White). As my analysis will show, although artists may be accused of racism, they deflect such accusations behind half-hearted apologies, or racial recovery rhetoric.

Although many country-rap musicians are White, Black artist Cowboy Troy has been releasing chart-topping work as a lead country-rap vocalist since the early 2000s. The Black country-rap performers discussed in this chapter, Lil Nas X and Cowboy Troy, sing lead vocals and also collaborate with White country stars who sing featured stanzas (Billy Ray Cyrus and Big and Rich, respectively). I focus on these Black country-rap artists because, despite their collaborations with White artists, they each develop techniques to challenge the historically White Nashville establishment and, while collaborating with White country singers, maintain their roles as lead vocalists in chart-topping cross-genre music. White country-rap artists like Colt Ford, Danny

---

16. Ching, *Wrong's What I Do Best*.
17. Mann, "Why Does Country Music Sound White?"
18. Fox, "White Trash Alchemies."
19. Rasmussen and Densley, "Girl in a Country Song."

Boone, and Bubba Sparxxx are each famous in their own right and collaborated in releasing the song "Country Folks" (2013); however, these artists are not frequently played on national country music countdowns as lead vocalists. Colt Ford, for instance, is well known for his country-rap collaborations with popular bro-country acts that make frequent appearances in national country music countdowns like Florida Georgia Line, Chase Rice, Toby Keith, Brad Paisley, and Tyler Farr.

Defined differently by fans, artists, and critics, bro-county is a subgenre typified by acts like Luke Bryan, Jason Aldean, Old Dominion, Thomas Rhett, and others. Bro-country songs and pop music are often indistinguishable to the untrained ear. Bro-country began to solidify as a subgenre in the 2010s and mixes traditional country, hard rock, hip-hop, and electronica; some singers like Sam Hunt and Chase Rice are also well known for their interplay between speech and song. The evolution of contemporary bro-country—particularly its militaristic, patriotic, and masculine elements—owes some of its current bravado to songs that emerged in response to the terrorist attacks of September 11, 2001, like Toby Keith's "Courtesy of the Red, White and Blue." After the national tragedy, there emerged "traditional working-class patriotic nationalism" exemplified in country music so much that "'country music' came to stand for 'working-class' (and 'White') identity, which was, in turn, a metonym for 'American' identity."[20]

Despite the rise in popularity of Lil Nas X, mainstream country music is still dominated by attractive, young, White men who espouse similar philosophies about the treatment of women, heterosexuality, party culture, and an appreciation of the working classes. The term bro-country is a neologism that, as I discuss further later in this chapter, is sometimes viewed as controversial as it deliberately evokes the hypermasculine performance and narrative of these songs whose branding appears produced, sung, and consumed by and for White men. Similarly, popular country-rap artists overwhelmingly identify as male. Even Lil Nas X mentions "boobies" and "cheating on my baby" in "Old Town Road." Scholars have found that the amount of sexism in country music increased with the rise in popularity of bro-country.[21]

---

20. Fox, "'Alternative' to What?," 173.

21. Rasmussen and Densley, "Girl in a Country Song." The colloquial term also provides an accurate image of contemporary country music more generally. On June 17, 2019—at the same time that the Billy Ray Cyrus and Lil Nas X remix of "Old Town Road" still ranked as the number 1 downloaded single—all ten of the top country albums on Apple Music were recorded by white men, or a group of white men (for example, Dan + Shay). Carrie Underwood's album "Cry Pretty" was the highest-ranking non-white-male album at number 11; followed by Kacey Musgraves's "Golden Hour" at 12; and Maren Morris's "Girl" at 13: all three of these artists are white women.

Third-Wave Whiteness and Musical Interpellation

Listening to music is an affective experience with both social and individual dimensions,[22] and music can produce cultural identities.[23] In his canonical work *The Country and the City*, Raymond Williams (1973) writes that "a contrast" between the city and country has existed since "classical times." To Williams, "country life has many meanings"; the term can be understood as "both a nation and a part of 'land'; 'the country' can be a whole society or its rural area"; and country "has gathered the idea of a neutral way of life: of peace, innocence, and simple virtue."[24] Aaron A. Fox (2005) adds to Williams's definitions and applies them to music. To Fox, the term "has a fiercely complex identity" that links "a nationalist ideology, and a structure of feeling that connects communities in places as diverse as South Texas, South Africa and urban Japan."[25] Similar to Williams, Fox understands a contrast between the city and country as "one of the major forms in which we become conscious of a central part of our experience and of the crisis of our society."[26] While researching hard country music, Barbara Ching (2001) underscores socioeconomic class and social capital, writing that "the long-standing distinction between the country and the city can be seen as a symbolic distinction between the sophisticated and the rustic: the possessors of cultural capital and the have-nots, the powerful and the dominated."[27]

Like Williams, Fox, and Ching, I am intrigued by the sociospatial implications of the term *country* and how the strategic use of the term can underscore class-based divisions among Whites. Despite a shared benefit of White supremacy across classes and geography,[28] not all Whites are equal. Country music scholars maintain that the strategic use of the term *country*, and the genre more generally, speaks to working-class struggles.[29] "Country" frequently signifies poor or working-class rural Whites who are sometimes dismissed as "White trash" or "redneck"—two terms, in addition to country, that I analyze later. Although country music is classed, the performers popular with Nashville-based labels, and even alt-country performers like Gillian Welch, are rarely working-class and often risk performing a parody of work-

---

22. Lipsitz, "Forward."
23. Morris, "Hick-Hop Hooray?"
24. Williams, *Country and The City*, 3, 1.
25. Fox, "'Alternative' to What?," 167.
26. Williams, *Country and The City*, 289; quoted in Fox, "'Alternative' to What?," 167.
27. Ching, *Wrong's What I Do Best*, 39.
28. Leonardo, "Color of Supremacy," 140.
29. Ching, *Wrong's What I Do Best*; Fox, "'Alternative' to What?"

ing-class identity[30]—a parody that I find social media audiences recognize and challenge.

Similar to chapter 2's discussion of female militant victimhood, I take a Third-Wave Whiteness[31] approach that resists "essentializing accounts of whiteness."[32] This method allows me to highlight how the socioeconomic and cultural fractures between Whites are revealed through a cross-genre analysis of racial rhetoric in song lyrics, artist profiles, and online fan communities.[33] To make the differences between Whites—and therefore the constructed nature of Whiteness—more visible, particularly to other Whites,[34] I foreground popular subgenres of country music that are often dismissed as (White) trash music: bro-country and country-rap. I argue that in contemporary Nashville establishment music, artists' repeated and often-nostalgic utilization of racially coded terms like "country" or "redneck" evokes a top-down *racialized cultural identity,* regularly unbound by geography, that maintains White habitus[35] and is articulated by largely wealthy, White, male artists.

Sound is racialized, but that does not make it racist. In asking why country music sounds White, Geoff Mann (2008) notes that it has always been "a complicated mix of musics, including those of Mexico, Africa, and African-Americans."[36] The attempt to mark country music as "white soul,"[37] "white man's blues,"[38] or as explicitly a White cultural product erases this history.[39] Rather, Mann asks us to consider how

> claiming the status of "white culture," something like a purportedly American whiteness—however historically baseless—is not *reflected* in country music, but is, rather, partially *produced* by it . . .—what John Mowitt calls "musical interpellation."[40]

---

30. Fox, "Alternative' to What?," 44.
31. Twine and Gallagher, "Introduction: The Future of Whiteness."
32. Twine and Gallagher, 12.
33. The importance of nuancing racial identities is stressed in the Third Wave of whiteness studies through emphasizing the intersectionality of white identities across many politically motivated vectors including race, class, gender, sexual identification, and geography (Twine and Gallagher, "Introduction: The Future of Whiteness," 12–13).
34. DiAngelo, "My Class Didn't Trump My Race."
35. Bonilla-Silva, *Racism without Racists,* 4th ed.
36. Mann, "Why Does Country Music Sound White?," 75.
37. Sample, *White Soul.*
38. Grissim, *Country Music: White Man's Blues.*
39. Mann, "Why Does Country Music Sound White?," 75.
40. Mann, 75.

Musical interpellation is the "notion that music is involved in producing the very bearer of an identity—that is its subject."[41]

For those who do not enjoy country music, common stereotypes of it are that it is trite, formulaic, lacking innovation, or just "bad music,"[42] with lyrics bemoaning "broken-home, drank-too-much, death-in-the-family, god-fearing content."[43] Nadine Hubbs (2014) sustains that country music tropes "can call up conservatism and racial, sex, and gender repression in a sweep, eliminating the need to name each one" and that scholars of country music should be careful to not recycle them.[44] From a Third-Wave Whiteness perspective, I am not concerned with the authenticity of "good country music" but in understanding the racial logics formed through musical interpellation and how these are classed.[45] Country music is no monolith; there are many subgenres, including bluegrass, Tex-Mex,[46] alt-country,[47] hard country,[48] and I would argue bro-country and country-rap.[49] Its content is profoundly diverse; there are queer country songs,[50] conservative and progressive songs,[51] songs rich with word play like puns and alliteration,[52] and scholars have written about the genre as a type of religion.[53] For some, the connection between country music and Whiteness makes it a dismissed genre, "trash" music. As Adam A. Fox writes, "The taint of whiteness in country aligns with the taint of rural ideocracy and working-class psychopathology."[54]

41. Qtd. in Mann.
42. Hubbs, *Rednecks, Queers, and Country Music*, 97; *Real Country*.
43. Mann, "Why Does Country Music Sound White?," 81.
44. Hubbs, *Rednecks, Queers, and Country Music*, 72.
45. In writing about hard country music—a subgenre that is typified by acts like Hank Williams and John Anderson who don't always focus of a romantic nostalgia for rural, pastoral landscapes—Barbara Ching traces the complexity of the use of the term "country" in lyrics beginning largely in the 1970s finding that hard country is "self-consciously low, and self-consciously hard, a deliberate display of burlesque abjection" (*Wrong's What I Do Best*, 17). When speaking of more popular music, like songs by Alabama, Ching argues that, when compared to insightful and lyrically complex hard country, "mainstream country songs offer no such complexity" in their deployment of the term "country" as it "aims to please just about any listener" (*Wrong's What I Do Best*, 36). Through musical interpellation the uncritical consumption of such songs can allow racialized tropes to seep into our subconscious, and this is particularly true for popular music.
46. Bebout, *Whiteness on the Border*.
47. Mann, "Why Does Country Music Sound White?," 78.
48. Ching, *Wrong's What I Do Best*.
49. Gussow, "Playing Chicken with the Train."
50. Hubbs, *Rednecks, Queers, and Country Music*.
51. Ferrence, *All-American Redneck*.
52. Mann, "Why Does Country Music Sound White?," 81.
53. Fillingim, *Redneck Liberation*.
54. Fox, "White Trash Alchemies," 44.

Popular songs are easy to *passively* hear rather than *actively* listen to.[55] However, if music has the ability to *produce* racialized working-class identities—while being written, produced, and marketed by a bourgeois Nashville establishment—it is essential that these pop country songs are given critical attention. As I have argued, a key strategy in policing country music as "White" is the willful forgetting of the Black roots of the genre.[56] Therefore, this chapter explores the oppositional marketing tactics and rhetoric of select Black country-rap artists and contrasts their lyrics and reception against songs by popular White male country artists that dominate US country countdowns. Given the genre's focus on narrative, I first compare the lyrics of Lil Nas X and Cowboy Troy, and then follow with a critical study of the strategic rhetoric of popular bro-country songs and online fan discussions.

Black Country-Rap

Calling his mix of country and rap "country trap"[57] to *Time Magazine,* Lil Nas X affirms that "Old Town Road" should be included on both *Billboard*'s Hot Country chart and its Hot R&B/Hip-Hop chart: "The song is country trap. It's not one, it's not the other. It's both. It should be on both." Lil Nas X was asked if his "removal from the country chart had racial undertones"? While noting that he was not the first artist to mix country and rap music, he resolves, "I believe whenever you're trying something new, it's always going to get some kind of bad reception, for example, when rap started, or when rock and roll began."[58] In his study of New England country music, Clifford R. Murphy (2014) finds that community memories related to music, similar to those recalled by Lil Nas X, are "misleadingly cheerful with regard to ethnic and racial relations."[59] Apple Music and Soundcloud classified "Old Town Road" as country music; yet, *Billboard* removed "Road" the very week it would have reached the top of the Hot Country Singles chart.[60] After Lil Nas X reached out to him on social media, country music veteran Billy Ray Cyrus collabo-

---

55. Douglas, *Listening In,* 27.
56. Hass, *Carried to the Wall.*
57. A subgenre of rap emerging from poverty-stricken areas in the Southern US in the early 2000s, "trap brought rap music to a new sonic dimension: with dark energy, a gothic feel, street culture (guns, drug houses, strippers) and an allover gigantic sound." Given the relatively light-hearted lyrics and feel of "Old Town Road," I often refer to the song as country-rap. Admin, "Trap Music under Lock and Key."
58. Chow, "Lil Nas X Talks 'Old Town Road.'"
59. Murphy, *Yankee Twang,* 7.
60. Adjei-Kontoh, "Lil Nas' Song was Removed from Billboard."

rated with the new artist in releasing the first "Old Town Road" remix, adding a single verse. Nearly twenty-seven years after his country-chart-topping hit "Achy Breaky Heart," Cyrus had his first number 1 hit with "Road"—and all thanks to the collaboration with the young social media star.

The Black history of country music, and the strategic forgetting of it, suggests a struggle over race, representation, and membership in the country music pantheon. Despite Lil Nas X's retort he was "trying something new," country-rap is nothing new to *Billboard*'s top country music charts. When Black country-rap star Cowboy Troy Coleman's *Loco Motive* album "debuted at #2 on *Billboard*'s Top Country Albums chart on June 4, 2005" it remained, yet it was not without controversy.[61] In spring 2005, Cowboy Troy's hit single "I Play Chicken with the Train" from this album was the number 1 song downloaded on iTunes.[62] Similar to Lil Nas X, Troy collaborated with established White male country singers in releasing his song; country duo Big and Rich sing the tune's chorus. Reminiscent of the cadence of classical country music, Lil Nas X's singing is at a slower speed than that of Troy. A comparison of "Old Town Road" with Troy's hit from fifteen years earlier works to better contextualize Lil Nas X's contributions to, and at times fraught, membership in the country music discography.

"Old Town Road" contrasts designer brands with working-class cowboy-aesthetics and self-aggrandizement, as Lil Nas X raps: "My life is a movie / Bull ridin' and boobies / Cowboy hat from Gucci / Wrangler on my booty." Unlike many bro-country and country-rap songs, "Old Town Road" doesn't reference drinking alcohol or partying. He sings about excessive wealth marked with defiance with the refrain "Can't nobody tell me nothin'/ You can't tell me nothin'" that implicates both the listener and society as the orator of dismissed advice. The young singer admits that these stanzas are about his parents' calls for him to go back to college after he dropped out to pursue his music career.[63] "Old Town Road" does embrace the traditional country tropes of heavy machinery and romance when he references "ridin' on a tractor" and disrespecting a romantic partner by "cheat[ing] on my baby."

"Old Town Road" references to infidelity are more about Lil Nas X's sexual prowess than his lover's beauty. He uses the androgynous term "baby" to refer to his romantic partner, yet in a gesture that reinforces heterosexism, Lil Nas X also mentions the "bull ridin' and boobies" that he enjoys because his "life is like a movie." Eric E. Rasmussen and Rebecca L. Densley (2017) found that, similar to Lil Nas X, "country music in the 2010s tend[ed] to objectify women

---

61. Gussow, "Playing Chicken with the Train," 43.
62. Gussow, 43.
63. Chow, "Lil Nas X Talks 'Old Town Road.'"

more and portray them as empowered less than in previous decades and that lyrics in country songs sung by male singers seem to be driving the trend towards objectification and less empowerment."[64] "Old Town Road" objectifies women, in part, by using a synecdoche (boobies) to refer to women.

Despite the song's thematic overlap with classic country songs, audience members have gone to a variety of lengths to police the place of "Road" in country music. In an attempt to use commercial pressures to define the genre, some country purists unsuccessfully called for a boycott of Wrangler jeans to protest the song. In the Apple Music comments section of the Lil Nas X-Cyrus remix of "Road" there is an ongoing debate about whether or not "Road" is a country song. Critical reviews often dismiss the song as "trash" and most of the positive reviews use fire emojis or simply describe it as "fire"—a colloquial term for giving praise—with other positive adjectives and emojis. A particularly interesting attribute of the Apple Music comments section is its inclusion of posts from listeners that the song should "win a Nobel Peace Prize" or that it "ended racism." Although possibly flippant comments, the frequency of these types of comments across social media commenting platforms warrants consideration. This trend in comments suggests that the "Road" remix "killed racism" through having a middle-aged White man add a single verse to a young Black man's already viral song. Giving too much agency to Cyrus—who owes his renewed success to Lil Nas X and acknowledges so in his social media posts—such comments assume that, by challenging *Billboard,* the institutionalized racism of the predominantly White Nashville country music industry somehow changed.[65]

"Old Town Road" is a song of youthful defiance of authority and a celebration of conspicuous consumption, whereas Troy makes timely social commentary through his hit song "Playing Chicken with the Train." Playing chicken is a game of confrontation where one's boastful and imposing nature seeks to make a challenger back down. A hypermasculine game of courage, playing chicken refers to a head-on race between two vehicles; the winner is the last to swerve away. Troy uses a similar theme of self-aggrandizement in "I Play Chicken with the Train," yet his lyrics also discuss a life-or-death battle between himself and the historically White Nashville establishment:

---

64. Rasmussen and Densley, "Girl in a Country Song," 199.
65. Nashville, Tennessee, is also home to the Country Music Association (CMA), which was founded in 1957 and selects the winners of annual awards; to help break up the power that the CMA has over country music, in 1965 the Academy of Country Music (ACM) was formed, yet "Nashville remains the center of public consciousness" when it comes to the genre (Sanjek, "Blue Moon of Kentucky Rising," 22).

Big black train coming round the bend
Go on kin folk tell your mom and them
Chugg a lugga, chugg a lugga, chugg a lugga

Who? The big black neck comin' through to you boy you done fell and bumped you head, uh huh
That's what they said
People say it's impossible, not probable, too radical
But I already been on the CMA's
Hell Tim McGraw said he liked the change
That he likes the way my hick-hop sounds and the way the crowd screams when I stomp the ground
Now, big and black, clickty-clack and I make the train jump the track like that

I play chicken with the train play chicken with the train, train.[66]

Elsewhere in the lyrics, Troy connects the imagery of the US South with the US frontier while rapping "Southern boy makin' noise where the buffalo roam." He alludes to how audiences and the country establishment view his mix of hip-hop sound and country swagger as "impossible, not probable, too radical" while Troy remains the defiant, "big black neck comin' through to you boy" as he plays "chicken with the train." A game of courage between a lone Black man and a roaring train does seem defiant and bold. Adam Gussow (2010) argues that Troy's song references a battle between an anthropomorphized "big black train comin' round the bend" meant to represent Troy against the "racist-Nashville-establishment train" that historically does not support Black country artists.[67] Similar to many country-rap performers who are featured in mainstream country music, Troy finds acceptance from the CMA (Country Music Awards) and country stars Tim McGraw, as well as Big and Rich and their Muzik Mafia artist collective[68]—John D. Rich is also listed as a cowriter of the song, along with Troy and Angie N. Aparo. Although Troy sings later in the song that his hick-hop, or country-rap, is a new creation "Rollin' like thunder on to the scene," the use of cowboy and frontier aesthet-

---

66. "I Play Chicken with the Train." Songwriters: Angie N Aparo / Troy Alvin Coleman / John D. Rich.
67. Gussow, "Playing Chicken with the Train," 44.
68. Termed by founders Big and Rich as "music without prejudice," the Muzik Mafia was founded in 2001 and includes the founders, Cowboy Troy, Gretchen Wilson, and Big Kenny (Gilbert, "Muzik Mafia").

ics are nothing new to rap music.⁶⁹ Blake Allmendinger (2005) historicizes rap recordings and films, like Ice Cube's "Westward Ho" (1996) or Bone Thugs' "Ghetto Cowboy" (1998), to make comparisons between rap, the West, cowboys, and the US frontier. Country and rap lyrics also bare linguistic similarities in their use of nonstandard grammar as marks of masculine authenticity.⁷⁰ Jane H. Hill (2008) studies the language of country and rap music, finding that both use the negative concord, or double negatives, a marker of nonstandard stigmatized language.⁷¹ Drawing these two genres together, linguist Hill finds "one of the reasons that double negatives are so common in song lyrics is that for working-class people the kind of grammar in which they are embedded can be a proud emblem of personal authenticity, of being an unpretentious and egalitarian person, and even more specifically, of being authentically masculine."⁷² What was perhaps distinct about Lil Nas X's and Troy's cross-genre musical stylings are their targeted audience: the country industry and mainstream country music fans.

"Old Town Road" and "Playing Chicken with the Train" embolden audiences to embody a cowboy persona of a boastful swagger laced with defiance of authority. Adam Gussow (2010) notes that what he calls "a multi-sourced, all-American tradition of vernacular self-aggrandizement" is a trope seen throughout American literature, noting the work of Mark Twain, folklore about Davy Crockett, as well as popular music including rap, traditional country music, and hip-hop.⁷³ Boasting of infidelity and rugged individualism, put differently, is a cross-genre US masculine tradition. Similar to Gussow's argument about Cowboy Troy, Lil Nas X and "Old Town Road" "demand that we understand ... musical traditions as *already* amalgamated." Both country-rap artists' work

> combines frontier brag-talk of the Davy Crockett variety with urban rap braggadocio in a way that forces us to acknowledge the shared, creolized history of both forms, a history that owes something to African praise song, something to blackface minstrelsy, and much to life on the Western frontier before and after Emancipation.⁷⁴

---

69. Gussow, "Playing Chicken with the Train," 51.
70. Allmendinger, *Imagining the African American West*.
71. Hill, *Everyday Language of White Racism*, 36.
72. Hill, 37.
73. Gussow, "Playing Chicken with the Train," 59.
74. Gussow, 46.

What makes Lil Nas X different from Cowboy Troy is not only the less political content of his lyrics, but also his apt use of social media (which did not exist in the same way fourteen years earlier) and his sexuality. Lil Nas X used social media to propel his success in a way that sidestepped the same White Nashville establishment that Troy critiques with his song. Put differently, in performing their own subgenre of country music, both Troy and Lil Nas X confronted similar systemic pressures from the White Nashville establishment but confront them using different methods that may influence the respective content of their lyrics. Troy directly confronted an establishment oppositional to his musical hybridizations with his art. Lil Nas X crafted his musical persona through social media, which allowed him to navigate a historically White star system in a way that gave him great autonomy over his musical and stylistic choices.

Unlike Lil Nas X and Cowboy Troy, White country artists' membership in the genre is rarely questioned. At this juncture, I transition to a critical analysis of the Nashville establishment's most profitable and iconic music, bro-country. As seen in the careers of Lil Nas X and Cowboy Troy, the artistic collaborations between country-rap and bro-country artists already puts them in conversation with one another. I seek to question the privilege of country membership automatically afforded to White male artists in hopes of understanding how this genre rhetorically (re)fashions itself as a historically White space, despite bountiful evidence otherwise.

The Bro-Country Controversy

According to "nearly every scholar of the genre," country is "produced by white people, consumed by white people, and apparently appealing almost exclusively to white people, at least in North America."[75] Such stereotypes erase the work of artists like Cowboy Troy; indeed, Lil Nas X and his collaboration with Cyrus, a White country music star, are not novel. Launched by social media, however, "Old Town Road" does challenge country's Whiteness in a new and unprecedented way; Lil Nas X sidestepped the Nashville establishment in marketing his own music on social media; almost overnight "Old Town Road" changed the perceived racial composition of country music stars and its broadening audiences. In her discussion of radio audiences, Susan J. Douglas (2004) finds that people reach a point in adulthood where

---

75. Mann, "Why Does Country Music Sound White?," 74; also see Murphey, *Yankee Twang*, 471.

new mental pathways cannot be drawn, at which point we can no longer find new genres of music enjoyable.[76] This understanding of listening would be an oversimplification of the controversy surrounding "Old Town Road"; rather, country music nostalgically reinvents itself—again and again—in part through strategic forgetting or "unwitnessing" complicated racial histories.[77]

When it comes to music, "country music occupies a privileged place in the pantheon of American musical badness, a place reserved for (white) trash."[78] Shannon Sullivan (2014) finds that upper-class White goodness is defined against a low-class White badness; within this relationship, "white trash operate[s] as the abject."[79] Although "white trash" helps show how White identities are stigmatized along class lines, country music embraces a low-class sensibility. In writing about how country music was racialized as a "bad" White music, Adam A. Fox (2004b) maintains that country is deliberately anti-elitist and "its badness is not only an index, but an icon of the abject status of its fans and creators," and many country genres reflect "a deeply complex musical style."[80] The anti-elitism of some contemporary country music can extend to what Fox terms a "minstrelsy of poverty" where artists who were born in the upper classes—like Thomas Rhett or Kid Rock—deliberately evoke working-class symbolism.[81] In other words, those who produce and make music are often of a different socioeconomic status than those who interpellate its messages.

Although country music has long been assumed to be a White cultural product, the lives of Whites are hardly uniform. Whites are diverse, and they discriminate against one another with terms like "white trash," "hillbilly," "redneck," "trailer trash," and other accusations of mental unfitness or incest.[82] John Hartigan Jr. (2003) suggests that class and geographically based fissures in normative White identity mark "one critical track to deconstruct whiteness [that] involves recognizing the complex and emotionally charged contests over belonging and difference that engage whites intraracially."[83] Accusations of racism are frequently scapegoated onto those who are White, uneducated,

---

76. Douglas, *Listening In*, 33.
77. Lopenzina, *Red Ink*.
78. Fox, "White Trash Alchemies," 43.
79. Sullivan, *Good White People*, 32.
80. Fox, "White Trash Alchemies," 44.
81. Fox, *Real Country*, 44.
82. Wray and Annalee Newitz, *White Trash*; Hartigan, "Who Are These White People?"; DiAngelo, "My Class Didn't Trump My Race"; Dunn, "Diggin In"; Hobson and Margulies, "Forgotten History of Eugenics"; Isenburg, *White Trash*; Sullivan, *Good White People*.
83. Hartigan, "Who Are These White People?," 111.

rural, working-class or poor, and Southern.[84] Annalee Newitz and Matt Wray (1997) write that "the white trash stereotype serves as a useful way of blaming the poor for being poor. The term white trash helps solidify for the middle and upper classes a sense of cultural and intellectual superiority."[85] Shannon Sullivan (2014) similarly finds that, for liberal middle-class Whites, "white trash" functions as an antipode to their "white goodness." Sullivan clarifies that "class difference within the group of white people make a meaningful difference to their race, and this is a constitutive, not an additive difference. . . . But the constitutive difference that class makes to race doesn't mean that race has been collapsed into class."[86] Robin DiAngelo (2006) also views "white trash" as one of the few slurs that makes Whiteness visible.[87] Through highlighting the divisions between Whites—in the case as seen in the difference between the producers and consumers of popular musical narratives—the constructed nature of Whiteness, and its intersection with neoliberal capitalism, is made clearer.

Despite working-class Whites embracing the "trashiness" of country music, many bro-country stars reject the term bro-country in part because of its connotations with formulaic storylines of working-class (read: low) culture. When asked how he felt about the term bro-country, artist Jason Aldean did not hold back his disdain:

> It's a fucking ridiculous term. . . . It's incredibly insulting to me. It's meant to describe guys whose songs are all about pickup trucks, drinking beer and

---

84. Goad, *Redneck Manifesto.*

85. Newitz and Wray, *White Trash*, 1. Nancy Isenberg reminds us that the history behind "white trash" has origins in the 1500s when British colonial officials resettled poor people who were "first known as 'waste people,' and later 'white trash'"; they were "marginalized Americans [who] were stigmatized for their inability to be productive, to own property, or to produce healthy and upwardly mobile children—the sense of uplift on which the American dream is predicated" (*White Trash*, xiv–xv). Isenberg argues that "white trash is a central, if disturbing, thread in our national narrative. The very existence of such people—both in their visibility and invisibility—is proof that American society obsesses over the mutable labels we give to the neighbors we wish not to notice" (*White Trash*, 321). Newitz and Wray contextualize that contemporary understandings of the term based on biological unfitness emerge from 1880 to 1920 when the US Eugenics Records Office "and affiliated researchers produced fifteen different 'Eugenic Family Studies,' wherein researchers sought to demonstrate scientifically that large numbers of rural poor whites were 'genetic defectives'" (*White Trash*, 2).

86. Sullivan, *Good White People*, 39.

87. Middle-class whites, according to DiAngelo, rarely interact with people of color and live in highly segregated neighborhoods; upper-class people may have people of color near to them, but in the role as laborers, "servants." Poor whites and people of color "tend to share poverty" and this "proximity of the people labeled as White trash to people of color is why; race becomes marked or 'exposed' by virtue of a closeness to people of color. In a racist society, this closeness both highlights and pollutes Whiteness" (DiAngelo, "My Class Didn't Trump My Race," 53).

girls. It's meant to talk down to us—me, Luke Bryan, Florida Georgia Line, all of us. They haven't bothered to listen to the body of work I've recorded over the years. At least take time to do your homework.[88]

These themes embody some of the stereotypes that Hubbs (2014) warns others against; it is precisely this overlap that causes many country purists—and artists like Aldean—to resist the term.

As an outspoken and popular performer of contemporary country music, Jason Aldean's star persona also helps define contemporary country music. Take, for example, his recent hit album *They Don't Know*, the title of which references his portrayal in the media, including TMZ publishing photos of him kissing Brittany Kerr while he was still married to his high-school sweetheart Jessica Ussery, with whom he shares two children. Aldean divorced Ussery and is now married to Kerr; they also now share two young children.[89] Aldean faced media controversy again in 2015 when photographs of himself in blackface dressed as Lil Wayne for Halloween surfaced online. Aldean offered a statement to *Billboard* magazine:

> In this day and age people are so sensitive that no matter what you do, somebody is going to make a big deal out of it. Me doing that had zero malicious intent. I get that race is a touchy subject, but not everyone is that way. Media tends to make a big deal out of things. If that was disrespectful to anyone, I by all means apologize. That was never my intention. It never crossed my mind.[90]

Aldean's statement is an example of what Michelle A. Holling, Dreama G. Moon, and Alexandra Jackson Nevis (2014) call racializing apologia, or "public statements by individuals (or, violators) who are called on their perceived racist comments and seek to redress and apologize."[91] Holling, Moon, and Jackson Nevis find that "while apologizing for microaggressive acts, offenders almost always committed additional microaggressions against the targeted group through denial, minimization, and/or employment of a white racial frame," all of which are clearly present in Aldean's statement.[92] For example, Aldean deflects and denies the intent of racism by saying that he was just trying to go out for Halloween without being identified and that "people are so sensitive"

---

88. Eldredge, "Jason Aldean Sticks Up for Blue Collar America."
89. Eldredge.
90. Eldredge.
91. Holling, Moon, and Nevis, "Racist Violations," 261.
92. Holling, Moon, and Nevis, 278.

(thereby blaming the victim); he minimizes the controversy through faulting the media making "a big deal out of things"; and he bolsters his own self-image through offering an apology to those offended. Indeed, these statements are very much from a White-centered view and experience of the world.[93]

To be completely fair, bro-country is not only defined by an artist's personal choices. It is important to also consider the content of the songs—as Aldean demands: "do your homework." The first hit single from the album *They Don't Know* was "Lights Come On," released on April 1, 2016, and is "an ode to blue-collar Joes letting loose on a Friday night"[94] that adheres to the partying stereotype of bro-country. His second single from the album was "A Little More Summertime," released on July 15, 2016, and is about a summer destination town closing for the winter season and the sadness that the singer feels: "They boarded up this water town / Ain't nobody hanging 'round / Another grey September day / Was I crazy to think she'd stay." This second single is about mourning the end of summer, a carefree time when "The Lights Come On" at parties. Country music has always focused on abjection and loss,[95] and this song very much fits that classical tradition, but is less stereotypical (unless one reads the anthropomorphized summer season, referred to as "she," as a woman). The third single, "Any Ol' Barstool," again fits tropes common in bro-country and is about drinking, abjection, and the demise of a failed relationship:

> Ask any ol' barstool in this town
> Ask my new found party crowd
> Sure I take more Jack in my Coke now
> A little more high in my smoke now
> Sure I stay 'til they're all long gone
> And I take the long way home
> But I ain't sittin' 'round
> Tryin' to drown the thought of you
> Ask any ol' barstool.

Music, including bro-country, cannot be minimized into a single formula. Aldean appears to reject the term because he views it as dismissing his art as trite. There are, however, examples of hard partying and sexism throughout Aldean's archive as an artist, and journalists have linked benevolent racism to his star persona. I take up the term bro-country, despite this controversy, not

---

93. Feagin, *White Racial Frame*.
94. Eldredge, "Jason Aldean Sticks Up for Blue Collar America."
95. Fox, *Real Country*.

out of disrespect for artists like Aldean, but in a recognition of working-class audiences. For middle-class liberal Whites, Shannon Sullivan's (2014) research finds that "white trash" refers to socially stigmatized, racist White people.[96] For working-class Whites, embracing what is perceived as abject about their lives can function as a carnivalesque inversion of middle-class mores. In an ethnographic study of working-class White country music fans in Texas, Adam A. Fox (2004b) notes audiences embrace country music's perceived "badness" as a point of pride:

> Country music's working-class fans *embrace* what is "bad" about the music's—and their own—cultural identity and meaning, as a way of discovering and asserting what is valuable and good about their lives and communities. This is what I mean by the apparently contradictory phrase "the abject sublime." Country is not only bad music—it is bad for you. Pathetic or foolish, it is meant to be hated, and it is loved for that, as a symbol of working-class experience. It's not just country's detractors, in other words, or those who would selectively subject the music to the discriminating gaze of the educated arbiter of authenticity, who hate country music. Nobody hates country more than a country music fan, as many great country songs acknowledge.[97]

Not only is country music a commodity,[98] artists blatantly advertise their favorite trucks, apparel, chewing tobacco, and libations in their songs. Many self-identified rural and country people feel misrepresented and dismissed by mainstream US culture and embrace the abject sublime—a dialogic wherein individuals claim what they imagine others believe to be the negative, or stereotypical, aspects of their culture. By claiming what you know others think may be bad about your culture as a point of pride, the abject sublime can provide affective support to those who are vulnerable, not because of their racial identity, but due to intersectional experiences of geography, class, and other factors. Yet, a true understanding of a working-class identity—what it means to be rural and working poor in the United States—is not inherently addressed in bro-country. Bro-country allows for a respite from reality, a romanticized version of a culture rarely thought of as commodifiable. Not every country music star overtly attempts to define White identity, and people of color can

---

96. Sullivan, *Good White People*, 32.
97. Fox, "White Trash Alchemies," 52.
98. Fox, 52.

contribute to White racial discourse.⁹⁹ Nevertheless, the latent nostalgia of the genre,¹⁰⁰ mixed with pop music flair, deploys colorblind tropes and messages meant to appeal to a celebrated, though mythic, sense of pan-US working-class White ways of being.

Bro-Country as (White) Culture

Scholars have written about country music's history of cultural appropriation,¹⁰¹ its practitioners' tendency to forget their music's origins in Black cultural traditions,¹⁰² and the at times overtly racist lyrics of White country stars.¹⁰³ Intersecting with these discussions is the narrative trope of White male desire for Black culture and women. As early as 1972, Merle Haggard's tune "Irma Jackson" "sympathetically tells the story of an 'interracial' love affair, in an effort to show that country music is not 'racist,'" and similar narratives are still popular today.¹⁰⁴ It is common for White country stars like Trace Adkins to sample hip-hop in their songs, like in his 2006 hit "Honkey Tonk Badonkadonk" that reached the ranking of number 2 on *Billboard*'s Hot Country Songs chart in February of that year.¹⁰⁵ In a markedly different reception than it had for "Old Town Road" and Lil Nas X, *Billboard* Magazine's Michael Paoletta (2006) wrote that Adkins's song "cleverly connects country, hip-hop and techno," thereby paving the road for future bro-country hits.¹⁰⁶ Capital Records' Senior Vice President of Marketing Fletcher Foster, who was responsible for marketing Adkins's album *Songs about Me* where the hit single appeared, reflected that, to sell a record, "you need a dramatic single or a dramatic performance" to reach consumers and noted that "because it [Honkey Tonk Badonkadonk] has a novelty element to it, we did not want the industry to take it seriously."¹⁰⁷

But, Black country-rap artists have something serious to say. Cowboy Troy's June 2005 album *Loco Motive*, discussed earlier, also reached number 2 on *Billboard*'s Top Country Album chart. This is an act of unwitnessing the

---

99. Ono and Cheung, "Asian American Performance"; Eguchi, "Queerness as Strategic Whiteness."
100. Fox, "White Trash Alchemies"; Mann, "Why Does Country Music Sound White?"
101. Morris, "Hick-Hop Hooray?"
102. Mann, "Why Does Country Music Sound White?"
103. Fox, "White Trash Alchemies."
104. Mann, "Why Does Country Music Sound White?," 76.
105. Morris, "Hick-Hop Hooray?," 467; Paoletta, "Adkins' Booty Romp," 10.
106. Paoletta, "Adkins' Booty Romp," 10.
107. Paoletta, 10.

success of Cowboy Troy, whose performance of country-rap was not a "novelty" but a serious art form with an element of social critique. As mentioned in the introduction, Cowboy Troy's breakout hit critiqued the White-dominated country music scene in Nashville.[108] Cowboy Troy's 2007 song "How Can You Hate Me" overtly acknowledges that he experiences racist threats from country music audiences because he is a Black country star. In this song, he draws comparisons between himself and fellow Black men who have also been victims of White mob violence. Troy bemoans, "People I've never met wanna take me body surfing behind a pickup," a line that references "the infamous dragging death of James Byrd Jr. in Jasper, Texas, at the hands of two white men."[109] Despite being a part of Big and Rich's Muzik Mafia, a musical collective producing "music without prejudice,"[110] it is clear that Troy's audiences are not without prejudices. "Old Town Road" makes no similar critiques of systemic racism or state-sanctioned violence that help embolden and support acts of domestic White terrorism.

This seemingly constant (re)fashioning of country's hybridity as "new"—despite bountiful evidence otherwise—strategically (re)scripts country as an always already White cultural and social space that has only recently opened its doors to artists of color. This White racial altruism is ahistorical. Adkins borrowed the term "badonkadonk" from Keith Murray, LL Cool J, and Ludacris's 2001 song "Fatty Girl," as well as Missy Elliot's 2002 song "Work It."[111] David Morris (2011) claims that Adkins's use of hybridity should be understood "not as a moment of communication and understanding, nor as a force for destabilization and uncertainty, but as a cultivated image that can comfortably co-exist with old essentialisms."[112] As Morris contends, the United States values its racial and cultural hybridity. This hybridity, often understood in terms of racial, sexual, and gendered diversity, is upheld through a myth of immigrant US America[113] and notions of neoliberal multiculturalism[114] that position the United States as morally and culturally superior to other nations for our (supposedly) embedded racial diversity and feminisms.[115] In reality, however, in the video for "Honkey Tonk Badonkadonk" "Adkins, his male friends, and the women in the video are overwhelmingly white."[116]

---

108. Gussow, "Playing Chicken with the Train," 44.
109. Gussow, 43.
110. Gilbert, "Muzik Mafia."
111. Gussow, "Playing Chicken with the Train," 62.
112. Morris, "Hick-Hop Hooray?," 468.
113. Honig, "Immigrant America?"; Behdad, *Forgetful Nation*.
114. Melamed, *Represent and Destroy*.
115. Douglas, *Listening In*.
116. Morris, "Hick-Hop Hooray?," 473.

David Morris (2011) critiques such "self-conscious hybridism" that gives the allusion of progressivism "while continuing twentieth-century efforts to downplay country music's racially hybrid roots."[117] Similarly, Sam Hunt's 2017 hit song "Body like a Back Road" references Black cultural traditions of hair braiding and a validation of curvy women while discussing his desire for a woman (of color). Hunt croons:

> Got a girl from the south side, got braids in her hair
> First time I seen her walk by, man I 'bout fell off my chair
> Had to get her number, it took me like six weeks
> Now me and her go way back like Cadillac seats.

A few verses later, the lyrics continue:

> The way she fit in them blue jeans, she don't need no belt
> But I can turn them inside out, I don't need no help
> Got hips like honey, so thick and so sweet
> It ain't no curves like hers on them downtown streets
>
> We're out here in the boondocks . . .

Hunt suggests his love interest is "from the south side" and not his domain of "the boondocks"—an implicitly White-dominated space—where there "ain't no curves like hers on them downtown streets." A White singer, Hunt makes sure to use verbal cues—including his Southern "twang"[118] and references to a woman's braids—to remind his listeners that he is a White man desiring a Black woman who is presumably just visiting his (White) boondocks home.

The geography of difference in White country music is mapped against historically marginalized groups, like Latinx and Black US Americans, as well as against the US–Mexican border. Using random Spanish-language phrases in their song "Toes" (2008), the popular country and Georgia-based Zac Brown Band fantasizes about leaving their home state—also known to have "tequila and pretty senoritas"—for a different land where "muchachas, they call me big poppa / When I throw pesos their way." Luke Combs's hit song "Moon over Mexico" (2019) recycles similar stereotypes of Mexico as a land he visits with a lover:

---

117. Morris, 466.
118. Mann, "Why Does Country Music Sound White?," 78.

> The second I left I was kickin' myself
> 'Cause I knew I should've stayed
> Still tequila love drunk, from us wakin' up
> Under the Cabo palm-leaf shade
> And it's crazy I know, but I'd give anything to go
> To you and me on that coast, in the midnight glow.

Lee Bebout (2016) finds that "today, romantic depictions of Mexico and Mexicanas are most prevalent in the discursive location of country music, forming a dominant and reoccurring thread in the subgenres of outlaw and Texas Country music."[119] These representations occur in greatest frequency in smaller labels but are also very present in the larger commercial labels of Nashville as seen in the Zac Brown Band's "Toes"[120] or Combs' "Moon over Mexico." They work to uphold White supremacy and "are bound to performances of white cowboy masculinity and neoconservative nostalgia."[121] Within country music, "this discursive and ideological tradition does not simply provide an intellectual map of anti-Mexican racialization. These discourses structure and shape behavior."[122]

This ideological tradition of bro-country extends to defining a pattern of behavior, supposedly embodied by working classes in the United States. While Lil Nas X is dismissed by some as not "real" country due to his sound, race, and urban Atlanta home, White male country artists actively (re)define country as a *way of being*, a culture, that exists across the United States. For instance, Brantley Gilbert's (2010) song "Country Must Be Country Wide" references "country" as a US Christian cultural value unbound by geography that is "in every state . . . from farm towns to big cities." Gilbert's song begins with the realization that a man from "O-hi-o" is country, reflecting what Craig A. Warren (2014) identifies as the "southernization of America."[123] He sings that country:

---

119. Bebout, *Whiteness on the Border,* 161.
120. Bebout, 161.
121. Bebout, 162.
122. Bebout, 174.
123. Warren, *Rebel Yell.* This concept refers to a "superficial expression" used by pundits that is "meant to acknowledge that many traditionally southern attitudes, beliefs, practices, and voices found currency within the larger nation during the last decades of the twentieth century," including country music, food, NASCAR, and "'southern' perspectives on society and government" (*Rebel Yell,* 132). Of course, the notion that country music is authentically Southern is a myth, yet these histories are strategically forgotten. Country music has never been a distinctly Southern tradition—as the 1965 hit song "A Tombstone Every Mile" by Dick Curless of Bangor, Maine, reminds us—yet, since the mid-1960s this rich history of working-class New England country and Western music history has largely been erased by the mainstream Nashville music establishment (Murphy, *Yankee Twang,* 13–36).

Ain't where, it's how you live
We weren't raised to take
We were raised to give
The shirt off our back
To anyone in need
We bow our heads before we eat
Before we start our day
'Cause in God we trust and we believe.

Asserting that country exists "in farm towns to big cities" signifies that Gilbert views country as more of a culture or way of life. Nevertheless, the literal meaning of "country" as a rural space stands in contrast to "urbanity" that is often racialized as non-White.[124]

Similar to the tradition in rap music to mention an artist's inspiration and musical mentors,[125] there is a trend for contemporary White male country artists also to reference their White male predecessors when discussing "country" as a culture, place, and as a musical genre. In the song, Gilbert reifies classical White male country artists: Johnny Cash, Hank Williams, Willie Nelson, and Waylon Jennings. Drawing even deeper discursive connections to White male artists, Gilbert's song is remarkably similar to Hank Williams Jr.'s song "Country Boy Can Survive" (1982), where Williams Jr. also defines country as a Christian concept unbound by geography:

Country folks can survive
'Cause you can't stomp us out and you can't make us run
'Cause we're them old boys raised on shotguns
We say grace, and we say ma'am
If you ain't into that, we don't give a damn
We're from north California and south Alabam'
And little towns all around this land.

Gilbert's tone and delivery is markedly gentler than Williams Jr.'s outlaw country tune that "don't give a damn"; nevertheless, both songs reference country as a national, inherited, and rural White cultural tradition. Such an inclusive definition of country is contrasted with the overtly White male lineage that Gilbert references.

Gilbert speaks to contradictory values of community and self-reliance. Interpellated through "Country Must Be Country Wide" are Christian neo-

---

124. Shabazz, *Specializing Blackness*.
125. Rose, *Black Noise*; Charnas, *Big Payback*.

liberal values that imply the "takers" of country folks' philanthropy are not observant followers of God; after all, the country people who "bow our heads before we eat / before we start our day . . . weren't raised to take." In his ethnographic work in country music clubs in rural Texas, Fox found that

> discourse of self-reliance is pervasive and elaborate, although of course many members of the community must seek "charity" (from both government and private sources). Out of respect for the recipient, however, charity must be given and received in secrecy, or else disguised as something else. The alternative is shame, a despised and feared condition.[126]

"Whiteness is an ideology and set of discursive and social practices" that dictate social behavior, including social decorum and stigma.[127] In an era of colorblindness where racial discourse uses coded and deracialized appeals,[128] Dreama Moon (1999) uses the term "whitespeak" to refer to racialized euphemisms ("we weren't raised to take") and platitudes ("We were raised to give"; "'Cause in God we trust and we believe") that effectively uphold White supremacy through covert discourse. Moon explains that "whitespeak functions to disrupt effectively full and direct engagement with white supremacy and its implications by providing white people with discursive and psychic distance from matters of race."[129] Gilbert does not discuss race, yet his words are racialized. While simultaneously joining the communities of the White rural North and South into a unified "country" (White) culture, such rhetoric relies on "dog whistle politics" that since the 1980s has relied on tropes that stereotype historically marginalized communities as "takers" (e.g., welfare queens) who don't need the public resources they supposedly receive.[130] Whites are conscious of the rhetoric that they and their targeted audiences use.[131] Racial dog whistles are deliberate as "the hidden message it seeks to transmit violates a strong moral consensus" because "the substance of the appeal runs counter to national values supporting equality and opposing racism [and] those blowing a dog whistle know full well that they would be broadly condemned if understood as appealing for racial solidarity among whites."[132]

---

126. Fox, "White Trash Alchemies," 57.
127. Bebout, *Whiteness on the Border*, 167.
128. Bonilla-Silva, *Racism without Racists*, 4th ed.
129. Moon, "White Enculturation and Bourgeois Ideology," 188.
130. Haney-López, *Dog Whistle Politics*, 4.
131. McIntosh, Moon, and Nakayama, *Interrogating the Communicative Power of Whiteness*, 1.
132. Haney-López, *Dog Whistle Politics*, 4.

Through lyrics that evoke nostalgia, songs like "Country Must Be Country Wide" encourage associated listening that "brings forth cognitive emotional notes."[133] US values are linked with White Christian culture, implicit racial signifiers, and all behind a catchy beat that nostalgically conjures images of childhood when one is "raised to give." Following Josh Kun (2005), country music creates an "audiotopia," or "sonic spaces of effective utopian longings" that reconcile "sites normally deemed incompatible"—like "farm towns and big cities"—producing an auditory space of transnational US White culture, strategically binding Whiteness and US Americanness.[134]

Not all popular bro-country artists assert country as an identity unbounded by Southern geography. Underscoring a difference in opinion, Chris Young's hit song "Raised on Country" (2019) directly references country as a specific genre of music, as well as culture, in the Southern US:

> Got a little southern drawl in my talk
> Little pickup truck on my highway
> Got a little boot stomp in my walk
> Little neon light in my Friday
> Got some Tennessee in my whiskey
> Raise a cup up if you with me.

Young follows many of the classic tropes of country music through emphasizing cowboy boots, a southern drawl, and a pickup truck, and then later sings:

> I was raised on Merle, raised on Willie
> Got my Honky Tonk attitude from Joe Diffie
> Daddy did too, it's family tradition
> If someone cranks it up, you can't help but listen
> My upbringing sounds like George Strait singing
> And I gotta give props to the radio
> 'Cause if you know me, I was raised on country.

Young notes only White, male country stars in his song—Merle Haggard, Willie Nelson, Joe Diffie, and George Strait, and his use of "family tradition" is strategic and references Hank Williams Jr.'s 1982 song of the same name. Williams Jr.'s famous song references inherited musical skills from his famous

---

133. Douglas, *Listening In*, 34.
134. Kun, *Audiotopia*; Bebout, *Whiteness on the Border*; Nakayama and Krizek, "Whiteness."

father (Hank Williams), as well as the family tradition of substance abuse.[135] Through stressing his "little southern drawl" and products like Tennessee whiskey, Young espouses a consciousness embodied south of the Mason-Dixon line. The song ends with the lyrics that play with the notions of country as both a culture and a type of music: "Yeah, I was raised on country / (Raised on country music) / I was raised on country / (Raised on country music)." Young's song is an ode to his "family tradition" of country music, suggesting—similar to Williams Jr.—that country culture is inherited and natural, rather than learned behavior. The notion that country is inherited—something biological—is similar to the folk understanding of race discussed in the introduction to this book.[136]

In his 2018 hit song "REDNECKER," artist HARDY links "country" to a distinct geography, "blue-collar" social class, and hard-drinking—and hard-partying—region of the United States. In contrast to "white trash," redneck is frequently defined as a term to refer to rural Southerners who are often seen as bigoted and violent.[137] Redneck is a common theme in country music[138] and "can negatively identify a person as Southern, racist, poor, and degenerate and positively define a person as self-reliant and patriotic."[139] HARDY's song is deliberately confrontational, obnoxious—similar to his use of all-capital letters for his name, song, and album titles—and relishes in this juvenile behavior. "REDNECKER" is a song about a one-sided verbal duel to establish country credibility between the singer, HARDY, and an imagined opponent:

> My town's smaller than your town
> And I got a bigger buck and bass on my wall
> Got a little more kick in my drawl
> Y'all I got little more spit in my chaw
> My truck's louder than your truck
> And my collar's a little more blue
> You might think that you're redneck
> But I'm rednecker than you
> Yes I am.

---

135. For example, Williams sings: "Country music singers / Have always been a real close family / But lately some of my kin folks / Have disowned a few others and me / . . . Stop and think it over / Put yourself in my unique position / If I get stoned and sing all night long / It's a family tradition."
136. Hill, *Everyday Language of White Racism*.
137. Goad, *Redneck Manifesto*, 21.
138. Goad, 21, 43.
139. Ferrence, *All-American Redneck*, 6.

The image of the college-educated HARDY on his album cover shows an average-looking blond White man with glasses in a red plaid shirt—not a macho-looking football star as a stereotypical reading of these lyrics might suggest. A generous interpretation of "REDNECKER" could view the song as a potentially subversive use of irony to challenge Southern "redneck" stereotypes like Confederate flag tattoos, cowboy boots, moonshine, and chewing tobacco.

As an identifier, redneck does not always connote political conservatism,[140] yet the toxic masculinity and aggressive nature of HARDY's song is typical of contemporary politicized discourses. For instance, another reading of this song is as one that furthers the White toxic masculinity that is frequently displayed in the bombastic rhetoric of Donald Trump.[141] Terry Kupers (2005) identifies toxic masculinity as a barrier for mental health treatment for men:

> Toxic masculinity is constructed of those aspects of hegemonic masculinity that foster domination of others and are, thus, socially destructive. Unfortunate male proclivities associated with toxic masculinity include extreme competition and greed, insensitivity to or lack of consideration of the experiences and feelings of others, a strong need to dominate and control others, an incapacity to nurture, a dread of dependency, a readiness to resort to violence, and the stigmatization and subjugation of women, gays, and men who exhibit feminine characteristics.[142]

The lyrics of "REDNECKER"—and even the type case—embody "extreme competition" and "a strong need to dominate and control others"; it appears at times that HARDY is even directly confronting his listener. Unlike the imagery of Gilbert, his toxic masculinity is located in the South through references in the song to "southern pride tattoos" and people who have "drawls," or slowed speech with prolonged vowel sounds characteristic of Southern accents that signify Whiteness in country music.[143] By saying that he is "more rednecker" despite being someone who visibly does not look the part, HARDY suggests that being redneck is a way of being that—although some may attempt to emulate it—one is born into. Again, country is framed as something almost biological and inherited.

The conflation of crassness, or the lack of social mores, with authenticity is a marker of White privilege. Within a framework of Whiteness, Rachel

---

140. Ferrence, 126.
141. Griffin, "Black Women's Intellectualism," 70.
142. Krupers, "Toxic Masculinity," 717.
143. Mann, "Why Does Country Music Sound White?," 78; Morris, "Hick-Hop Hooray?," 467.

E. Dubrofsky writes that perceptions of Donald Trump as unconventional and brash make him appear authentic. Rather Trump's "authentic-seeming presentation of self" is "key in understanding Trump's popularity"; however, "Trump is normative, particularly in his racism, sexism, homophobia, islamophobia, and xenophobia."[144] This authenticity "is a marker of White privilege and makes Whiteness usefully visible at a moment of intense White fragility, enabling him . . . to leverage his toxic masculinity to embolden other White Men to do the same."[145] From crassness to ungrammatical speech, HARDY—similar to Trump—portrays White, working-class sensibilities as uneducated, confrontational, violent, and heteropatriarchal.

Fans also debate the interpretation of "REDNECKER" in the comments section of the official video's YouTube page. The video shows HARDY with a group of White male friends in a flat field in front of an upper-middle-class home riding on a mattress that is dragged by a large, and seemingly new, Ford truck. Other shots show the men "piss[ing] where they please" in a pond where they are also fishing, doing donuts in the mud, chewing tobacco, and drinking Busch beer. HARDY, originally from Philadelphia, Mississippi, wears a White baseball cap with a red silhouette of his home state; a blue workman's shirt; and a blue pair of shorts with flip flops. In Neshoba County, Philadelphia has a violent racial history of settler colonialism and White terrorism that is overlooked in the revelry of this video. It is located on the Mississippi Band of Choctaw Indians Reservation, yet this diversity and living history is unwitnessed in the video. Philadelphia is also where White supremacists murdered and dumped the bodies of Civil Rights organizers Michael Schwerner, James Earl Chaney, and Andrew Goodman in 1964. Early in his 1980 presidential campaign, Ronald Reagan also infamously appeared at the Neshoba County Fair where he gave a states' rights speech designed to be a dog whistle to White Southern Democrats.[146]

The comments section of the official video on YouTube is particularly fascinating as some commenters view the video as satire, while others take it seriously. "Wild Boar," with 816 likes and 43 replies,[147] says, "I love how half the people do not even get the message he is trying to get across. Country music has become a competition to see who is more country." This sentiment

---

144. Dubrofsky, "Monstrous Authenticity," 159.

145. Dubrofsky, 158.

146. Thank you to Dr. Joshua Haynes for these useful insights on Southern history. Also see Haney-Lopez for a more comprehensive overview of the "Southern strategy" that used racial dog whistles to win over White Southern Democrats using racially coded language (Haney-López, *Dog Whistle Politics*).

147. This post was the most liked comment at the time of this writing.

is echoed by many other commenters like "Somewhere Virginia" who, with 495 likes and 13 replies, reflects:

> I'm pretty sure this songs [sic] is actually taking a hit at the current crowd of "country" music artists. Many of which are constantly in a pissing contest to see who's more country. Ironically, the majority sound nothing like country anymore. That's how I took it, maybe I'm wrong.

With 212 likes, "Henry Seales" also sees HARDY intervening on the "what is and what is not country" debate when he writes, "You know this song is about luke Brayan's [sic] what makes you country 😂😂😂😂😂." Others remark on how the juvenile behavior looks like "fun" or even plays into the competitive rhetoric of the video directly challenging HARDY's "county line cred" through ridicule, particularly of HARDY and his choice of attire: clean—rather than dirty—clothing. For example, a top post by "Marc Flores" with 700 likes and 41 replies reads "bet that ain't the loudest truck at sonic," referring to the popular fast-food chain. "Carlos" reflects on what country means to him and how country people are frequently misrepresented:

> Too perfect to NOT be satire lol. Rural communities believe it or not are super nuanced. I live in a town of close to 200–300 people and all we have is a volunteer fire department with two pop machines out front. Nobody locks their doors and generally would give the shirt off their backs to help a person in need. All that being said, few match the description of "country" that modern country artists seem to keep telling everyone is REAL country. Country people aren't monolithic and come in all sorts of shapes, sizes and styles. Love thy neighbor, wave at every passing car with a smile and always help others in need of you can.

Carlos is voicing a distaste for establishment country music's tendency to define country in ways that don't reflect his rural lifestyle. Despite an ever-present desire to define "country," Carlos writes, "country people aren't monolithic." Similar to rejections of the terms *White trash* or *redneck,* they are rejecting blanket stereotypes of rural aesthetics and ways of life.

Hearing Whiteness

The two-part dialectic of deflective Whiteness occurs in contemporary country music with (1) the appropriation of Black musical traditions throughout the country genre and also in the blending of bro-country and country-rap musical stylings. This musical borrowing happens in tandem with (2) the policing, or deflection, of the so-called authenticity of the genre by country music traditionalists. Lil Nas X and Cowboy Troy each faced backlash from historically White music establishments. Lil Nas X used social media to sidestep the Nashville establishment that Troy "played chicken with" in the early 2000s. Troy's lyrics directly critiqued systemic racism and police brutality and were invested in the causes of social justice. Despite this nimble self-promotion, *Billboard* still questioned Lil Nas X's validity as a country artist by removing him from their Hot Country chart. Frequently borrowing elements of country-rap, bro-country musicians were divided in their support for Lil Nas X's musical hybridization. Meanwhile, through musical interpellation bro-country artists articulated a distinctively White way of being, or culture, tied to working-class values through their nostalgic narrative-focused songs.

Media headlines remind us that White, poor, and rural US communities are often glossed over in popular culture, and some bro-country artists assert a pan-rural solidarity that crosses the Mason-Dixon Line. When writing of hard country music, Barbara Ching finds that "our identities are shaped by the cultural tastes and practices that surround us and, hence, with which we feel comfortable, with which we feel 'at home.'" The genre "sounds out the logic of 'distinction' as it operates in the realm of country music and in post-modern American Culture."[148] An exercise in escapism, these songs frequently paint rural life as a constant vacation—sometimes that starts only after the plow has been put away. In reality, the lives of the working classes in the United States are hardly a carefree vacation. When one is struggling to pay bills and working multiple jobs, it's no wonder that music that glorifies their communities and provides support for their stories of abjection are appealing.

Country music has long relied on the musical talents of historically marginalized groups, often without due attribution, and male artists frequently romanticize "exotic" destinations and women. Although rural Whites may seek temporary escape from their own abjection by listening to popular music that glorifies the working classes and objectifies marginalized identities, the terrors of US White supremacy are inescapable.

---

148. Ching, *Wrong's What I Do Best*, 41.

PART 2

INFERENTIAL DEFLECTIVE WHITENESS

CHAPTER 4

Brand Liberal

*Ethical Consumption and
Latina Representation under Racial Capitalism*

Throughout the 2000s and early 2010s, American Apparel Inc.'s retail clothing stores populated urban shopping districts near college campuses. The corporation marketed its retro-hipster fashions and form-fitting t-shirts as socially conscious (sweatshop-free) clothing made in downtown Los Angeles, a city with a garment industry employing mostly Latinas. American Apparel's national media presence frequently had little to do with the company's urban-chic apparel and accessories and more to do with immigration reform and transmigrant labor.[1] Such issues occupied the core of the company's proimmigrant rights and t-shirt marketing campaign, "Legalize LA," that promoted a seemingly liberal agenda for comprehensive immigration reform. Advertisements for Legalize LA in newspapers and on billboards regularly contained images of Latinx workers, or Canadian former CEO Dov Charney's resident alien card.[2] American Apparel used "Legalize LA" to further a marketing

---

1. Following Jennifer F. Reynolds and Caitlin Didier and other social scientists who study new immigrant groups, I use the term "transmigrant" to refer to groups of transnational migrants throughout the American hemisphere. I choose this term, over undocumented, to emphasize the humanity and migratory patterns of these diverse communities across a multitude of national and social boundaries. Most Latinx workers do have some form of documentation, albeit perhaps not from the United States (Reynolds and Didier, "Contesting Diversity and Community.")

2. American Apparel's media attention is also attributable to Charney's history of alleged sexual harassment of employees (*No Sweat*, directed by Amie Williams).

agenda that promoted the core tenants of the economic, political, and social system of neoliberalism—namely, deregulation, privatization, and personal responsibility.[3] Neoliberal ideologies are often deceptively complex and can deliberately, and in some cases unwittingly, employ the rhetoric of personal responsibility to mask deep-seated, systemic social inequality. In the case of American Apparel, this marketing agenda was partially enacted through colorblindness and ethical capitalism embodied by the advertisements attached to the Legalize LA brand.

An ethical capitalist branding campaign uses an ethos of morality—in this case regarding immigration reform—to sell a product. This chapter further explores how White deflection manifests in more liberal-leaning ethical capitalist advertising crafted by corporations that, despite pronouncements of being socially aware, exploit their workers. The two-step dialectic of White deflection operates differently than more conservative examples discussed previously in this book, as there is a superficial empathy expressed by the corporation toward the workers. In its ethical advertising, the corporation recognizes that individual workers and their communities are oppressed—however, the corporation is not faulted in this exploitation. The corporation speaks *for* its workers, co-opting employees' organizing efforts as a liberal brand agenda. What is missing in an ethical campaign is context: the treatment of workers (salary, health benefits) and how an ethical branding campaign—that advertises an awareness of systemic problems regarding US immigration policies and practices—effectively challenges such oppressive structures when the branding campaign itself is embedded within a larger framework of racial capitalism. Ethical advertising is an insidious type of White deflection that appropriates the identity politics of workers, who under racial capitalism are frequently members of historically marginalized communities, to make a profit. In this two-step process, the business owner *recognizes* that his workers are exploited and, rather than change dynamics of exploitation in the workforce, uses this as a media advertising spectacle to garner a profit. Put differently, the victims in this liberal variety of White deflection are members of historically marginalized communities; however, the corporations co-opt this marginalization as a brand strategy, using it as advertising to market its brand as liberal, open-minded, and socially aware—regardless of the actual treatment of their workforce.

Branding a corporation's core ethos as "ethical" to sell a product obscures the vital role that labor and labor exploitation play in capitalist corporate profit. Using marginalized identities to market ethically branded goods in

---

3. Schaeffer-Gabriel, "Flexible Technologies of Subjectivity," 898.

this way is an example of what Cedric Robinson refers to as racial capitalism. Capitalism requires power disparities and racial capitalism refers to the ways that historically White institutions, and some Whites, exploit the labor, history, and culture of historically marginalized communities in accruing wealth. Charles W. Mills finds that racial capitalism is ubiquitous and terms the global exploitation of Blacks and historically marginalized people under capitalism as the often unspoken "racial contract" of White allies. Rather than overt racism, liberal White deflection relies largely on the less obvious inferential racisms, or "those apparently naturalized representations of events and situations related to race, whether 'factual' or 'fictional,' which have racist premises and positions inscribed in them as a set of unquestioned assumptions."[4] In their study of critical racial rhetoric, Michael G. Lacy and Kent A. Ono (2011) argue that overt acts of racism become "media spectacles," but it is inferential racism embodied in "mundane, everyday, and routine cultural practices"—like ethical marketing—that often goes unchallenged and that, while working with overt racism, "affect[s] us in [its] commonplace and taken-for-granted forms."[5] Liberal White racism is commonplace yet often goes unnamed, unmarked, and in the case of ethical consumption, is sometimes coveted by Liberal consumers who feel good about buying "ethically."

In the case study of American Apparel, I explore how dynamics of misrepresentation used in advertising wittingly conceal Latina labor exploitation while implicitly marketing goods toward a racialized and classed demographic: upper-class liberal Whites. I am interested in how ethical consumption operates as a form of neoliberal social regulation—a mechanism of racial capitalism whose pronouncements of being socially aware deflect attention from the actual lack of worker voices in advertising campaigns supposedly supporting transmigrant workers. In uncovering these ideologies marketed under racial capitalism, I perform a cross-media discourse analysis of advertising campaigns, print journalism, a documentary film, and select American Apparel website content between the period of 2008 to 2012.

Liberal White deflection is particularly insidious as it recognizes, then co-opts the identity politics of historically marginalized groups in the service of racial capitalism and individual corporate profit. This type of White deflection provides ethical consumption choices without context. First, I explicate my theoretical framework for analyzing Latina (mis)representation at American Apparel: "ethical consumption" and "ethical advertising." As a political and rhetorical tactic[6] to disrupt the willful forgetting of Latinx labor in Ameri-

---

4. Hall, "Whites of Their Eyes."
5. Ono and Lacy, *Critical Rhetorics of Race*, 3.
6. Nakayama and Krizek, "Whiteness"; de Certeau, *Practice of Everyday Life*.

can Apparel's advertising, this chapter first situates labor issues at American Apparel within a century-plus history of Latina labor in LA prior to my analysis of the corporations' advertisements. This placement of Latinx labor history is a politically significant act as it grounds my critique in the labor history of Latinas who are relatively absent from most of American Apparels branding. To undo dynamics of misrepresentation present in advertising, it is essential to first understand the history that is strategically absent *before* I discuss the ads. In the same vein, I then discuss Latinas and labor issues at the LA-based corporation. Finally, I offer a cultural studies reading of material from American Apparel's corporate websites that works to differentiate Latinx "workers" from young White liberal "consumers." Ethical consumption is a marketing tactic designed to target White liberal guilt, yet, in this case study, ethical consumption does little to eradicate the exploitation that historically marginalized groups face under racial capitalism.

Ethical Advertising

Branding a product as "ethical," as evidenced in the company's trademarked phrase "Made in Downtown LA—Sweatshop Free," conceals American Apparel's unethical practices like the illegal hiring of transmigrant workers and its antiunion policy. Stemming from a fear of the unsustainability of capitalism and prevailing consumption patterns, ethical consumption assumes that consumers are educated about the exploitation of historically marginalized groups under capitalism, both in the United States and internationally. Ethical consumption occurs when issues including sustainability, environmental conservation, and the equitable and safe working conditions of laborers impact consumer choice.[7] This chapter privileges the term "ethical consumption" because, as Nicki Lisa Cole (2014) contends in her study of ethically produced coffee, ethical consumption does not dictate that the act of consumption is inherently political or one of civic virtue.[8] Put differently, when worn or consumed, the often-blatant branding of "ethical" products does not necessarily denote a consumer's political ethos. Some scholars view consumption as an

---

7. Ethical consumption is similar to, but different from consumer citizenship and political consumption. Political consumption mandates that an overt political meaning or message is asserted through a consumption choice, whereas consumer citizenship emphasizes a relationship between civic participation and consumption patterns. In my discussion of citizen brand in chapter 1, I present a more comprehensive discussion of consumer citizenship (Cole, "Ethical Consumption in the Global Age," 320).

8. Cole, 320.

individualized process that cannot be considered a form of collective action.[9] Others critique this viewpoint, asserting that ethical consumption can lead to "networks of global solidarity."[10] While this case study of American Apparel suggests that networks of global solidarity are important, a singular focus on the global may ultimately ignore the exploitation of "Third World" labor in the "First World."

Previous scholarship about American Apparel focuses on how ethical consumption, Neo-Fordism,[11] and the idea of the celebrity CEO are all the result of contemporary capitalism.[12] To Jo Littler (2007), CEO Charney's frequent presence in the headlines garners him a celebrity status that also works to cross-promote the American Apparel brand. Littler explains that Charney's media persona as a hipster-chic rule-bender extends to American Apparel's brand identity. She writes: "Many contemporary celebrity CEOs are trying to turn 'fat cats' into 'cool cats' by employing or appropriating discourses of bottom-up power and flaunting them across an expanded range of media contexts."[13] This approach to the study of American Apparel, while acknowledging the exploitation of a predominantly Latina labor force, posits the CEO and capitalism as the central subjects of analysis, and therefore does not provide a critical reading of Latinx representation (or lack thereof) in advertisements that espouse *ethical* capitalism.

But Charney is more than a celebrity CEO, and this chapter expands on Littler's argument by suggesting that American Apparel's advertising campaigns are manifestations of a US neoliberal business model that is also a form of White identity politics. I argue that the ethical consumption corporate model operates in the ethos of personal responsibility espoused by the gesture of "buying moral" that is endemic to many affluent and liberal-minded subjects under US neoliberalism. From the viewpoint of working-class Los Angeles Latina labor history, American Apparel's neoliberal marketing agenda of ethical consumption perpetuates a dynamic of misrepresentation in service of racial capitalism. In this context, a "dynamic of misrepresentation" denotes representations that simplify or obscure structures of exploitation behind ostensibly progressive corporate politics that ultimately benefit wealthy consumers racialized as White. In this way, wealthy consumers' ability to purchase

---

9. Newholm and Shaw, "Studying the Ethical Consumer," 260.
10. Barnett et al., "Consuming Ethics," 15.
11. Neo-Fordism describes US manufacturing that relies on the exploitation of a workforce of disenfranchised people of color, similar in ethnic/racial composition to those present in the "Third World."
12. Littler, "Celebrity CEOs"; Moor and Littler, "Fourth Worlds and Neo-Fordism."
13. Littler, "Celebrity CEOs," 236.

goods affords them added social capital. Worker voices are absent and their consumption choices implicitly judged.

As a part of racial capitalism, American Apparel's ethical advertising is not a new corporate advertising technique. While American Apparel markets itself as socially aware, the corporation is actually recycling longstanding discourses of consumer responsibility with origins in the United Kingdom during the 1800s.[14] Ethical-minded consumption possesses multiple dimensions. For example, when discussing the citizen-consumer hybrid in the case of Whole Foods Market, Josée Johnson (2008) asserts that contemporary ethical consumption has its origins in the 1970s when the environmental movement hastened people into the belief that their current consumption patterns were not sustainable.[15] Similarly, American Apparel's "Sustainable Edition" organic cotton line should be understood as fitting into a second commercial and corporate wave of ecofashion that appeared in the 1990s and followed the leftist revolutions of the mid-1970s.[16] Not coincidentally, the 1970s is the same time frame that scholars, such as David Harvey, indicate as key to the development of contemporary neoliberal thought.[17]

American Apparel's garments and accessories also fit into an ethical consumption model founded on a "Buy American" ethos. Since the September 11 terrorist attacks, the United States has experienced a resurgence of jingoistic patriotism that often seeks out immigrants as scapegoats for US social, economic, and political problems.[18] This nationalism has in turn fueled a "Buy American" movement that is both xenophobic and global in scope. Some of the progressive motivations behind this post-9/11 "Buy American" movement are tied to green solutions: buying locally made goods reduces carbon emissions during transport, "American-made" goods give the consumer the peace of mind that they are not buying toxic or contaminated goods from "Third World" countries, and it addresses a concern that inexpensive imported goods will hurt the US economy by putting national corporations out of business.[19]

Ethical consumption, like that embodied by the American Apparel brand, perpetuates the logic that "morally minded" corporations have the propensity both to steward individual consumption patterns as well as their consumers' politics. From a corporate marketing perspective, this is the idea that a corpo-

---

14. Nicholls and Opal, *Fair Trade*, 181.
15. Johnson, "Citizen-Consumer Hybrid," 238.
16. Black, *Eco-Chic*, 19.
17. The origins of neoliberalism are often indexed as beginning at the end of World War II and the beginnings of the Cold War.
18. Chavez, *Latino Threat*.
19. Williams, "Check the Label."

ration's purported politics in turn sells not only a product but also an ideology and a lifestyle. Linked to that ideology, as Naomi Klein (1999) argues, corporations like American Apparel endeavor to market a brand of corporate social responsibility through ethically minded marketing campaigns, if not directly through their services. This new image of corporate social responsibility is no longer achieved directly through corporate philanthropy, but is deregulated and realized through individual consumer's spending patterns. These spending patterns in turn mark the corporate brand as "ethical."

As a liberal type of White deflection, ethical consumption allows a consumer—coded as White—to purchase a product with a positive affective benefit—but without necessarily investing time and energy into the cause of supporting historically marginalized groups. Put differently, ethical consumption makes White liberals feel good as they brand themselves—through the purchase and performance of goods—as liberal on matters of race, ethnicity, and social justice. As Clive Barnet et al. (2005) assert, "Ethical consumption works through a set of subtle interpellations that turn upon ambivalent forms of inducement as well as the provision of practical devices that enable action."[20] These "subtle interpellations" are what Sarah Barnet-Weiser and Roopali Mukherjee (2012) define as "neoliberal ideas about self-reliance, entrepreneurial individualism, and economic responsibility."[21] Ultimately, this dynamic could be understood as a nuanced rendering of the notion of "personal responsibility," or a variation of the ideal that deregulated economic and political conditions better allow an individual to actualize their own versions of the "American Dream." A key strategy of opponents of systemic racism theory is to turn racism into an individual failing, rather than focus on the reality of racist institutions, structures, and practices that undergird nearly every vector of the modern world. Social justice struggles, however, are collective and racism is systemic. Through turning social justice issues into consumer choices, the neoliberal subject superficially feels good about their politics and purchases without fighting systemic and institutional racism—including racial capitalism with which they directly engage.

Under this neoliberal business model, the ideology of "ethical consumption" is not a contradiction. From the perspective of the neoliberal CEO, advertising campaigns may constitute the visual embodiment of the CEO's cult of personality, but also the exploitation of historically marginalized groups to sustain corporate profit is presumed and therefore part of "business as usual." Advertising and the Legalize LA immigration initiative codes

---

20. Barnett et al., "Consuming Ethics."
21. Mukherjee and Banet-Weiser, "Introduction," 2.

American Apparel as a predominantly White consumer space, and American Apparel manufacturing as an exclusively Latina space. This chapter decenters the notion of the celebrity CEO and the study of American Apparel's corporate model. I attempt to undo the dynamics of misrepresentation through grounding my analysis of Legalize LA and ethical consumption from the historical perspective not of privileged consumers and business owners, nor the branding of White public spaces, but from Latina labor history in Los Angeles. I also add to existing scholarship through my inclusion of a close reading of Latinx absence in differently branded and marketed American Apparel advertisements, notably Legalize LA.

Josée Johnson (2008) argues that ethical consumption is culturally pervasive, in part because ethically marketed products are not just sold at expensive stores like Whole Foods but also at low-budget retailers like Walmart.[22] Similarly asserting the cultural dominance of morally based consumption, Cole (2008) finds that ethical capitalism is "emerging as a new dominant mode of capitalism."[23] Such ethical consumption patterns are informed by what Frederic Jameson terms "the cultural logic of late capitalism."[24] Jameson (1984) argues that feelings of crisis and feelings of an end or a catastrophe motivate contemporary late capitalism, wherein "the new social formation in question no longer obeys the laws of classical capitalism, namely the primacy of industrial production and the omnipresence of class struggle."[25] As my analysis of American Apparel elucidates, ethical capitalism detracts attention from the physical labor of historically marginalized communities used to manufacture goods and instead focuses on a nebulous "ethical" standard. Before Homeland Security raided American Apparel in 2009 and fined the corporation for knowingly hiring undocumented workers, American Apparel successfully used the framework of ethical consumption to detract attention from their illegal practice of hiring transmigrant workers without US work permits who occupy the lowest social class in the US labor market. Consumers were able to feel good about their apparel purchases while Latinxs on the shop floor labored for unionization, higher pay, and immigrant rights.

Ethical consumption is a mechanism of racial capitalism that marks affluent Whites as moral while relying on the labor of historically marginalized groups to produce those ethical goods. Ethical consumption, then, can function as an everyday mechanism of White supremacy that brands those with surplus capital as moral. Ethical consumption operates under the assumption

---

22. Johnson, "Citizen-Consumer Hybrid," 257.
23. Cole, "On the Cultural Logic," 2.
24. Cited in Cole, "Ethical Consumption in the Global Age," 320.
25. Jameson, "Postmodernism and Consumer Society," 55.

that consumers are educated about how their goods are produced, and thus spend based on morality. The assumption of an informed consumer constituency may at first appear to assert an aura of political correctness but in fact often enables more nuanced and covert forms of exploitation hidden behind a purportedly moral and educated façade. Moreover, the class privilege attached to some ethical consumption choices does not signify that marginalized and poor groups are somehow immoral.[26] In fact, marginalized groups are also educated about moral consumption choices; however, the predominance of consumption spaces as "white spaces" wherein Whites make rules and regulations, deters certain racialized groups from partaking in some instances of ethical consumption.[27]

Ethical consumption occurs in both local establishments and larger chain corporate stores. Furthermore, ethical consumption manifests differently depending on an individual's social class,[28] racial or ethnic identity,[29] and gendered identity.[30] In their study of the LA economy, Rebecca Morales and Paul M. Ong (1993) find that "wage discrimination and such institutional impediments as unequal access to education and a history of disrupted community formation have combined with structural factors to severely disadvantage this segment [LA Latinx garment workers] of society."[31] In other words, structural impediments and discrimination in the labor force, which in part result in large numbers of Latinxs employed in low-wage jobs, render ethically branded consumption choices impractical or even impossible for the individuals that manufacture those very products. As already noted, the inability to consume ethically branded goods does not mean that low income and historically marginalized populations are not moral. Although low-income and racialized groups are less likely to engage in the dominant repertoire of ethical eating, for example, they are knowledgeable and do care about moral eating choices.[32]

In their analysis of Neo-Fordism, Fourth Worlds,[33] and American Apparel, Liz Moor and Jo Littler contend that American Apparel's overtures to ethical

---

26. Johnson, Szabo, and Rodney, "Good Food, Good People."
27. Often actions of consumption are gendered as feminine, and the processes of production are gendered as masculine. See Cairns, Johnston, and MacKendrick, "Feeding the 'Organic Child'"; Guthman, "Fast Food/Organic Food."
28. Johnson, "Citizen-Consumer Hybrid," 256.
29. Johnson, Szabo, and Rodney, "Good Food, Good People," 311.
30. Cairns, Johnson, and MacKendrick, "Feeding the 'Organic Child,'" 100.
31. Morales and Ong, "Illusion of Progress," 57.
32. Guthman, "Fast Food/Organic Food"; Guthman, "'If They Only Knew'"; Johnson, Szabo, and Rodney, "Good Food, Good People," 313.
33. Moor and Littler use the term "Fourth World" to refer to "zones of exclusion" present in every nation, regardless of "First World" or "Third World" ranking (Moor and Littler, "Fourth Worlds and Neo-Fordism").

consumerism are tempered by its staunchly antiunion politics. They explain the contradictions of American Apparel's purported politics and corporate actions:

> American Apparel contributes at a usefully high-profile level to the discourse against sweatshops/unfair labour conditions, and demonstrates manufacturer responsibility towards paying the minimum wage. . . . Yet, as its anti-union stance demonstrates, it clearly also trades on anti-exploitation policies not being enforced throughout the industry, and in doing so mitigates against the international policies which have been increasingly pursued by clothing trade union the International Ladies' Garment Workers' Union (ILGWU) since the 1990s.[34]

Moor and Littler astutely recognize that ethical consumption works within the American Apparel brand as a type of smoke screen of "caring capitalism." However, though their essay posits that this is a problem, it does not seek to offer suggestions as to how to undo these processes, nor present a history from a laborer's point of view. In this analysis, laborers are seen as pawns of neoliberal capitalism, forever stuck in "zones of exclusion." Such a simplistic representation posits people within systems of exploitation as complacent with their own subjugation. It does not consider the tactical choices that working class people make when faced with systems of oppression, like racial capitalism and sexism, including the calculated choice to be seen yet not speak.

The choice to address the majority of laborers at American Apparel as Latina is based on the historical reality that Latinas have remained the dominant labor pool in LA for over a century.[35] Although knowledgeable about labor unions, I explain in my next section how these workers make tactical choices based in part on sexism and racism felt in US institutions—both capitalist corporations and labor unions.[36] This history of calculated tactical maneuvers by Latinas against patriarchal White supremacy gives a deeper meaning to the power of silence and the choice to be seen or photographed for American Apparel ads.

---

34. Moor and Littler, 719.
35. Fernández-Kelly and García, "Informalization at the Core," 258; Laslett and Tyler, *ILGWU in Los Angeles*, xiv.
36. Nakayama and Krizek, "Whiteness."

Latinxs in the LA Garment Industry

The global garment industry, predominantly located in Latin America and Asia, relies on a largely female and feminized workforce in free trade and export processing zones.[37] In representations of American Apparel's seamstresses on its website, and in the 2006 documentary, *No Sweat,* the majority of laborers appear to be darker-skinned Latinas. Scholarly discussions of Latina labor and the LA garment industry have predominately focused on sweatshop conditions, apparel subcontracting, immigrant labor, the informal economy, and homework.[38] In more recent years, scholarship about Latina labor offered a more comparative and transnational scope.[39] This research frequently critiques global capitalism and explores the intersection of race and gender.[40] Other emergent scholarship traces more recent migratory destinations such as to the rural Midwest or the Southeast,[41] and has focused on the education, labor, and the work at home of teenage and adolescent Latinxs.[42] Scholars contend that technology enables transnational flows, as well as the migration of more privileged middle-class and aspiring middle-class labor migrants.[43] This literature does not address, however, how a company's liberal, ethical, and neoliberal marketing toward an affluent, implicitly White, consumer base works to erase and perpetuate the exploitation of Latinas and other racialized laborers within the United States. A failure to address how the complexities of colorblindness and ethical marketing operate together as a form of social control in effect overlooks the legacy of structuralized racism that still impacts poor and marginalized populations in the United States today.

Feminist scholars argue that to understand the reasons why Latinas are not often involved in labor organizing we must first understand the historically patriarchal and racist organization of labor unions. Prior to the 1920s, the LA garment industry also employed immigrants from Europe in large numbers. In 1907, these European laborers organized the first labor union in the city. Again, race, citizenship, and gender play important roles in understand-

---

37. Bonacich and Appelbaum, *Behind the Label*; Browne and Misra, "Intersection of Gender and Race"; Gereffi, Spencer, and Bair, *Free Trade and Uneven Development*; Whalen, "Sweatshops Here, Sweatshops There."

38. Homework is the practice where employers give their workers material to take home to finish sewing and assembling for additional pay.

39. Chavez et al., "Undocumented Latina Immigrants," 88; Whalen, "Sweatshops Here and There," 45; Meyler and Peña, "Walking with Latinas," 97.

40. Browne and Misra, "Intersection of Gender and Race," 487.

41. Williams, Alvarez, and Hauck, "My Name Is Not María," 563.

42. Cammarota, "Gendered and Racialized Pathways," 53.

43. Schaeffer-Gabriel, "Flexible Technologies of Subjectivity," 903.

ing Latinas' configuration in the LA economy. For instance, Rebecca Morales's (1983–84) research has shown that employers in the city divide laborers into different groups based on citizenship status and race, paying non-White laborers and laborers without citizenship a lower wage.[44] Such hierarchies are duplicated within labor unions where, particularly within the male leadership, many European Americans assumed that Mexicans and Chicanxs were not familiar with labor unions. María Angelina Soldatenko (1991) has since proven that this was not the case. Soldatenko writes that Latinas have long been aware of a complex web of unions and prolabor organizations, both in their home countries and in the United States, and that they are also informed regarding US labor laws.[45] Simplistic portrayals of Latinas who did not want to organize due to their ignorance of labor unions or US practices perpetuated the racism and sexism that permeated the era's labor unions.[46] In her discussion of Latinas in the garment industry, Patricia Zavella (1991) reflects, "We need to research women's and men's lives in ways that identify the sources of diversity without resorting to the mechanistic conclusion that class, race, or gender alone gives rise to difference."[47] Indeed, Soldatenko (1991) responds to this call when she argues that Latinas have resisted unionization in the LA garment industry partially because they occupy unstable positions within shops, perform homework, work in private homes, are involved in the informal economy, lack US citizenship papers or work permits, and encounter issues with child care.[48]

This is not to say that Latinas have never successfully organized in LA. Under the leadership of Russian Jewish anarchist Rose Pesotta, the ILGWU sought to organize Latinas. With a growing Mexican and Chicanx membership, the ILGWU successfully launched a dressmakers strike in the spring of 1933 against workplace violence and abuses at a time when 75 percent of union members were women or girls of Mexican descent.[49] Like their economic stratification, workplace abuses also affected workers differently depending on their gender, race, citizenship status, ethnicity, and/or social class. Labor violations included employers who expected "kickbacks" from workers' salaries and employees who were forced to "speed up" or increase the quantity of

---

44. Morales, "Undocumented Workers," 576.
45. Soldatenko, "Organizing Latina Garment Workers," 83.
46. Soldatenko, 73.
47. Zavella, "Mujeres in Factories," 313.
48. Soldatenko, "Organizing Latina Garment Workers."
49. Durón, "Mexican Women and Labor Conflict," 149.

work produced in a given period of time. Many employees were also expected to work a double day and take work home.⁵⁰

During the 1933 dressmakers strike in LA, dressmakers protested because they were paid at a piece-rate scale for the time they spent working on a garment, not for total time spent in the factory. For example, one Mexican dressmaker involved in the 1933 strike, María Flores, explained: "I come in the morning, punch my card, work for an hour, punch the card again. I wait for two hours, get another [fabric] bundle, punch card, finish bundle, punch card again. Then I wait some more—the whole day that way."⁵¹ For Flores being paid by the piece led to cyclical highs and lows in production that rendered her labor both monotonous and stressful, as her job security and daily pay rate varied. Significantly, such a system could also make workplace organizing difficult because workers might be forced to compete against one another to receive subsequent fabric bundles.

Despite considerable technological advances over the past century, the nature of garment work has not significantly changed. Similar to the lack of significant change in the gendered division of labor in the garment industry, industry executives have also remained hostile to labor organizing for over a century. The LA garment industry did, however, become more antiunion when unions lost strength after the auto industry succumbed to the recession of the late 1970s and 1980s.⁵² During the same time period that the auto industry vanished in LA, the garment industry was able to maintain a place and profit in the city in part due to a large pool of transmigrant workers without US work permits,⁵³ many of whom were recent arrivals from Central America.⁵⁴ These garment workers often labored for below minimum wage at home, in sweatshops, or cottage industry settings.⁵⁵

American Apparel's choice to open a garment factory in LA was a strategic decision, as the city has remained the nexus of profitable West Coast garment manufacturing since the early 1900s. Over the past century, multiple factors have guided production in the LA garment industry, in part resulting in economic growth that has fueled Latinx migration. Pushed by a poor economy

---

50. Durón, 149–50.
51. Durón, 149.
52. Morales, "Undocumented Workers," 574; Kristin M. Zentgraf, "Through Economic Restructuring," 52–53.
53. Fernández-Kelly and García, "Informalization at the Core," 259–60.
54. Hamilton and Chinchilla, *Seeking Community in a Global City*, 70. In the 1980s, people from Central America, principally Salvadorians and Guatemalans, migrated to Los Angeles in order to escape violence in their home countries and often sought employment in the LA garment industry.
55. López-Garza, "Study of the Informal Economy," 145.

at home and the Mexican Revolution, over 1 million Mexicans immigrated to LA in the early twentieth century.[56] The influx of Mexican labor, restrictions on Asian migration, and a rapidly growing manufacturing sector helped render Mexicans and Chicanxs a desirable labor pool for an industrializing LA economy.[57] In fact, even before female full-time wage labor was common, many Latinas worked part-time in the garment industry.[58] Today, 75 percent of all garment laborers in LA are Mexican women or US Chicanas, and less than 2 percent of workers are unionized.[59] Despite efforts, American Apparel employees have failed to organize a labor union. This history of antiunion sentiment in the LA garment industry helps contextualize current labor struggles at American Apparel. Since its emergence as a manufacturing base at the turn of the twentieth century, LA has remained staunchly antiunion. As a consequence, the garment industry boomed in LA during the 1920s, partially because manufacturers developed businesses in the Sunbelt City to avoid union organizing in New York City.[60] Nevertheless, labor unions have existed in California also since the early twentieth century, but in the early years they had little interest or desire in organizing Mexican and Chicanx workers.[61]

Although a predominantly Latinx workforce may be responsible for garment production at American Apparel, their voices remain largely absent from branding material and even a documentary film about working conditions at the plant. In fact, American Apparel's branding strategy of ethical consumption foregrounds a corporate voice—frequently with quotations from the celebrity CEO—under the image of Latinx workers. As I discuss in the next section, this dynamic attempts to mimic worker opinions, giving the allusion to consumers of a progressive and fair workplace, while speaking *for* workers. These workers remain silent in the ads and function as a backdrop while corporate policies that supposedly help workers are explained.

Latinas and American Apparel

According to *No Sweat*, American Apparel pays its garment workers for the number of products that they help to assemble and compensates them in

---

56. Durón, "Mexican Women and Labor Conflict," 147.
57. Durón, 158.
58. Laslett and Tyler, *ILGWU in Los Angeles*, 18.
59. Kessler, "Impact of North American Economic Integration," 91.
60. Fernández-Kelly and García, "Power Surrendered, Power Restored," 137.
61. In the 1920s, LA labor leaders tried to unsuccessfully organize Mexican American women (Laslett and Tyler, *ILGWU in Los Angeles*, 20).

modules, or small groups of workers, who are managed by a supervisor or captain that constantly forces laborers to "speed up" their efforts. Christina Vásquez, a spokesperson for the Union of Needletrades, Industrial, and Textile Employees (UNITE!) in LA (a union that has failed to unionize American Apparel workers), reflects that at American Apparel "the number-one issue for the workers was the pressure . . . so this is a piece rate world. They are producing the work of two or three people."[62] Cynthia Guillén, a former American Apparel employee, explained the pressure of working in modules: "Everyday [sic] they [workers at American Apparel] worked so hard. I remember that they encouraged people to drink energy drinks like Red Bull and different things like that. . . . They have captains on each floor and they were almost formed into like small little gangs."[63] *No Sweat* director Amie Williams conducts only one interview with an anonymous Spanish-speaking current employee in her documentary.[64] This employee contends that at first s/he thought American Apparel offered a unique business model, but soon discovered many abuses at the company:

> Perhaps the owner is really cool, but the supervisors humiliate the workers. And that's the pressure that exists in the modules. People can't even go to the bathroom because the work accumulates. There are a lot of workers that have gotten sick. People have had nervous breakdowns and headaches. If you don't do enough work, you run the risk of another worker producing more and you could get shoved aside. Always day-to-day I have that in my head. That one-day [sic] there's work and another day, who knows?[65]

The interviewee ends by telling Williams that American Apparel's human resource department ignores worker complaints. Given the gendered nature of the garment industry, this laborer, whose gender has been omitted by Williams, is nevertheless feminized due to the type of work s/he does: sewing and garment assembly. In this vein, Clementina Durón (1984) writes that within the garment industry "women's alleged docility and immunity to the tedium of routine household tasks were characteristics seen as vital to the perfor-

---

62. *No Sweat*, directed by Amie Williams.
63. Between 2004 and 2006, Amie Williams compiled the footage for and released a documentary film titled *No Sweat* that compared Ben Cohen's failed sweatshop-free labor cooperative "Sweat X" with American Apparel.
64. Throughout the documentary, Williams interviewed many employees of the now defunct "Sweat X," but American Apparel employees were reluctant to talk with her.
65. This interview occurs in the second half of the documentary. When the interviewee speaks, the image is just of his/her hands on a table, a directorial decision that leaves the location of the interview and the interviewee's gender suspect.

mance of monotonous tasks of the unskilled industrial sector."[66] Similarly, Anne Phillips and Barbara Taylor (1980) note that throughout the history of the garment industry, work done by men has been classified as "skilled" while work done by women has been classified as "unskilled."[67] These designations are largely arbitrary and result from resistance to the idea of women as breadwinners, a desire to maintain patriarchal control, and stereotypes about the gendered nature of labor.[68]

The feminized American Apparel workforce maintains their silence because of a fear of their own disposability and a desire not to add work or stress to their coworkers. Melissa Wright (2006) documents what she terms the "myth of the disposable Third World woman" that is particularly applicable in understanding the experiences of Latinas at American Apparel. The myth references a key paradox of global capitalism in which a feminized laborer's dexterous work creates wealth for multinational companies at the expense of the laborer's health. Once the repetitive work renders the laborer no longer effective, she loses her job and as a result faces more compounded physical, psychological, and economic exploitation.[69] In the interview of the anonymous American Apparel worker quoted above, the myth of Latina disposability is alive and well, and constitutes a daily threat that affects the physical, economic, and mental well-being of herself and her coworkers.[70] The work of Alejandra Marchevsky and Jeanne Theoharis (2006) underscores the harsh reality that low-wage jobs like those typical in the LA garment district simply do not provide women with enough money to support their families. Rather, Marchevsky and Theoharis obliterate the stereotype of Latinas as "welfare queens" by nuancing our understanding of Latina economic experiences as a dynamic of "interdependency between welfare and work," even for women who have child care and other networks of support.[71]

American Apparel employees' realities of economic need in the onslaught of this supposed disposability are further supported by corporate policies. The company's practice of paying workers according to the number of garments produced by modules was developed in 2003 to help streamline production. Katherine Macklem of *Maclean's Magazine* makes the following observation about American Apparel's manufacturing:

---

66. Durón, "Mexican Women and Labor Conflict," 148.
67. Phillips and Taylor, "Sex and Skill," 85.
68. Phillips and Taylor, 84.
69. Wright, *Disposable Women*, 2.
70. Although the pronoun of choice of the interviewee is not known, I am using female pronouns to highlight his/her feminization.
71. Marchevsky and Theoharis, *Not Working*, 8.

Instead of rows of workers on an assembly line, sewing machine operators now complete garments in teams. One will attach a sleeve, another the neckline binding. Their machines are placed almost in a circle so the item is passed—flung really—from one to the next. When the change was first made, workers staged a mini factory-floor revolt, stopping production for a couple of hours. But after the system was better explained—including how they could make up to US$20 an hour—workers returned to their machines. Now, because operations are paid in volume, needles fly at top speed.[72]

One could interpret being "paid in volume" as being paid a piece-rate wage. American Apparel employs the allure of more money and capitalist values of worker competition to entice its workers to become more "productive." This new production model, along with a $15 million upgrade in machinery, resulted in hundreds of employee layoffs in December 2008, a time when the corporation was very profitable. In response, American Apparel spokesman Elliot Sloan explained to the *Los Angeles Times,* "As a result [of changes in manufacturing], employee productivity is up, the need for the same numbers of employees decreases."[73] Sloan's statement ultimately contradicts American Apparel's claim in 2009 on its website that "most importantly, we guarantee job security and full-time employment; this is an anomaly in the garment industry."[74]

Rebecca Morales and Paul M. Ong (1993) argue that the LA economy was built on a surplus labor market that works to depreciate wages. They find that racial capitalism impacts the economic status of Latinxs in the city due to a combined legacy of racial prejudice, lack of education, gender bias, citizenship discrimination, and social class.[75] This legacy is no doubt still at play in American Apparel's factory. Take, for example, American Apparel's stance on progressive immigration issues that has been challenged on the national stage. On September 29, 2009, the *New York Times* reported that American Apparel headquarters was "firing about 1,800 immigrant employees in the coming days—more than a quarter of its work force—after a federal investigation turned up irregularities in the identity documents the workers presented when they were hired."[76] In an email correspondence with the newspaper, Charney openly questioned the reasons why Immigration Customs and Enforcement (ICE) targeted American Apparel as one corporation, among the 654 other

---

72. Macklem, "Doing the Rag Trade Right."
73. Chang, "LA Apparel Firm Lays Off Hundreds."
74. American Apparel, Inc., 2009, www.americanapparel.net.
75. Morales and Ong, "Illusion of Progress," 57.
76. Preston, "Immigration Crackdown with Firings."

companies that were investigated, for employing undocumented workers. It can be assumed that Charney was insinuating that the immigration investigation might have been triggered by his liberal immigration politics and the Legalize LA brand. Charney argued that the firings at his company "will not help the economy, will not make us safer." Charney continued to write that "no matter how we choose to define or label them, they [undocumented workers] are hard-working, taxpaying workers."[77] It is a matter of public record that American Apparel hired transmigrant workers in their factory who lacked legal US work permits. The corporation was also not unionized, and the exact details behind these laborers' payment and treatment remain unclear.

American Apparel has not unionized because, like most LA factories over the past century, the corporation is staunchly antiunion. In an interview in *No Sweat*, CEO Charney contends that capitalism is based on the idea that "no one wants to be associated with a loser" and that he wants his company to "maintain a high level of independence," an independence that he maintains would be eliminated by a union. This desire for "independence" is likened to a version of individual success that erases the role that labor plays in corporate profit. In the documentary, Charney states that his business acumen led to American Apparel's success: "I'm the corporation expert. That's why the union couldn't penetrate my company. . . . I'm an expert entrepreneur. I am, you know what? I am one of the best hustlers of my generation, man!"[78] The CEO's individualized notion of success obfuscates the vital role that a cheap and renewable labor force has played in his ability to become a corporate entrepreneur, a gesture that "hustles" both money from consumers and justifies paying his easily replaceable workers a fluctuating piece-rate wage.

In reality, within American Apparel, factory workers were active in immigrant rights movements prior to Charney's Legalize LA campaign; for example, workers were already organized against the Sensenbrenner Bill[79] prior to the Legalize LA campaign. Moreover, the campaign does not provide a close reading of American Apparel's exploitation of discourses of immigration through their Legalize LA brand. In the next section, I perform a critical discourse analysis of American Apparel's advertisements and images on its corporate website to shine light on the underbelly of so-called "caring capitalism."

---

77. Preston.
78. *No Sweat*, directed by Amie Williams.
79. The Sensenbrenner Bill failed to pass in the Senate in 2006. It sought to greatly increase the militarization of the border, made being undocumented a felony, and criminalized contact with undocumented people.

American Apparel's Advertisements

In American Apparel's advertisements, White public space is often clearly delineated from Latinx public space. Take, for instance, the images of Latina factory laborers who function as a backdrop behind the focal point of a slender White woman in the ad titled "Vertical Integration" (see fig. 1). This ad elucidates the ethnoracial and classed divisions of labor between the predominantly slender White female models and the extensive Latina female labor force. The actions of these Latina workers—looking around at the camera and not at their work—suggests a disruption in normal work activities. These subtle movements by the workers foreground the constructed and artificial staging of the ad. In the ad, one could imagine the Latina laborers might be constructing an American Apparel dress for around $12/hour, an inconsistent pay rate that is above the minimum wage, but that is also within pennies of the national average for a garment worker's hourly wage. Such seamstresses would not likely purchase that same dress, which they helped to make in a matter of seconds, at a cost of around fifty dollars. Furthermore, these Latina seamstresses hardly fit the "ideal" body type, race, or class embodied by the inordinately slender model featured in the advertisement. The economic value of the model to the corporation is greater in that, according to its 2008 website, she earns more than four times the hourly salary of the seamstress, or about fifty dollars per hour.

"Vertical Integration" depicts a White model in three distinct rectangular snapshots stacked on top of one another: she is alone and shopping at American Apparel at the bottom, walking the shop floor in the middle frame, with Latinas working behind her, and again alone and wearing an executive-type outfit at the top. The American Apparel model thus embodies the persona of the ideal clothing consumer: young, well-to-do, slender, White, and female. Additionally, this ad attempts to place the viewer/consumer in the position of the model; you too could work at, model for, and buy American Apparel clothes! It also represents American Apparel consumer and executive roles as individualized White public spaces. These representations work together to further a notion that through personal responsibility and hard work, anyone can equally consume and become a corporate CEO—very much an incarnation of the American Dream. Such a construction of an executive's accomplishments as an individualized achievement mirrors Charney's own view of himself as a "hustler" who alone is responsible for American Apparel's economic success. In her work on colorblindness in California's alternative food industries, Julie Guthman (2008) reflects that farmers' markets and community-supported agriculture are historically White-marked spaces that

FIGURE 1. American Apparel, "Vertical Integration," 2009, http://americanapparel.net/advertising

people of color are not likely to frequent, where "whites continue to define the rhetoric, spaces, and broader projects of agro-food transformation."[80] In a similar colorblind dynamic, the cumulative impact of the majority of American Apparel's advertisements containing predominantly White women marks the consumption of the American Apparel brand as a White public

---

80. Guthman, "'If They Only Knew,'" 395.

space whose marketing agenda is overseen by White executives. In practice, economic success, particularly in the LA garment industry, is dependent on the hard work of women of color and not solely a strong consumer market.

Ethical consumers choose to buy ethically marketed clothing because they are concerned with the quality and production of the garment as well as the social recognition that they receive from wearing it. Ethical consumers list the following values when they rationalize their consumption choices: the purchase furthers their personal and emotional well-being, and the purchaser believes all people deserve equal treatment and opportunity, to care for the weak and share wealth more equitably, to promote conservation of resources and to help end pollution, to provide for future generations, to feel self-confident, to receive social recognition from others, to ensure the safety of the products they consume, to have an immediate influence on the environment, to help local interests, to help them live a healthy life, to feel unique, and because they want to live in harmony with nature.[81] American Apparel appeals to a multitude of these values through its American-made products that also promote overt political messages on liberal causes such as immigration.

American Apparel's Legalize LA campaign published advertisements on billboards in downtown LA and in full-page *Los Angeles Times* and *New York Times* ads in January 2008 (see fig. 2), claiming "It's time to give a voice to the voiceless." The text at the base of the newspaper advertisement explains:

> Migration and economic experts generally agree that the productivity and hard work of immigrants improves the economy. . . . Immigrants not only increase the wealth of the nation, they have contributed significantly to major scientific, medical and industrial advancements, as well as the arts. Many of them have become great entrepreneurs, too.

Contemporary scholarship contends that consumption is not a binary "ethical" versus "unethical" practice, but instead a dynamic choice mediated by a variety of social, political, cultural, and ethical factors.[82] Likewise, an individual's views on comprehensive immigration reform cannot be completely articulated through wearing a "Legalize LA" t-shirt. Mediating factors, such as socioeconomic status, fashion style, or a reluctance to engage with a corporation with antiunion politics may all impact an individual's fashion choice. Recycling neoliberal rhetoric of individual success and personal responsibility, some advertisements for this campaign elaborate on immigrants

---

81. Jägel et al., "Individual Values and Motivational Complexities," 384.
82. Johnson, "Citizen-Consumer Hybrid," 233.

FIGURE 2. American Apparel, "American Apparel on Immigration," 2009, http://americanapparel.net/advertising

who "become great entrepreneurs, too" and contain an image of American Apparel's former CEO's resident alien card on a White background (see fig. 3). Ironically, this second ad series, promoting the May 1, 2006, March for Immigration Reform against the Sensenbrenner Bill, was meant to equate the CEO with undocumented workers, but in reality accomplished the inverse. Through the reproduction of proper legal documents, the ad validates the former CEO's privileged legal immigration status as a White, male, Canadian resident alien, as well as his wealth and entrepreneurial skills. Many state-level immigration policies, such as Arizona's S.B. 1070, contain provisions mandating that individuals suspected of being undocumented must "show me your [immigration status] papers." A historically grounded fear of people of Latinx descent being forced to produce documents on command, regardless of legal status, to prove that they are citizens, dates back to the massive repatriation campaigns of the 1930s.[83] Whereas the immigration status of Charney's workers was left suspect in the aforementioned newspaper ads, Charney literally showed everyone his papers. This gesture is profoundly steeped in White

---

83. Balderrama and Rodríguez, *Decade of Betrayal*, 312.

deflection and White privilege—Charney is assuming an achieved status as an immigrant, but unlike his workers, he is White, wealthy, and well documented. He both asserts his victimhood and ignorance by showing he does not understand what it means to be without US legal paperwork in the United States. Despite his rhetoric to the contrary, this advertisement is an example of how profoundly entrenched in late capitalism American Apparel is: the focus remains on a CEO who demands "independence" from, yet is dependent upon, Latinx workers.

The Legalize LA ads in the *Los Angeles Times* and the *New York Times* contain Latinx workers from American Apparel's factory. Foreshadowing his company's ICE investigation, these ominous black and white advertisements suggest that the corporation hired undocumented workers, all of whom are of Latin American origin. It is significant that American Apparel hired undocumented workers because it provides reasons behind why the corporation may support immigration reform. Hiring undocumented workers in the US is against the law, and the Immigration Reform and Control Act (IRCA) of 1986 established sanctions to punish employers who hire, and often exploit, undocumented workers. The law itself cannot be "ethical"; however, committing an act that is illegal challenges any simplistic renderings of American Apparel as a "moral" brand. By claiming to "speak for the voiceless" in its advertisements, American Apparel paradoxically is taking the voice away from its documented and undocumented workers by speaking for them—a voice that had been previously clearly articulated during the May 1, 2006, immigration protests in LA. This is another example of White deflection and White rhetoric—positing that transmigrants have no voice and that it is the responsibility of White liberals to educate everyone about racial matters; Eduardo Bonilla-Silva also terms this White racism as "abstract liberalism."[84] If all undocumented people were granted US citizenship, like "Legalize LA" promotes, American Apparel would not have had to fire around 1,800 undocumented workers in 2009. The company might have also had to pay workers a higher wage, which would depreciate profit margins. American Apparel has long offered immigration assistance to its employees yet at the same time asserted that all its workers have proper documentation, a claim proven false. In a *New York Times* article about Legalize LA, Charney said:

> These people [undocumented residents] don't have freedom of mobility, they're living in the shadows. . . . This is at the core of my company, at the core of my soul. Let me be clear who makes our clothes. It's a collaboration

---

84. Bonilla-Silva, *Racism without Racists*, 4th ed.

FIGURE 3. American Apparel, "Legalize LA," 2009, http://americanapparel.net/advertising

between American-born people and non-American-born people. . . . I don't think supporting immigration reflects negatively on the brand, and in fact, it makes it look like we're a responsible business. I think my Latino workers are American workers. . . . They're from the Americas. We're all here together.[85]

Charney believes in a hemispheric definition of America; that is why he named his company "American Apparel" and not "United States Apparel." When Charney attests that "Latino workers are American workers, they're from the Americas," he may be calling for a more expansive definition of "America," but at the same time he paternalistically marks "these people" as potentially undocumented. The placement of American Apparel ads in major newspapers, on billboards, and the CEO's own use of provocative language in interviews constitute deliberate attempts to create a brand based in ethical capitalism and garner media attention. Although the ads do critique failed US immigration policies, they do not offer any real suggestions for changing the current system. American Apparel began its Legalize LA campaign in support of its workers, some of whom were politically active around issues of immigration reform. In this way, it can be argued that the Legalize LA ads

---

85. Story, "Politics Wrapped in a Clothing Ad."

to some extent took public focus away from the acts of organized protest by American Apparel workers and instead focused attention on the corporation and its celebrity CEO.

It is important to recognize that the representations of Latinx workers on the American Apparel website featured subjects who appeared to enjoy their work; the company is no doubt more humane than other manufacturers globally and in LA. For example, the company website lists that it offers employees "parking, subsidized public transport, subsidized lunches, free onsite massages, a bike lending program, a program of paid days off, ESL classes and much more."[86]

The *New York Times* journalist Julia Preston reports that many of the employees fired after the ICE investigation had become a close community while employed at American Apparel. Interestingly, Preston does not interview Latina seamstresses, only their relatively higher-paid male supervisors. She cites the case of "Jesús, 30, originally from Puebla, Mexico, [who] said he was hired 10 years ago as a sewing machine operator, then worked and studied his way up to an office job as coordinating manager . . . [but] who would not reveal his last name because of his illegal status."[87] Jesús tells the journalist that prior to the raid, he had health and life insurance, and made around $900 pretax dollars per week.

The Legalize LA blog contains a page of a longer letter purportedly given to Charney by a former employee during an immigration rights march (see appendix 2). The touching letter reveals that its writer was notified by ICE to leave her/his job, and concludes with: "Thank you American Apparel for giving us hope, and thank you to all the people who understand us." However, upon contextualizing American Apparel's support of immigration reform as a process of its "ethical, socially responsible" self-branding efforts, a political statement actualized through consumption constitutes a self-gratifying and individualizing gesture. When focused on goods or services, a trusting ethical consumer may not question the reasons and methods a company utilizes in constructing its corporate image of social or moral responsibility. For instance, ethical consumption does not guarantee that the individual who made the "Legalize LA" t-shirt does not face exploitation in the workplace.

---

86. The website for this information is no longer active. However, the original link is here: http://www.americanapparel. net/aboutus/verticalint/workers/.
87. Preston, "Immigration Crackdown with Firings."

Conclusions: The Brand Liberal Paradox

American Apparel's corporate conduct and business practices do not deviate dramatically from the national norm. The ethos of the brand provides a case study in liberal White deflection that exploits historically marginalized groups in selling a brand image and product. The corporation long acted as a manifestation of Dov Charney's cult of personality by reifying his entrepreneurial skill as the reason behind corporate revenue. The individualized construction of the US American Immigrant Dream narrative embodied in Charney, however, is deceptively complex. His resident alien card does not liken him to his immigrant workers, many of whom have been or currently are undocumented. It further highlights his privileged status as a White, North American, heterosexual man from a relatively affluent Canadian family. American Apparel's use of mostly Guatemalan laborers in its ads in the *New York Times* and the *Washington Post* promoting proimmigrant activism in 2006 did not "give a voice to the voiceless." In fact, these paternalistic ads ignore the now more-than-one-century-long history of Latina labor organizing in Los Angeles, as well as the CEO's successful attempts at silencing labor organizing at American Apparel.

The history of Latinx labor is essential to understanding how racial capitalism has differentially exploited Latinx laborers in LA for well over one hundred years. According to testimonies in the documentary *No Sweat,* Latina seamstresses at American Apparel are, in effect, paid a piece-rate wage. These workers labor for an antiunion corporation in modules where they are constantly coerced by male supervisors to drink energy drinks in order to "speed up" their labor. As a result, these workers sometimes forego bathroom breaks and undergo constant mental and physical stresses. Although laborers may be offered a twenty-minute massage by a masseuse,[88] the aforesaid shop floor dynamics and gendered divisions of labor are conditions witnessed in LA sweatshops for well over a century.

The case study of American Apparel provides us with multiple representations of the core neoliberal tenet of personal responsibility and how the focus on the individual over the collective serves deflective Whiteness. The celebrity CEO sees himself as responsible for his own and his company's successes. The marketing strategy of ethical consumption speaks to affluent consumers whose individualized acts of consumption purportedly display liberal politics. What these two representations have in common, however, is a latent narcissism that applauds the individual for his or her selflessness and heightened

---

88. Preston.

social consciousness. These two representations do not seek to deconstruct or decenter traditional power dynamics that have long existed in the LA garment industry, or the position women of color continue to hold as the lowest and most exploited workforce. This study reoriented the main subject of analysis in current scholarship on the corporation away from articulate and smart analyses of individualistic modes of capital and ego accumulation, and instead asserts the importance of the collective labor pool through making these workers' history, voices, and representations (or lack thereof) the primary subject of analysis.

I argued that the case study of representations of American Apparel's websites and advertisements embody a US-based form of neoliberal social regulation, enacted through ethical and often-colorblind representations, that unproblematically champion notions of individual success, the private regulation of corporations, antiunion politics, and consumer choice, while marking ethically based consumption as a White public space. The corporation's progressive immigrant-rights marketing campaign "Legalize LA" is an example of deflective Whiteness and uses images of these workers to promote a brand agenda. Sociologists who study the motivational values behind the consumer choice to buy ethical clothing recognize that the multiple supply chains needed in manufacturing clothing and accessories make ethical consumers particularly weary and uncertain about their clothing consumption choices.[89] Such feelings of hesitation and doubt are well founded under dynamics of ethical capitalism that perhaps unwittingly deploy a covert form of colorblindness that inferentially marks consumers as young, White, middle-class hipsters and laborers as likely undocumented Latinxs.

---

89. Jägel et al., "Individual Values and Motivational Complexities."

CHAPTER 5

Framing Immigration

Legal Violence in NPR's Coverage of the Postville Raid

On May 12, 2008, Immigration and Customs Enforcement (ICE) raided Agriprocessors Inc., a Kosher meatpacking plant in Postville, Iowa, for allegedly hiring transmigrant laborers. One week following, National Public Radio's (NPR's) first syndicated news report about the immigration raid, "Deportation Hearings Follow Iowa Raid," debuted on the evening news program All Things Considered.[1] The report features an interview with *Chicago Tribune* journalist Antonio Olivio conducted by NPR's Michele Norris. Occurring under Bush Administration immigration policies, the Postville raid remains the largest single immigration raid in US history[2] during which, to quote Norris, "roughly 10 percent of the town's population . . . almost 400 people were arrested."[3] The interview opens with a description of the raid by Olivio: "Fleets of helicopters and federal government busses came racing into Postville . . . surprising a lot of residents out there, and [ICE officials] went in to the plant,

---

1. Norris, "Deportation Hearings Follow Iowa Raid."
2. During the Trump Administration, a total of 680 people were apprehended at multiple facilities across the state of Mississippi in the largest state-wide immigration raid; however, Postville remains the largest raid at a single work location (Housloher, "ICE Agents Raid Miss. Work Sites").
3. Quotations from National Public Radio broadcasts are taken from official NPR transcripts. Inconsistencies in spelling, grammar, or wording are found in the transcripts that are produced under tight deadlines by subcontracted labor.

which is about a six-acre facility, and started picking people up."[4] Such large-scale "shock and awe" immigration raids that targeted businesses were typical of Bush Administration immigration enforcement policy yet ultimately did not deport as many people as Obama Administration tactics.[5] Olivio informs NPR's listening community that the workers rounded up in the raid "were taken to a makeshift detention center about 77 miles away in Waterloo, Iowa, inside the National Cattle Grounds. . . . It's a place, essentially, for festivals and for some livestock exhibition shows and so forth. And they [ICE] had brought in trailers and set up a temporary court inside the trailers."[6] This first interview highlights the national diversity of the detained transmigrant workers who hailed from Guatemala, Mexico, Israel, and the Ukraine. This diversity is represented only in the May 19, 2008, broadcast and thereafter remains invisible throughout the seven months of NPR's coverage of the raid in which laborers are labeled only as "Latino," "Hispanic," or "illegal."[7]

This chapter nuances the inferential and taken-for-granted ways that deflective White rhetoric shapes liberal-minded and historically White discourse communities. NPR's coverage of the Postville raid relies on episodic coverage, framing mechanisms, and discursive shifts within stories that strategically remind NPR's listening public that US citizens are the real victims—the victims of potential identity theft. Further still, NPR's own reporting and statistics, along with the coverage and framing mechanisms, racialize and police NPR's listening community as overwhelmingly White, well educated, and liberal minded. Nevertheless, through airing humanizing coverage of Latinx transmigrants NPR seeks to co-opt and further its brand as a liberal-minded and unbiased media outlet.

There is a narrative disconnect between the diverse populations represented in this initial broadcast with Ludden and Olivio mentioned above and the discursive erasure of diverse Latinx workers in subsequent coverage. Immigration journalist Roberto Suro (2011) observes three tendencies common in immigration journalism, and all three appear in the NPR Postville raid coverage. First, there is a focus on stories that break seemingly out of nowhere. Second, they are driven by episodic coverage that grabs media attention for a

---

4. Norris, "Deportation Hearings Follow Iowa Raid."
5. I borrow the phrase "shock and awe" as an allusion to the Bush Administration's "Bush Doctrine" for foreign policy and military action in the Middle East.
6. Norris, "Deportation Hearings Follow Iowa Raid."
7. Another interesting aspect of this story is that the reporter, Antonio Olivio, is never interviewed or referenced again during the Postville Raid coverage, and no other individual with a discernibly Latinx sounding name is the reporter for any subsequent installments of the Postville Raid coverage. Additionally, it should be noted that in an email interview with Jennifer Ludden in 2012, NPR had no standard when it came to labeling Latinxs as "Latino," "illegal," or "Hispanic" (Jennifer Ludden, email interview by author, May 21, 2012).

short period of time and then fades away; this makes immigration appear as a constant crisis. Third, immigration journalism tends to focus on individual immigrant stories and lawmakers, rather than on transnational labor flows and the corporations that recruit transmigrant labor.[8] On NPR, the Postville story appears to break out of nowhere; there is no in-depth history of immigration law to provide context as to how, legally, workers could be corralled in makeshift prisons. The atrocities and human rights abuses detailed in Olivio's interview are never questioned, followed up with subsequent facts, or adequately fact-checked. This initial story presents information about the raid, and neither Norris nor Olivio offer any commentary or context. The report does not question, for instance, the ethics of ICE corralling individuals like cattle by sentencing and temporarily interning them inside the National Cattle Grounds. The report does not make connections between the impromptu imprisonment of individuals in cattle fields and the War Relocation Authority's repurposing of horse stables during World War II as temporary holding centers for Japanese and Japanese Americans following Executive Order 9066. In its subsequent nationally syndicated coverage on the Postville raid, NPR never informs its listening community about what happened to these workers *after* they received their sentences and left the makeshift internment. We are also not given the added context that the interning of immigrants in private prisons is commonplace.[9] NPR's subsequent episodic coverage does not follow the plight of these workers through immigration courts and into federal prisons. We do learn that many transmigrant workers were issued five-month to two-year federal prison terms for utilizing false documents and stolen Social Security numbers.[10] The coverage does attempt to humanize workers through focusing, in one interview, on the stories of two apprehended workers. However, this humanization operates within the context of unquestioned state violence. Similar to the example of deflective Whiteness and ethnical consumption discussed in the previous chapter, a focus on the individual (particular transmigrant workers, token community or religious officials, etc.) misdirects attention from the greater issue at hand: systematic human rights abuses by US Immigration Customs and Enforcement and the longstanding pattern of the exploitation of transmigrant labor in agricultural industries under US racial capitalism.

---

8. Suro, "Introduction," 8.

9. Hernández, "Pursuant to Deportation."

10. Although never mentioned by NPR in their Postville coverage, many transmigrants who are sentenced to a US prison term, like those temporarily imprisoned in Iowa, serve out their sentence in one of the many private prisons in the United States. The privatization of the prison industry is a neoliberal economic and social change wherein a once-government service is outsourced to the contractor that can most cheaply build and staff the prison system.

After first discussing NPR's framing of its demographic audience in the section "Framing Immigration," I unpack key framing mechanisms present throughout NPR's coverage of the Postville raid. I analyze how White rhetoric in the radio broadcasts constantly refashioned itself as unbiased, normative, and US American—and liberal—while at the same time associating marginalized groups with criminality and fear.

NPR's National Public

Through its own naming as "National Public Radio," NPR posits itself as the voice to and for the *national public,* yet NPR's own demographic profile recognizes that not all citizens are equally likely to be listening in. In its broadcasts and digital publications, NPR constructs and maintains an image of its listening publics as White, middle class, liberal minded, and well educated. During an episode of On the Media, Brook Gladstone reports on a five-hundred-page 2006 demographic self-study of NPR's listening audience's consumption patterns, attitudes, behaviors, and personal politics. Gladstone reflects that the commonplace stereotype in American culture of NPR listeners as progressive is accurate. She narrates to NPR's listeners that they

> really do like Starbucks. . . . You are 173 percent more likely [than a non-NPR listener] to buy a Volvo and 210 percent more likely to read *The Sunday Times.* . . . Now, as far as left wing goes, you are more likely to live in the coasts, which tend to be blue, and you definitely like "The West Wing" more than average, but then again, you were 13 percent less likely to watch "Will and Grace," so go figure. . . . You are *more* likely to describe yourself as liberal.[11]

On NPR's website the page titled "Audience" contains updated demographics of NPR's listening publics for, presumably, the consumption of NPR's digital public.[12] These 2012 demographics inform us that the average NPR listener is 24 percent more likely to have a graduate degree, 40 percent more likely to have a bachelor's degree, 22 percent more likely to read books for a leisure

---

11. Gladstone, "Listeners of National Public Radio."
12. I am referring to the listeners of NPR on the internet as well as radio listeners. Although a good topic for a subsequent seminar paper, the exploration of the convergence of media and the multiple lives of radio broadcasts (whether on your iPod, car radio, or computer) is not the objective of this chapter. By "digital public" I am referencing the portion of NPR's listening community that listens to NPR, or gains more information about NPR's reporting, from visiting their webpage.

activity, and 22 percent more likely to have voted in federal, state, and local elections than the general US population.[13] Although such generalizations may describe the "average" NPR listener, Gladstone is quick to report that they do not adequately describe *every* listener. She muses that some members of the listening audience "are broke, plenty of you are conservative, and quite a few of you are young and 20 percent of you are not white." The phrasing of "20 percent of you are not white" defines NPR by what it is not, rather than what it is—80 percent White. In their discussion of White rhetoric, Nakayama and Krizek (1995) argue, "Whiteness eludes essentialism through this multiplicity and dynamism, while at the same moment containing within it the discourses of essentialism that classify it scientifically or define it negatively."[14] A goal of White rhetoric is to remain normative; practitioners racialize others, while seeking to make their own racial identity normative.

Gladstone's report seeks to problematize assumptions that NPR listeners are "white, over-educated, latté drinking, *New York Times*-reading, Volvo-driving, 'West Wing' watchers" while nevertheless reinforcing them. Overstepping the differences of class, gender, race, and sexual orientation, Gladstone reflects that she was "struck most by [the audience's high] self-esteem" and that NPR listeners are "more curious than average, more eager to spend time in other countries. Thirty percent of NPR News listeners are more likely to want to, quote, 'understand how the world works.'" Both Gladstone's report and the website's demographics suggest that NPR's national public is composed of well educated, relatively affluent, and civically engaged White people with an open curiosity and willingness to make the world a better place. The composition of this presumed listening audience is noteworthy while considering possible framing mechanisms in the Postville raid coverage.

Something that all members of NPR's audience have in common is that they are imagined as White, affluent, well educated, and liberal citizens. By covering stories about non-US citizens for a presumed audience of wealthy, White, and well-educated US citizens, NPR's Postville coverage inferentially "others" populations who are not White, English speaking, well educated, and liberal minded.[15] The intent of this chapter is to uncover how a self-identified "liberal" media outlet, while producing racially sensitive reporting for a well-

---

13. Gladstone, "Listeners of National Public Radio: On the Media."
14. Nakayama and Krizek, "Whiteness," 303.
15. Hispanic marketing research suggests dominant representations of Latinxs homogenize diverse ethnic, racial, and national communities into a monolithic group to sell goods as well as ideologies (Dávila, *Latinos, Inc.*; Dávila, *Latino Spin*). This corporatized homogenization performs the ideological work of marking all Latinxs as brown-skinned, indigenous-featured, Spanish-speaking, and Mexican (Santa Ana, *Brown Tide Rising*; Chavez, *Covering Immigration*; Chavez, *Latino Threat*).

educated, civic-minded audience, can simultaneously reproduce exclusionary logics through media framing, such as the notion that Latinxs are "illegal" and threatening. These ideologies of exclusion work to render Whiteness as normative and Latinxs as threatening, foreign, and also outside of NPR's mainstream, English-language listening audience. Such a dynamic sustains a form of racialized capitalism that serves elites of both the "conservative" and "liberal" variety.[16] Economic and social factors impact consumer choice for individuals of all backgrounds. Scholars assert that some members of historically marginalized groups choose not to frequent historically White spaces, for example, some farmer's markets or clothing establishments, because of a lack of representation.[17] Although marginalized communities remain knowledgeable about ethical and sustainable consumption choices, they may not choose to frequent historically White social spaces or even liberal-minded auditory spaces—like NPR—due in part to the implicit framing mechanisms I discuss here.[18]

Immigration is framed in media as well as in political and social discourses in ways that influence both news reporting (e.g., content of stories, questions asked, interviewees selected, editing of audio pieces, selection of background noise) and our collective abilities to imagine alternative futures (e.g., building walls, criminal charges for immigration violations, increased border surveillance). Suro (2011) emphasizes that repeated narratives in journalism shape the ways the public views transnational migration; that "journalism does exercise a framing function that can have a cumulative effect on the way that the public interprets events."[19] In the following section, I outline key frameworks present in NPR's coverage. These frameworks are not exclusive to NPR's coverage of immigration and that is precisely the point. Although NPR may attempt to humanize historically marginalized people in its Postville coverage, it repeats familiar media frameworks and tropes about transmigrants.

Framing Immigration

Erving Goffman (1974) finds two broad categories of frameworks, natural and social, that shape our cognitive processes. Natural frameworks have their

---

16. Racial capitalism is the dynamic wherein capitalism depends on the exploitation of racialized groups, for example, transmigrants. Under new types of racial capitalism, certain groups are deemed "good" and "bad"; these "bad" workers are individuals whose labor is exploited while simultaneously justified, for instance, by the group's illegality (in the case of transmigrants), "culture of poverty," or "lack of initiative" to find better jobs. For a more thorough engagement with racial capitalism, see Melamed, *Represent and Destroy*.

17. Guthman, "Fast Food/Organic Food," 395; Noel, "Branding Guilt."

18. Guthman, "Fast Food/Organic Food," 395; Noel, "Branding Guilt."

19. Suro, "Introduction," 7.

genesis in the "physical and biological sciences," for example "the state of the weather as given in a report." Social frameworks, the subject of study here, "provide background understanding for events that incorporate the will, aim, and controlling effort of an intelligence, a live agency, the chief one being the human being. Such an agency is anything but implacable; it can be coaxed, flattered, affronted, and threatened."[20] Without our conscious recognition, frameworks shape how we see and understand events and influence our ability to imagine solutions to complex social issues. In the following section, I explain some of the dominant social frameworks that influence NPR's coverage of the Postville raid. These overlapping frameworks interact with one another and include the Latino Threat frame, the crimmigrant frame, and the White racial frame.

Latino Threat Frame

The framing of immigration in journalism as a constant problem influences public perception of transmigrants and limits the scope of possible policy proposal. Building on Goffman's work, George Lakoff and Sam Ferguson (2006) further explain the influence of frames in relationship to immigration: "[Frames] are pre-linguistic—in the realm of concepts, not words. Framing is about characterizing values, concepts, and issues. . . . Frames structure the way we think, the way we define problems, the values behind the definitions of those problems, and what counts as 'solutions' to those frame-defined problems."[21] The authors argue that the "immigration problem frame" informs the way we engage with and comprehend the immigration debate. Under the immigrant problem frame, "the problems are the immigrants and administrative agencies," which therefore limit "all solutions [to] involve those parties"—for example, building walls and increasing border militarization.[22] The problem of immigration is often tied to a specific geography: the US–Mexico border. Nicholas De Genova (2004) theorizes that the rhetoric of "illegality" relies on the spatial construction and militarization of the US–Mexico border as a "theatre of enforcement 'crisis'" that works to discursively inscribe Mexican as the shorthand for "illegal."[23] Tangentially, media representations

---

20. Goffman, *Frame Analysis*, 22.
21. Lakoff and Ferguson, "Crucial Issues Not Addressed."
22. Lakoff and Ferguson.
23. De Genova, "Legal Production of Mexican/Migrant 'Illegality,'" 171.

and US law reinforce the stereotype that all Latinxs are "Mexican."[24] Statistical data suggests that federal law enforcement presumes "illegality" to be akin to "Mexicanness" or "Latinxness." Latinxs make up about 81 percent of the nation's estimated unauthorized population but represent 97 percent of those deported.[25] Put differently, law enforcement differentially targets those ethnoracially classified as Latinx American for deportation at a rate of frequency that is about 16 percent greater than their overall composition of the total undocumented population. As I discuss in my next section, through strategic absence (e.g., interviewing US citizens to speak for transmigrates), framing (e.g., background noise associated with the Spanish language), and naming (e.g., "illegal," Mexican), NPR's coverage relies on old tropes that all Latinx migrants are Mexican transmigrants.

The immigrant problem frame, therefore, cannot be divorced from rhetoric of racialized Latinx threat. Leo R. Chavez (2008) defines the "Latino Threat Narrative" as historically situated and evolving alarmist discourses in the media, public policy, and society that construct Latinxs as immigrant threats. He argues that narratives depicting historically marginalized racial/ethnic groups as "threatening" are pervasive throughout US history; however, the specific racial or ethnic groups labeled as "threats" have changed. The Latino Threat Narrative was preceded by "the German language threat, the Catholic threat, the Chinese and Japanese immigration threats, and the southern and eastern European threat."[26] Within this racialized history of threat, many groups have assimilated into Whiteness or into the damaging "model minority" stereotype, yet Latinxs are persistently associated with new migrant threats.[27] Chavez finds that this "narrative show[s] that what might appear as random or idiosyncratic comments, characterizations, traits, images, and other representations about Latinos, both immigrants and US-born, are actually part of a more cohesive set of ideas."[28] The Latino Threat Narrative performs the ideological work of normalizing tropes about diverse Latinxs as resistant to assimilation, Spanish speaking, Mexican, Catholic, tremendously fertile, members of large families, noncitizens, and terrorist threats to the nation-state. Such tropes frame discourse and can inform journalism. These

---

24. Ngai, *Impossible Subjects*, 71; De Genova, "Legal Production of Mexican/Migrant 'Illegality,'" 171; Chavez, *Latino Threat*, 23.

25. Lopez, Gonzalez-Berrera, and Motel, "As Deportations Rise."

26. Chavez, *Latino Threat*, 177.

27. As a counterpoint, for instance, consider German Americans who were once considered linguistic and national threats in the early part of the twentieth century, but have now assimilated into "whiteness."

28. Chavez, *Latino Threat*, 3.

tropes frame and shape popular discourse about Latinxs, and immigration—forever binding them together in the national imagination.

Crimmigrant Frame

If Latinx Americans are presumed Mexican, this not only contributes to their racialization but also scripts them as not US American. Stuart Hall (2001) maintains that dominant groups (e.g., Whites) understand themselves and justify the oppression of marginalized groups through rudimentary binary oppositions; for example, through rhetoric of law and order. Lee Bebout (2016) finds "US whiteness is constructed against a Mexican Other," and through such binary understandings "Mexicanness is also juxtaposed to and fashions Americanness." US identity, in other words, constructs itself through demarcating national and racial others. Bebout shows how "the ideological and discursive characteristics of whiteness and Americanness are conterminous" and "as such, the innocence, benevolence, fears, anxieties, fantasies, and desires of whiteness may be expressions of not simply a racial imagination but also a nationalist one."[29] These *nationali*st sentiments are overtly reinforced by *National* Public Radio, whose funding comes, in part, through donations from NPR's imagined nation. Chavez and Bebout remind us that frameworks that shape discourse are racialized. As I will show, a discussion of transmigrant criminal behavior, and the individualization of responsibility for acts deemed criminal, is pervasive throughout NPR's coverage of the Postville raid.

Writing about immigration, Julie A. Dowling and Jonathan Xavier Inda (2013) find that US neoliberalism's framing of individual responsibility as virtuous creates a racialized binary between the "proper neoliberal citizen," whose personal acts secure their own safety, and the mostly Black and Latinx "deviant anti-citizens" who include criminals, the poor, and welfare recipients.[30] Colorblind immigration discourses focus on this question of "legality"[31] as opposed to race, which marks Latinxs as racially "other" (read: not White), not US American, and criminal.[32] The framing of transmigrant Latinxs as criminal, or as "deviant anti-citizens" in the words of Dowling and Inda, cannot be divorced from so-called "crimmigration," or the dynamic of govern-

---

29. Bebout, *Whiteness on the Border*, 3.
30. Dowling and Inda, *Governing Immigration through Crime*, 4.
31. Dowling and Inda, 5.
32. Today, a "post-race" discourse about Latinxs, the nation's largest non-White ethnic group, is propelled in part by the shifting demographic reality that infants of color outnumber White infants. For more information, see Siek and Sterling, "Census: Fewer White Babies Being Born."

ing immigration through an ever-expanding definition of what constitutes a crime.³³ This concept is particularly significant in contextualizing the framing mechanisms at play in the Postville raid coverage, as many of the apprehended non-US citizens received jail sentences that are the direct result of such policies.³⁴ The widening definition of criminality as it applies to noncitizens is not a new concept. The 1996 Illegal Immigration Reform and Immigrant Responsibility and Control Act (IIRICA) signaled the broadening of the definition of what constitutes a felony and an expanding of the range of deportable offences for noncitizens.³⁵ As the hybridization of criminal and immigrant law, the term "crimmigration," or the individualized "crimmigrant," also performs a framing function that reinforces a false assumption that transmigrants and immigration are inherently criminal.

Offering a different set of terminology to shape discourse, Cecilia Menjívar and Leisy J. Abrego (2012) label the "increasingly fragmented and arbitrary field of immigration law gradually intertwined with criminal law . . . *legal violence.*" For Menjívar and Abrego, legal violence is "a theoretical lens that makes visible different forms of violence inherent in the implementation of the law, particularly when these become normalized and accepted."³⁶ As a theoretical lens, legal violence encompasses the frames of "immigration problem" and Latino Threat. The binary understandings discussed above by Hall (2001) also impact legal violence with the construction of "good immigrants" versus "bad immigrants."³⁷ Building on Menjívar and Abrego's work, Alfonso Gonzales (2013) maintains that the discourse surrounding immigration is set by an "anti-migrant bloc" that encourages the criminalization of transmigrants. The language used by the anti-migrant bloc to criminalize transmigrants fluctuates depending on the context (e.g., the media, popular culture, the state department, or other government bodies). Nevertheless, the anti-migrant bloc frames popular, mediated, and political discourses about immigration. Gonzales finds that the most dangerous impact of the anti-migrant bloc is this framing against which all others feel compelled to respond:

> The most insidious consequences of the criminalization of migrants is that it allows the anti-migrant bloc to set the boundaries of the immigration debate

---

33. Stumpf, "Crimmigration Crisis," 376.
34. Camayd-Freixas, "Interpreting after the Largest Ice Raid"; Dowling and Inda, *Governing Immigration through Crime*; Reynolds and Didier, "Contesting Diversity and Community"; Valerio-Jiménez and Whalen, *Major Problems in Latina/o History*, 469.
35. De Genova, "Legal Production of Mexican/Migrant 'Illegality,'" 176.
36. Menjívar and Abrego, "Legal Violence."
37. Hall, "Spectacle of the 'Other.'"

within a binary opposition, in which they advance a one-dimensional image of "the bad immigrant" who, based solely on a few "exaggerated, simplified, and naturalized characteristics," deserves to be detained and deported and in which the traditional opposition attempt to counter with more simplified images of the immigrant who deserves to stay. This simplistic characterization forces Latino migrant activists and their allies into a false binary opposition [in] which the rights of the "good immigrant"—the poster child image of the palatable assimilated American kid who came to the United States—as a child may potentially stay at the expense of the "bad immigrant." The latter of whom . . . may have made a few mistakes in their lives, [and so] must be policed, detained, and deported.[38]

Gonzales's claims about an anti-migrant bloc, including popular White conservatives like radio personality Rush Limbaugh and conservative institutions like the Heritage Foundation, the CATO Institute, and others, remind us of vertical power relations where dominant groups set the rules for social and political action, as well as discourse.[39] Although positioned from a different ideological space that emphasizes humanistic representations, NPR, I contend, similarly shapes discourse by relying on a framework of good versus bad immigrant.

White Racial Frame

By utilizing restrictive frameworks like crimmigration or good immigrants versus bad immigrants to organize discussions of US transmigrants, and immigration more generally, popular rhetoric is shaped from a strategic location of racial, social, and political dominance. Thomas K. Nakayama and Robert L. Krizek (1995) use the work of Michel de Certeau (1984) in arguing that strategic rhetoric maintains systems of inequity, and tactical rhetoric challenges these dominant ideologies. I liken strategic discourses to those of the anti-migrant bloc that Gonzales identifies, and tactical discourse to those who reject and disengage with the bloc's framing of the immigration debate. Nakayama and Krizek find that this dominant rhetoric is racialized as White, yet this White-allied rhetoric can be used by individuals of any racial or ethnic identity(ies). The authors view "whiteness as a rhetorical construction" and "avoid searching for any essential nature to whiteness" while they "seek an

---

38. Gonzalez, *Reform without Justice*, 6–7.
39. Gonzalez, 23.

understanding of the ways that this rhetorical construction makes itself visible and invisible, eluding analysis yet exerting influence over everyday life."[40] In this chapter, I view Whiteness as a rhetorical construction that makes itself visible, in part, through deploying colorblind frames of immigrant problem and Latino Threat.

As defined in the introduction of this book, colorblindness is a racial ideology that posits that race no longer has a tangible impact on people's lives, and that to "see color" is therefore a racist act. Eduardo Bonilla-Silva (2018) finds that there are numerous frames through which colorblindness operates. In the NPR coverage of the Postville raid, the frame that Bonilla-Silva identifies as "abstract liberalism" is particularly apparent. Informed largely by liberal rhetoricians, he finds that "the frame of *abstract liberalism* involves using ideas associated with political liberalism (e.g. 'equal opportunity,' the idea that force should not be used to achieve social policy) and economic liberalism (e.g. choice, individualism) in an abstract manner to explain racial matters."[41] As mentioned previously, Roberto Suro (2011) identifies a focus in immigration journalism on individual stories of transmigrants—divorced from context. This tendency in the journalistic coverage of immigration and transmigrant stories frequently evokes the abstract liberalism frame of colorblindness. Particularly as my analysis below suggests, I find that the frame of abstract liberalism is used to shift rhetoric toward discussion of law and order (e.g., questions of stolen Social Security numbers, labor violations), thereby discussing Latinx transmigrants using the frames of immigration problem and Latino Threat, but using colorblind terms.

In the section that follows, I explore how historically White media, no matter the political affiliation or perceived journalistic rigor, employ a White racial frame. I do not seek to brand NPR or its listeners as somehow racist, but to emphasize that, no matter how vigilant we are, the national White racial frame impacts journalism about historically marginalized groups. Joe Feagin (2009) defines the White racial frame as a centuries-old assemblage of ideologies, discourses, media, and behaviors that privileges Whites. He writes:

> Over time white Americans have combined in it a beliefs aspect (racial stereotypes and ideologies), integrating cognitive elements (racial interpretations and narratives), visual and auditory elements (racialized images and language access), a "feelings" aspect (racialized emotions, and an inclination to action to discriminate). Moreover, over centuries of operation this

---

40. Nakayama and Krizek, "Whiteness," 293.
41. Bonilla-Silva, *Racism without Racists*, 4th ed., 58.

dominant white framing has encompassed both a strong positive orientation to whites and whiteness (a pro-white subframe) and a strong negative orientation to racial "others" who are exploited and oppressed (anti-others subframes). Much research shows that this dominant white frame is often negative towards racial others, that it is full of anti-others subframes. . . . Early in this country's history this overarching racist framing includes a central subframe that assertively accents a positive view of white superiority, virtue, moral goodness, and action.[42]

For example, homogenizing diverse Latinx groups as "Mexican" is a framing mechanism and discursive maneuver of strategic White rhetoric that maintains a White racial frame. It minimizes the complexity of marginalized groups at risk from state-sanctioned violence, as well as their unique migratory experiences that could impact asylum claims, while remaining—ostensibly—race-neutral.

Borrowing from the frames of Latino Threat, immigration problem, Whiteness, and legal violence, I analyze how the broadcasts and transcriptions function as framing mechanisms for how NPR's listening community interprets not only the entirety of NPR's Postville coverage but also transnational migration more generally. Taken together, these framing mechanisms perform a type of liberal White deflection; though ostensibly humanizing coverage, these mechanisms of othering are covered by a veneer of left-leaning egalitarianism. However, listeners are formulaically reminded throughout the Postville coverage that they are victims of transmigration and transmigrants. For instance, as I will show in the sections that follow, at the end of broadcasts are repeated discursive shifts from humanistic coverage to discussions of transmigrant criminality that threaten White US citizens, such as accusations of aggravated identity theft. This chapter also challenges Suro's notion that the "narrative of illegality," or the criminalization of transmigrants without proper US work documents, does not have a corollary in the progressive or liberal press.

NPR'S Agriprocessors Coverage

To uncover the power dynamics and framing mechanisms in NPR's coverage of the Postville raid, I perform a critical discourse analysis (CDA) of these

---

42. Feagin, *White Racial Frame*, 10.

broadcasts and transcriptions.[43] CDA shows how social cognition is influenced by framing mechanisms found throughout NPR's raid coverage.[44] Particularly during times of economic insecurity, like the Great Recession that occurred during the Postville coverage, Otto Santa Ana (2002) finds that the US public readily accepts, internalizes, and espouses stereotypical language, or "textual images," that cast Latinxs as relentless "brown tides" assaulting the nation. In turn, discursive representations influence policy, for example California's Proposition 187, that specifically targeted transmigrant women and children's access to government benefits including health care and education.[45] Building on scholarship that views Whiteness as a discursive construction, I find that NPR's coverage frames transmigrants, and immigration law and policy, as a threatening problem. This is done, in part, through a strategic absence of nuance behind legal violence, transmigrant journeys, transnational labor recruitment, and transmigrant experiences in the US prison industrial deportation complex.

Following the frame of legal violence, criminality is discursively linked with Spanish-speaking Latinxs throughout NPR's coverage of the 2008 immigration raid. Take for example the aforementioned May 19, 2008, report that began this chapter. This report details a shocking case of alleged employee abuse at the meatpacking plant. Citing this case, Olivio explains that "A worker was—had his eyes duct-taped with a blindfold and then was hit in the head with a meat hook."[46] This outrageous act of physical violence is never mentioned again in NPR's ongoing coverage, although subsequent reports discuss other, less extreme incidents of workplace abuse, such as failing to pay workers overtime, or forcing individuals to work while ill and against doctor's orders.[47] Norris does not ask any further questions of Olivio about this violent abuse; for example, was this atrocity committed by a supervisor or another worker? Norris's next question immediately following Olivio's description of

---

43. Although I reference information from the NPR radio shows *Morning Edition, Talk of the Nation, Tell Me More, Day to Day,* and *All Things Considered,* my second section, "NPR's Agriprocessors Coverage," contains close textual readings from six sets of *All Things Considered* and *Morning Edition* broadcasts and transcripts. This section contains an analysis of the following: "Deportation Hearings Follow Iowa Raid" (May 19, 2008), "Iowa Plant Charged with Hiring Minors" (September 1, 2008), "Immigration Raid Leaves Mark on Town" (June 9, 2008), and "At Iowa Meatpacking Plant, New Workers Complain" (September 2, 2008). I chose to analyze this set of broadcast coverage because shows air during drive-time traffic (*All Things Considered* airs from 4:00 to 6:30 p.m., and *Morning Edition* airs from 5:00 to 9:00 a.m.) and therefore have large listening audiences.

44. Van Dijk, "Critical Discourse Analysis."
45. Santa Ana, *Brown Tide Rising,* 7.
46. Norris, "Deportation Hearings Follow Iowa Raid."
47. Ludden, "Immigrant Rights Groups."

the violent scene is about the fraudulent identification cards used by the workers.[48] This framing technique is a type of deflective White discourse: (1) The news coverage focuses on decontextualized episodic acts of workplace abuse to garner an empathetic listening audience, while not expressing a sincere concern about the innate humanity and ongoing treatment of the mostly Guatemalan workforce. (2) The discursive shift at the end of the report reminds this audience that the *real victims* are NPR's largely White, liberal, and well-educated listening audience—not the transmigrant workers.

Rather than contemplate these abusive acts by plant employees, the audience is keenly reminded at the end of the story that these transmigrant workers were working under stolen Social Security numbers. Significantly, listeners are not told who committed the act of theft, but, without context, listeners are left to assume that those in possession of the stolen property are culpable. The broadcast's final statement, therefore, performs a significant discursive shift. It locates responsibility for criminal behavior not with the physically abusive working conditions overlooked by plant management but rather onto the bodies of the transmigrant laborers.[49] This rhetorical posturing uses the colorblind frame of abstract liberalism to place the culpability for breaking US law on individual transmigrants. NPR's predominantly White audience is reminded that their Social Security numbers could also be vulnerable; it is a racial dog whistle to make Whites fear without context.[50] Furthermore, the reoccurrence of this framing mechanism in stories about Latinx transmigrant workers perpetuates a narrative of Latino Threat and the frame of immigration problem: no matter how humanizing a story, audience members are reminded, in the end, that Latinx transmigrants face federal criminal charges for stealing citizens' private identification numbers.

On June 9, 2008, *All Things Considered* reporter Tim Belay issued the report "Immigration Raid Leaves Mark on Town" about Postville. This story begins by explaining that, prior to the raid, "about half of them [Postville residents] were Hispanic"; however, after the raid Postville faced the negative side effects of an overnight population shortage.[51] Belay predicts that "Mexican-Americans from Texas" will most likely fill the jobs now left vacant at Agriprocessors. In the meantime, he informs NPR's audience that Post-

---

48. Particularly during the Bush Administration, after 9/11 there was a sharp increase in massive raids in the Midwest and Southeast frequently targeting food-processing plants (Lopez, Gonzalez, and Motel, "As Deportations Rise").

49. For more information about labor abuses, please see the court cases *USA v. Juan Carlos Guerrero-Espinoza* (US District Court, Northern District of Iowa, July 2, 2008) and *USA v. Martin De La Rosa-Loera* (US District Court, Northern District of Iowa, July 2, 2008).

50. Haney-López, *Dog Whistle Politics*.

51. Belay, "Immigration Raid Leaves Mark."

ville's schools, churches, and businesses are suffering due to a nearly 18 percent decrease in population. The report is structured into two main parts: Belay narrates the reasons behind the current economic and community crisis in Postville, and then he interviews community members who testify to the negative side effects of the raid on the overall economy, industry, and community of the small town. Belay interviews a Catholic minister, a librarian who discusses how the decrease in population hurts the school system,[52] a leader of the Orthodox Jewish community, a successful Mexican restaurateur, and a local radio station manager whose station broadcasts in English, Spanish, and Hebrew.

Belay's text creates a layered image of a detained transmigrant community by interviewing community members who were not apprehended. Before the immigration raid at Agriprocessors, Belay reflects that the "plant brought diversity and prosperity to a town with three central streets and no stoplight. But after the raid, many here are wondering if the future of the town is in jeopardy." Beginning in 1998, NPR began reporting on the demographic changes brought to Postville by the Kosher meatpacking plant, a business that transformed a once largely White and Protestant Midwestern town of 1,500 into a larger and more diverse community with many Jews from Brooklyn and Israel, and later Latinx transmigrants who came to fill the lower-level jobs at the plant.[53] Given Postville's history, Belay's choice to interview a Catholic minister is significant, as Latinxs are largely presumed to be Catholic,[54] and in Postville, St. Bridget's Catholic community was the only church to have bilingual Spanish and English services, as well as transmigrant outreach programs.[55]

After Belay's prelude, the piece transitions into the background vocalizations of Catholic priest Father Paul Ouderkirk, a linguistic shift that the official transcript notes as "Speaking Spanish." Belay then explains, "Father Paul Ouderkirk leads the Spanish mass on Saturday nights at St. Bridget Catholic Church. He says the immigrant raid wounded the town." The Spanish lan-

---

52. Elementary schools, in particular, worked to welcome new transmigrants to Postville, hiring new teachers, expanding existing facilities, and even offering sign language classes in Spanish and English (Reynolds and Didier, "Contesting Diversity and Community," 184).

53. For historical context, please see the following reports: "Orthodox Jews in Rural Iowa," December 7, 1988; "Changing Face of America: Iowa Immigrants," March 28, 2001; "Changing Face of America: Postville, Iowa," March 29, 2001; "Changing Face of America: Postcards from Postville," November 29, 2004; Allen, "PETA Footage Puts Kosher Slaughterhouse on Defensive," January 10, 2009; "Faith Matters: Kosher Slaughterhouse Raises Ethical Dilemma," August 8, 2008; "Faith Matters: Religion a Big Story in 2008," January 2, 2009.

54. Chavez, *Latino Threat*.

55. Reynolds and Didier, "Contesting Diversity and Community."

guage in Belay's piece is termed "ethnic noise," a phrase that appears elsewhere in the transcriptions and neither Belay nor Father Ouderkirk translates it. Functioning similarly to the musical interludes often used by *All Things Considered*,[56] "Speaking Spanish" in this case functions as a sound bite or melody connecting disjointed pieces of the story.[57] In terms of audience reception, the literal meaning of the Spanish text is rendered irrelevant to the monolingual English speaker and is also absent in the transcript for a bilingual audience. As xenophobic English-only state-level legislation gains increasing support in states like California, Arizona, and Florida, the highly politicized communicative burden to learn a new language is differentially leveled on English-language learners.[58] From the point of view of some Spanish-speaking audience members, acts of simultaneous translation could be seen as potentially transgressive; if monolingual English speakers want to understand the broadcast, they must learn Spanish.[59]

In a similar mode of representation, the willingness of individuals to make the effort to learn the Spanish language becomes a sort of "brand identity" that marks a space or individual as Latinx or as sympathetic to transmigrant interests. When Father Ouderkirk speaks in Spanish, he foreshadows his later statements that he is empathetic to the plight of the transmigrant community, particularly after the immigration raid:

> FATHER OUDERKIRK: First it's in the hearts of people. They're frightened. They're not sure. They had roots here. They liked it here because Postville was about the same size of areas that they came from. It's unsettled. The wound also has hurt this parish because it's so deep, we don't know what the long-term effects are going to be.

Father Ouderkirk describes Postville's undocumented community as assimilated into the Iowa town with "roots," and with religious and community ties that resemble their own upbringing in rural Spanish-speaking (Latinx) America. He humanizes the Latinx and Latin American population in Postville through highlighting their likeness to longtime White residents based on shared small-town lifestyle and religious family values. This well-

---

56. For more information about NPR and a discussion of its use of musical accompaniment, please see Douglas, *Listening In*.

57. On September 2, 2008, Jennifer Ludden used the same strategy of using non-English-speaking people as "background noise." In this case it is the "foreign language" of Somali refugees.

58. Lippi-Green, *English with an Accent*.

59. I am indebted to Dr. María Elena Cepeda, in particular, for her insight here.

meaning gesture intended to minimize difference promotes a model cultural pluralism wherein only cultures similar to the dominant (White) rural culture of Postville are legitimated. Such a model does not assume that the older White population should adjust to Postville's changing demographic profile, but instead highlights how only cultures similar to the dominant culture are allowed to survive, albeit in a new US-Americanized form. The romanticization of a shared rural upbringing and religious heritage is a simplistic rendering of the complex reasons why Latin Americans and Latinxs choose to move to the Midwest. As scholars of Latin American and Latinx migration to the Midwest recognize, these factors have historically included labor recruitment, family networks, economic need, domestic and international policy, and a desire to establish a more settled lifestyle to improve the quality of their children's education.[60]

Every location visited by Belay is linguistically associated with the Spanish language, either through music or speech.[61] The report mentions one nationality—Mexican—linking the absent transmigrant workers with a Mexican heritage. Also, in the May 19, 2008, *All Things Considered* piece mentioned earlier, Michele Norris tells NPR's listening public: "Among the hundreds detained, [were] people from Mexico, Guatemala, Israel and the Ukraine."[62] Although it appears as the first nation in Norris's list, more specifically, most of the apprehended workers were not from Mexico. In actuality, the *Washington Post* reported that "those arrested include 290 Guatemalans, 93 Mexicans, 2 Israelis and 4 Ukrainians, according to the US attorney's office for the Northern District of Iowa."[63] However, the tendency to label all Spanish-speaking undocumented Latinxs as predominantly "Mexican" is not idiosyncratic but rather part of a cohesive set of ideas, linked with the militarization of the US–Mexico border and legal violence, that mark diverse Latinx groups in the US context as always already foreign.[64]

---

60. Loucky and Moors, *Maya Diaspora*; Millard, Chapa, and Burillo, *Apple Pie and Enchiladas*; Allegro and Wood, *Latin American Migrations*; Kanter, "Faith and Family."

61. There are three other instances in the text where music is used as background accompaniment to Belay's report. The first occurs as a "sound bite of choir" in the official transcription, as the St. Bridget Catholic Choir sings religious music in Spanish as background noise following Father Ouderkirk's interview. The second occurs when Spanish language music plays in the background in Sabor Latino, a Mexican restaurant and grocery store, prior to Belay's interview with the establishment's owner. The last instance of music is an instrumental piece of blue grass music that provides the "sound bite of music" that introduces Jeff Abbas from "KPVL Radio, a local non-profit station [that] . . . broadcasts in English, Spanish, and Hebrew" (Belay, "Immigration Raid Leaves Mark").

62. Norris, "Deportation Hearings Follow Iowa Raid."
63. Hsu, "Immigration Raid Jars a Small Town."
64. De Genova, "Legal Production of Mexican/Migrant 'Illegality.'"

Given Belay's use of the Spanish language as background noise, and the absence of people from Latinx marked spaces, it would appear as if the individuals apprehended from Israel and Ukraine never existed. This is striking as NPR had also been reporting on the large Hasidic Jewish population of Postville, relocated from Brooklyn due to jobs at the Kosher plant as early as 1988 with the story "Orthodox Jews in Rural Iowa" that aired on *Morning Edition*. More recent to the 2008 immigrant raid, NPR aired a series of stories about Postville's demographics in 2001 on the segment "Changing Face of America" during the program *All Things Considered*.[65] After interviewing local librarian Julie Heitland about how, in the wake of the immigration raid, the local school system projects a loss of essential funding because of the decrease in "immigrant families" who attended the local schools, Belay interviews Aaron Goldsmith. Goldsmith "is a leader in the Orthodox Jewish community [in Postville], and he's worked hard to bring these very different cultures together." Goldsmith's comments to NPR: "Who's running to get packing jobs? I don't know. I don't know if there's going to be people that are good community members. Are they going to be people that have jumped from job to job? What kind of people are they going to be?"[66] As a representative of the Orthodox Jewish community, Goldsmith's testimony that he does not know who will take the vacant jobs at Agriprocessors implies that they will not be members of the Jewish or Israeli community. Belay's statement that Goldsmith has "worked hard to bring these very different cultures together" additionally suggests that the people who once held these packing jobs were also not Jewish. Goldsmith's interview confirms, in other words, that the hazardous and labor-intensive jobs were performed largely by Latinx transmigrants. Subsequent coverage confirms these workplace dynamics where transmigrant laborers express resentment for their supervisors for forcing them to come to work regardless of physical injury or illness.

According to Chavez, the Latino Threat Narrative includes the xenophobic fear that Mexicans and Mexican Americans want to "re-conquest" the US Southwest, to take back land that was originally taken from Mexico with the signing of the Treaty of Guadalupe-Hidalgo in 1848 following the Mexican-American War.[67] This re-conquest, reimagined when labeling heterogeneous Latinx groups as singularly "Mexican," is significant because, throughout the NPR coverage, Latinxs are depicted as newcomers to once rural, White, and Protestant Postville. After a short period of time, the Latinx transmigrant

---

65. See the "Changing Face of America" segments: "Changing Face of America: Iowa Immigrants," March 28, 2001; "Changing Face of America: Postville, Iowa," March 29, 2001; "Changing Face of America: Postcards from Postville," November 29, 2004.
66. "Changing Face of America: Postville, Iowa," March 29, 2001.
67. Inda, "Value of Immigrant Life"; Chavez, *Latino Threat*.

workforce nearly doubled the town's population. Latinxs are portrayed not only as desiring to re-conquest the Southwest, but also as expanding their territorial reach into parts of the United States that, since the forceful removal, genocide, and relocation of Indigenous Americans, have been historically White and rural spaces. The reality that the overwhelming majority of apprehended undocumented individuals actually came from Guatemala, as well as the significance behind this growing diaspora, is not explicitly recognized in any of NPR's coverage of the immigration raid.[68] Jonathan Xavier Inda (2007) finds that once a narrative of threat becomes socially pervasive the political ramifications are both material as well as symbolic. Inda writes that narratives depicting immigrants as threatening, such as conquest and re-conquest narratives, have structural implications in the form of restrictive state and federal immigration policies, as well as a fixation on the border as a site of crisis, militarization, and foreboding Latinx criminality. These exclude Latinxs from public discourse and limit transmigrant mobility and quality of life through a logic of prevention through deterrence.[69] A part of this exclusion from public discourse extends to the story itself—transmigrants are talked about, but not interviewed.

Regardless of the terminology that its reporters use, NPR's national public decodes these linguistic cues that link criminality with transmigrants. On June 10, 2008, NPR's Michele Norris and Melissa Block read listener letters responding to Belay's Postville coverage:

> NORRIS: Listener Rodney Nilan (ph) of Greenville, South Carolina, was one of several people who wrote to say the story missed an important point. Tim Belay story's [sic] fails to mention that those detained and deported are undocumented, illegal workers. This is just another example of a failed immigration policy from both parties.
>
> BLOCK: And Sam Longstreet (ph) of St. Louis wonders why was NPR so sympathetic to Agriprocessors in Postville, Iowa? Agriprocessors had to knowingly hire illegal immigrants. Postville schools gladly took the government funding that came with the illegal immigrants' children. What both did was wrong, and they deserve what is coming to them.[70]

---

68. Loucky and Moors, *Maya Diaspora*; Fink, *Maya of Morganton*; Millard, Chapa, and Burillo, *Apple Pie and Enchiladas*.

69. Inda, "Value of Immigrant Life," 134.

70. Block and Norris, "Letters." This is the text written exactly as it appears in the official NPR transcript. I believe that the (ph) after the names means that they are spelled phonetically. Also, Agriprocessors was incorrectly spelled in the official transcript. This highlights the hasty production of NPR official transcripts that one has to pay to gain only limited access to for a forty-eight-hour period.

Both letters perpetuate the Latino Threat and Immigration problem frames; the listeners blame transmigrants and Agriprocessors while critiquing the report's word choice. In the piece, Belay's report never mentions "illegal immigrants" or "illegal aliens." In a gesture that reminds listeners of the predominantly White listening community of NPR, the letters also assume the standpoint of a US citizen; an identity linked with Whiteness.[71] By reading Longstreet's and Nilan's commentary aloud, Norris/NPR and Block/NPR literally become conduits for the voices of their listening audiences, linking the radio station with the audience statements.[72]

In the "Letters" segment, criminality is therefore disproportionately levied on transmigrants rather than on corporations and labor contractors who are discussed in subsequent coverage. Norris and Block do not provide their listening publics with the key knowledge that rural food processing factories have an extensive history of using outside labor contractors to directly recruit transmigrant workers from Mexico and the US Southwest. Rural meatpacking plants in the Midwest have even purchased billboards in Mexico advertising US employment opportunities in efforts to cut costs and increase revenue.[73] These jobs developed in rural locations because, to cut costs, corporations restructured the food processing industry by moving processing plants out of cities and nearer to the rural locations of the crops and animals that they process.[74] Neither the original nationally syndicated reports nor the "Letters" segment of *All Things Considered* ever question whether or not outside labor contractors were used to recruit undocumented workers prior to the raid. They remind audience members of the Latino Threat Narrative as well as the assumption of NPR's audience as predominantly English-speaking White US Americans. Subsequent reports discuss the use of outside labor recruiters to replace the apprehended workers, busing in homeless people from Texas, Somali refugees, and finally flying in US nationals from Palau to fill the vacant jobs.[75] In the subsequent coverage, the use of outside contractors, who are never specifically named by NPR, to bring in laborers with regularized statuses is the subject of two different stories. The apparent focus on labor con-

---

71. Bebout, *Whiteness on the Border.*

72. As in the case of Ludden's translation piece, here again is an example of two "standard English-speaking" women embodying the voices of other people. This provokes the possibility of a gendered analysis of, in the case of the Postville raid, the use of women as linguistic translators.

73. Millard, Chapa, and Burillo, *Apple Pie and Enchiladas.*

74. Broadway and Stull, "Meat Processing and Garden City, KS; Kandel and Parrado, "Restructuring."

75. Ludden, "After Raid, Iowa Meatpacker Seeks Palau Workers"; Ludden, "At Iowa Meatpacking Plant, New Workers Complain"; Ludden, "Iowa Plant Charged with Hiring Minors."

tractors in these reports notably underscores the failure of NPR reporters to discuss the individuals responsible for labor recruitment by Agriprocessors prior to the ICE raid, particularly for longtime listeners. At the very least, and if it were in fact the case, the reports might have included a disclaimer explaining that NPR was unable to uncover any information regarding the initial recruitment of transmigrants to Agriprocessors. In effect, transmigrant Latinx worker exploitation is presented in the Postville coverage as an anomaly, rather than as a common occurrence. This is in part because it is not examined or analyzed in comparison to any other large-scale immigration raid. This missing context proves integral, as labor recruitment is rarely an individualized process. Rather, corporations directly recruit both Latinx and Latin American workers, many while they are still in their home countries, to fill jobs in the food processing industry throughout rural America.[76]

On July 24, 2008, *Morning Edition* aired Jenifer Ludden's first report about the Postville Raid[77] titled "Immigrant Rights Groups Challenge ID Theft Arrests."[78] *Morning Edition*'s Deborah Amos introduces the story:

> DEBORAH AMOS, HOST: Today, Congress joins those questioning a controversial immigration raid on a meat-packing plant in Iowa. Traditionally, illegal immigrants swept up in such raids have faced administrative charges and swift deportation. But in Iowa, the Bush administration brought criminal charges and sent hundreds of immigrants to prison. NPR's Jennifer Ludden reports.
>
> JENNIFER LUDDEN: Iowa immigration attorney Dan Vondra says he was stunned to see immigrant workers from the Agriprocessors Packing Plant charged with aggravated identity theft. Congress created that law in 2004 to toughen penalties for what is a growing problem.[79]

From its beginning, this story is shaped through the immigrant problem frame that, as discussed earlier, shoulders the "blame" on transmigrants and policy makers. The Bush administration created tough penalties for transmigrants as a preventative legal mechanism. The report details that, after workers were charged with aggravated identity theft, their attorneys and a state representative from California planned to refute it. Other workers did not plead guilty

---

76. Stull and Broadway, "Meat Processing and Garden City, KS."

77. In NPR's nationally syndicated coverage, Ludden issued the most reports about the raid, a total of six pieces; the first and last airing on *Morning Edition* and the remainder airing on *All Things Considered*.

78. Ludden, "Immigrant Rights Groups."

79. Ludden.

to aggravated identity theft, the report explains, because a conviction carried with it a mandatory two-year prison term. Under a plea agreement, however, the NPR reporter clarifies that many workers plead guilty to lesser charges.

Ludden interviews immigration attorney Dan Vondra who relays that, in a different facility that was raided by ICE, "The mainly Guatemalan immigrants he encountered had no idea what a Social Security card was, let alone that the numbers belonged to real people."[80] Vondra's argument—that many transmigrant workers do not know what Social Security numbers are and therefore could not be charged with aggravated identity theft—became a legal precedent for other immigration lawyers. Although he is speaking of a separate case, Vondra's statement implicitly alludes to the accurate national heritage of most of Postville's detained workers—Guatemalan—and the changing composition of the transmigrant US labor force that includes individuals from Central America. Nevertheless, the overt mention of the detained workers' diasporic history and ethnicity remains absent in this report. Erik Camayd-Freixas (2009), a translator for the transmigrant workers at Postville, recounted that many of the workers had similar Mayan last names and were likely extended family members.[81]

The story transitions to the statements of Iowa immigration attorney Gary Koos who utilized Mr. Vondra's argument in court while trying another case in Iowa, also not connected to Agriprocessors. Koos argued that his client's act of buying an identification document to fill out employment forms at a concrete company did not fit the crime of aggravated identity theft in Iowa, yet he did so unsuccessfully:

> MR. GARY KOOS, ATTORNEY: If you want to think of it in legal terms, it would be that a person has to be put upon notice of what the crime is. And in this case, it's knowingly to use someone else's identity. My client didn't know he had someone else's Social Security number. He just had a number.
>
> LUDDEN: Koos lost the case on appeal, and his immigrant client is now serving five years in federal prison. But other appeals courts have agreed with Koos, and he thinks the Supreme Court may well step in to resolve the dispute.[82]

After explaining legal precedent in Iowa for the argument that immigrants without US citizenship cannot plead ignorance when charged with the theft of

---

80. Ludden.
81. Camayd-Freixas, "Interpreting after the Largest ICE Raid," 124.
82. Ludden, "Immigrant Rights Groups."

identity documents, the piece moves to an interview with the spokesman for the US Attorney's office, Bob Taig. Reiterating a subtle point made earlier by Ludden, Taig explains, "The statute is not just designed to punish. The statute is designed to prevent."[83] The NPR coverage applies the frame of abstract liberalism in the way it individualizes the issue of aggravated identity theft charges while effectively sidestepping the greater systemic factors of workplace and labor subcontractor exploitation of a transmigrant workforce.

Immigration attorney and Democratic Congressmen Zoe Lofgren of California is then interviewed. The report details how Rep. Lofgren called a federal hearing to discuss if Agriprocessers workers were coaxed into pleading guilty to a lesser charge when faced with the two-year prison term that comes with an aggravated identity theft conviction:

> REPRESENTATIVE ZOE LOFGREN (DEMOCRAT, CALIFORNIA): Hundreds of people were convinced to plead guilty to a crime without really an adequate opportunity to see whether they had any remedy under immigration law. And, of course, now that they've pled guilty to a crime, they have no remedies that they might otherwise have had.[84]

These legal issues that Rep. Lofgren brings to light, that Agriprocessors employees may have been coerced into pleading guilty, are never again discussed in NPR's subsequent coverage. The report briefly discusses the collective plea agreement, but we are left with little knowledge of the trial proceedings, or how people were tried in small groups in makeshift facilities at the National Cattle Congress in front of a judge.[85]

Although the plight of the transmigrant workers is nuanced throughout Ludden's piece, it ends with a reminder that the workers at Agriprocessors are criminals who break the law through illicit migration and then break the law again by stealing the identity of US citizens. Ludden interviews Julie Myers from ICE:

> LUDDEN: Not all arrested immigrant workers are being sentenced to jail time, but federal immigration officials say incarceration can be an important deterrent. And Julie Myers, head of Immigration and Customs Enforcement, says some victims of this kind of ID theft do suffer financial and legal hardships.

---

83. Ludden.
84. Ludden.
85. Camayd-Freixas, "Interpreting after the Largest ICE Raid."

MS. JULIE MYERS (IMMIGRATION AND CUSTOMS ENFORCEMENT): We think it's tragic and unfortunate when people break the law by coming here and then break the law again by actually stealing the identity of US citizens.

LUDDEN: So far this year, the immigration agency has made more than 900 criminal arrests. Jennifer Ludden, NPR News, Washington.[86]

In this final exchange, Ludden concludes by recognizing that the citizens whose identities were stolen are the "victims . . . [of] financial and legal hardships." Again, in this exchange the culpability of Agriprocessors and labor subcontractors in illegally acquiring these documents is not explored. The tendency to remind the listening audience of the supposed criminality of transmigrants who lack proper US work permits at the end of broadcasts is pervasive throughout the breadth of NPR's coverage of the immigration raid. Ludden does successfully document two sides of the argument for and against charging those individuals apprehended at Agriprocessors with aggravated identity theft. However, the effect of ending the story with this ICE interview offers NPR's listening public a concluding reminder that these workers are fundamentally double criminals, criminals for "stealing" Social Security numbers and criminals for crossing a border without proper documentation. This discursive technique leaves a final thought in listeners' imagination that works to undue the argument put forth in the beginning of the story where workers were portrayed as ignorant of US labor laws. The NPR audience is left remembering rhetoric of Latino Threat—the idea that transmigrants hurt US citizens who are the real "victims . . . [of] financial and legal hardships."

What is missing in this broadcast is a greater context of legal violence, a result of the confluence of immigration and criminal law. After Erik Camayd-Freixas (2009) helped to translate for Agriprocessors workers, he wrote a testimonial about his experience that underscores the impact of legal violence on the workers. I reference Camayd-Freixas's personal account at length here to emphasize the experiences of laborers while in federal detention, as well as their linguistic and ethnic differences; such accounts are absent from the Postville NPR coverage:

> Driven single-file in groups of 10, shackled at the wrists, waist and ankles, chains dragging as they shuffled through, the slaughterhouse workers were brought in for arraignment, sat and listened through headsets to the interpreted initial appearance, before marching out again to be bused to different

---

86. Ludden, "Immigrant Rights Groups."

county jails, only to make room for the next row of 10. They appeared to be uniformly no more than 5 ft. tall, mostly illiterate Guatemalan peasants with Mayan last names, some being relatives (various Tajtaj, Xicay, Sajché, Sologüí . . .), some in tears; others with faces of worry, fear, and embarrassment. They all spoke Spanish, a few rather laboriously. It dawned on me that, aside from their Guatemalan or Mexican nationality, which was imposed on their people after Independence, they too were Native Americans, in shackles. They stood out in stark racial contrast with the rest of us as they started their slow penguin march across the makeshift court. "Sad spectacle," I heard a colleague say, reading my mind. They had all waived their right to be indicted by a grand jury and accepted instead an *information* or simple charging document by the US Attorney, hoping to be quickly deported since they had families to support back home. But it was not to be. They were criminally charged with "aggravated identity theft" and "Social Security fraud"—charges they did not understand . . . and, frankly, neither could I. Everyone wondered how it would all play out.[87]

The charges of aggravated identity theft are the result of changes to immigration policy where transmigrants were, for the first time in US history, put through the federal criminal justice system and into prisons rather than simply being deported. In December 2005 in Del Rio, Texas, as a part of Operation Streamline the US government began criminally prosecuting transmigrants for illegal entry. This pattern quickly spread through the idea of "prevention through harsh penalties"; an assumption that posits that migration is always a choice. When caught during their first illicit crossing, transmigrants are charged with misdemeanors and given six months in jail. Repeat offenders face a felony charge and a maximum of 20 years in federal prison.[88] Through choosing a frame of legal violence to understand the convictions, rather than one that focuses on supposed criminality, the wider systemic changes that facilitated the criminal charges become clearer. The Bush Administration charged the transmigrant workers at Agriprocessors with aggravated identity theft using a broad definition of a federal statute (18 USC SS 1028A (a) (1)) usually applied to credit card theft and terrorist activity. This needed context is left vague, although Ludden does try to nuance the ways that various attorneys, in individual cases, tried to challenge the federal statute.

By focusing on individual immigrant cases and rationalizing Iowa state law, while interviewing only representatives associated with the US justice

---

87. Camayd-Freixas, "Interpreting after the Largest Ice Raid," 124.
88. Dowling and Inda, *Governing Immigration through Crime*, 10, 17.

system and government, this piece applies the frame of abstract liberalism. Eduardo Bonilla-Silva (2018) explains, "By framing race-related issues in the language of liberalism, Whites can appear 'reasonable' and even 'moral,' while opposing almost all practical approaches to deal with de facto racial inequality."[89] The NPR story creates a binary between US citizens (ICE agents, lawyers, and politicians) and the transmigrants who are spoken *for* by the citizen experts—even in ways that support migrant rights—but are not interviewed. After the Postville Raid, and Ludden's report, in *Flores-Figueroa v. US* (May 2009) the US Supreme Court unanimously ruled that, when charged with aggravated identity theft, the court needs to prove that the defendants *knew* that the documents belonged to other people, and that they were *deliberately* attempting to defraud those people.[90] In this first *Morning Edition* segment, Ludden and her interviewees suggest that the detained workers were not culpable for their acts because many transmigrant people simply do not know that Social Security numbers are stolen property. This suggestion further creates a binary between US Americans, who are coded as implicitly White, being associated with law and order and the transmigrants, who are associated with ignorance, criminality, and threat. While this point of view of transmigrant ignorance implicates a third party who actually stole and/or sold the Social Security numbers—a point left unexplored—it also brands laborers as less knowledgeable of US law than those coded as citizens.[91] Social scientific research proves that many Latinxs in Los Angeles without legal papers allowing them to be in the US are not only informed about US labor laws, but they are frequently aware of labor unions and prolabor organizations.[92] At best, the story posits transmigrants as ignorant individuals who, without their conscious knowledge, committed federal crimes and who cannot speak for themselves. Criminality is still disproportionately leveled on transmigrant workers.

As we learn from Ludden's later interviews, some transmigrant workers were not fluent in English yet obtained false documents at the direction of Agriprocessors. This dynamic implies vertical power relationships within Agriprocessors where English-speaking supervisors held more social and managerial power. On the October 31, 2008, broadcast of *Morning Edition*,

---

89. Bonilla-Silva, *Racism without Racists*, 5th ed., 56.

90. Dowling and Inda, *Governing Immigration through Crime*, 26.

91. For example, in the Guatemalan Mayan Diaspora to the United States, three main locations of settlement—Indiantown, Florida; Houston, Texas; and Los Angeles, California—were all chosen by individuals when in Guatemala because of preexisting community ties, along with potential employment that was secured because of these ties (Fink, *Maya of Morganton*).

92. Soldatenko, "Organizing Latina Garment Workers."

Ludden elucidated these power relationships. In this piece, Ludden details the reasons for CEO Sholom Rubashkin's arrest:

> Dozens of plant workers were told their social security numbers were no good. They [Sholom Rubashkin and Agriprocessors] would have to buy new fake documents, so that [the] company could rehire them under different names. The complaint describes a meeting near a barn on company property where Rubashkin is told that some workers don't have the $200 for a new identification and he offers to loan them the money. Federal prosecutors allege he then called employees in to process these supposedly new applicants the Sunday before the raid.[93]

Meat-processing facilities throughout the US have long practiced inscrutable labor practices by hiring transmigrant laborers in poor working conditions. While writing about Postville, Jennifer F. Reynolds and Caitlin Didier (2013) find that "Agriprocessors is also identical to other rural industrial plants in the way it has recruited new immigrants for the most labor-intensive, low-paying jobs."[94] In the story, there is no context of a larger pattern of recruiting transmigrant labor existing in rural industrial processing plants throughout the Midwest, or Agriprocessors' role in helping workers acquire fraudulent documentation.

On September 1, 2008, Ludden's second nationally syndicated report on the Agriprocessors Raid aired during *All Things Considered*. Although this second report spends a majority of its airtime implicating Agriprocessors in hiring and exploiting workers who were *not* explicitly underage, the report is provocatively titled: "Iowa Plant Charged with Hiring Minors."[95] This news segment has three discernable parts that each address distinct issues at Agriprocessors: (1) workplace abuse of two Spanish-speaking transmigrant employees, (2) the hiring of an underage, and frequently transmigrant, labor pool, and (3) past worker and Rabbi initiated protests against Agriprocessors for various abuses that upper management committed against laborers (though not exclusively underage).

The first third of this report begins with Ludden's interview of two laborers, Cruz Rodriguez Moncada and Bartolo Bustamante, who faced workplace abuses at the kosher meatpacking plant, and not tales of underage labor like

---

93. Ludden, "Kosher Slaughterhouse Former Manager Arrested."
94. Reynolds and Didier, "Contesting Diversity and Community," 174. By new immigrant the authors mean laborers who have recently come to the United States; I use transmigrant to evoke a similar sentiment.
95. Ludden, "Iowa Plant Charged with Hiring Minors."

the segment's title suggests. Ludden does not tell NPR's listening community the age of these two employees, rather Ludden focuses on the different types of abuses that they each faced at the hands of plant officials. Complying with the standards and practices of NPR to report all news in English,[96] Ludden's English language translation overlays Rodriguez Moncada's Spanish language testimony:

> MS. MONCADA (EMPLOYEE): (Spanish spoken)
> LUDDEN: We suffered many humiliations under my supervisor, she says. He'd shout at us to move faster. If we arrive five or 10 minutes later, he'd dock us a day's pay. And if we complained, he'd say, go on then. There are 20 others waiting to take your place.[97]

Rodriguez Moncada is described as an apprehended worker "under home detention and her former supervisor has reportedly skipped the country to avoid arrest, [so] Moncada figures she has nothing to lose" from giving her testimony to NPR.[98] Immediately following Rodriguez Moncada's testimony, Ludden translates the testimony of Bartolo Bustamante who cleaned turkey and chicken trailers for Agriprocessors. When a doctor told Bustamante that he could not work after falling on the job and injuring his back, Bustamante forced himself to go to work despite his debilitating pain. Again, Ludden translates Bustamante's testimony as his Spanish words fade into the background:

> MR. BARTOLO BUSTAMANTE (EMPLOYEE): (Spanish spoken)
> LUDDEN: My boss has told me, if you don't show up, we won't pay you. So, I had two days where my sisters had to help me stand up. They put my shirt on for me. They practically had to carry me into the plant so that I could work.[99]

Bustamante is not directly labeled as not a US citizen, yet his testimony is also given in Spanish, which linguistically associates him with Rodriguez Moncada. Bustamante and Rodriguez Moncada each testify to workplace abuses they felt they could not address while employed at Agriprocessors, particularly due to their fear of losing their jobs. Such a reporting strategy works to contain and pacify the transmigrants as nonthreatening and in fact as safe, awaiting deportation, and as complacent workers who do not affiliate

---

96. Ludden interview with author, 2012.
97. Ludden, "Iowa Plant Charged with Hiring Minors."
98. Ludden.
99. Ludden.

with organized labor. This suggests that, although Ludden may be sympathetic and wishes to present workers at Agriprocessors in a humanizing way, NPR's listening community may be less willing to stay tuned to a story that only discusses how adult transmigrant laborers faced abuse at Agriprocessors. Given the provocative naming of this story, the NPR listening audience was, in a sense, lured into sympathizing with transmigrant workers if they listened in based on the story's title and were therefore expecting a report that explicitly focused on child labor violations.

After these two testimonies of workplace abuse, Ludden reports that, following the immigration raid at Agriprocessors, government officials found that "at least 57 underage workers were at the plant, some as young as 13 in violation of state law."[100] The placement of the first two testimonies of workplace abuse *before* any mention of child labor use makes the title of the report, "Iowa Plant Charged with Hiring Minors," not explicitly representative of the initial third of the interview. Similarly, only about the middle third of Ludden's report focuses on brief interviews with an Agriprocessors spokesman and a Lutheran minister about the tendency for children in the community to work at a young age. The report also briefly mentions that Agriprocessors had policies against child labor use. The choice to interview a representative of the Lutheran Church is perplexing as St. Bridget's Catholic Church was well known for its established transmigrant community outreach programs and became a safe haven for transmigrants and their families after the ICE raid. The church raised money to support impacted families. Additionally, St. Bridget's was the first church in Postville to offer bilingual mass once a month and had a Hispanic Ministry that reached out to both Mexican and Guatemalan nationals.[101]

The final third of the report discusses past workforce protests about labor abuses. Ludden interviews Elver Herrera, who speaks accented and broken English. Herrera worked at Agriprocessors for seven years, during which time he remained an advocate against poor working conditions and complained about such conditions to his supervisors:

> MR. ELVER HERRERA (EMPLOYEE): I told with [sic] a lot of people. The problem is people never listen.
>
> LUDDEN: Herrera says he personally told the plant manager about the mistreatment of employees. Conservative rabbis and the United Food and Commercial Workers Union had raised alarm bells about the kosher slaughterhouse. And last year, workers staged a protest walkout.

---

100. Ludden.
101. Reynolds and Didier, "Contesting Diversity and Community," 183.

MR. HERRERA: When you have a lot complains, you have to know something is wrong. And the complain [sic] started like what, 2001, 2002, '03, '04, '05, '06, what are you waiting for?[102]

The first third of the report is about two cases of transmigrant abuse; it shifts to an explicit focus on employing minors in the middle third of the report; and the final third narrows attention to the general culture of abuse toward Spanish-speaking or accented-English-speaking Latinx workers employed at Agriprocessors. Ludden's strategic composition of her second report lures listeners into staying tuned with the idea that the listening audience will hear a report exclusively about child labor at Agriprocessors; notably, the citizenship of the minors is never discussed. By interviewing workers about abuses they faced, Ludden humanizes the transmigrant Latinx laborers and implicates the corporation as a violator of human rights.

Again, a backdrop of the history and context legal violence is omitted from the stories of labor abuse. ICE knew about allegations of labor abuse at Agriprocessors even before the immigration raid. The United Food and Commercial Workers International Union (UFCW) had been attempting to unionize the plant since 2006. Jonathan Inda and Julie Dowling (2013) found that "on May 2, 2008, a week before the raid, the UFCW had sent a letter to ICE in charge of carrying out operations in Iowa." The UFCW letter stated "that the union was in the middle of an organizing campaign, that various local and federal labor agencies were investigating the plant, and that any immigration enforcement action would have detrimental impact on labor rights."[103] Inda and Dowling's research found that, in the past, ICE had responded to such letters by not interfering and therefore detrimentally compromising workers' rights; however, this was not true in Postville.

In her September 2, 2008, news piece titled "At Iowa Meatpacking Plant, New Workers Complain," Jennifer Ludden outlines the progression of low-wage workers who filled the jobs vacated after the immigration raid. The transmigrant workers detained during the raid disappear from subsequent coverage. Despite Belay's report, the first laborers were not "Mexicans from Texas." Ludden explains Agriprocessors' employment problems:

LUDDEN: There isn't much local labor in this tiny town in Iowa farm country. Since Agriprocessors was accused of knowingly hiring illegal immigrants, it turned over its hiring to outside labor contractors. The first

---

102. Ludden, "Iowa Plant Charged with Hiring Minors."
103. Dowling and Inda, *Governing Immigration through Crime*, 21.

busload brought in included people recruited at a homeless shelter in Texas. That didn't go over well, and some were sent back. The next wave of workers were Somali refugees.[104]

After discussing the bad working conditions, low wages, and tendency for Agriprocessors to perhaps unfairly dock workers' wages, Ludden interviews volunteers at a local Lutheran-administered food pantry that "essentially subsidizes Agriprocessors' low wages." Throughout her report, Ludden interviews new laborers brought to Agriprocessors. She ends by informing NPR's national public that the homeless people from Texas, as well as the Somali refugees, both left their jobs at Agriprocessors. In their wake, Agriprocessors' labor contractors brought in other people, some with criminal histories, from the Midwest. Ludden ends her report with the suggestion that the meatpacking plant may soon bring workers from the Pacific Island of Palau to fill the jobs once again left vacant.

Ludden details that these more recent waves of replacement workers at Agriprocessors experienced conditions similar to those that workers discussed during Ludden's September 1, 2008, piece, "Iowa Plant Charged with Hiring Minors." For example, Ludden interviews two new employees, Ricky Joe Rapier and Ariel Jimenez, in the housing afforded to them by the company while working at Agriprocessors, about the poor treatment they received:

> LUDDEN: They sleep on mattresses on the floor crammed into the dining room, utility room, and they're told will soon have another roommate in the dank concrete basement. There's no furniture. The upstairs shower doesn't work. And in the living room and kitchen, ceiling leaks have left rotted-out holes.
>
> MR. RAPIER: I mean, they treat us like illegal immigrants, right? You crowd a bunch of people in one house, you know? And see, illegal immigrants couldn't complain because they're illegal.
>
> LUDDEN: Others in town say they've heard similar stories of substandard housing. But a spokesman with Rapier's staffing company, One Force, says he's heard only one complaint. And he says the contract workers signed strongly recommends they find their own accommodations. Meantime, the workers have $100 a week deducted from their checks for rent, plus other deductions for travel and cash advances. It's left some, like Ariel Jimenez (ph), nearly penniless their first weeks here.

---

104. Ludden, September 2, 2008, news piece titled "At Iowa Meatpacking Plant, New Workers Complain."

MR. JIMENEZ: They promised me $700 a week. And my first check was $42. They ripped me off. I want my money back.

LUDDEN: Again, the contractor says all the deductions are clearly spelled out in the contract.[105]

Mr. Rapier is correct that "illegal immigrants couldn't complain because they're illegal" as verified by the translated testimony of Mr. Bustamante, who injured his back and came to work against doctor's orders. Ms. Rodriguez Moncada testified that she was not paid overtime and repeatedly had her wages docked if she arrived five or ten minutes late for work. A notable difference between Ludden's two stories is that the Latinx transmigrant workers never felt empowered to vocalize these abuses to NPR while still employed by Agriprocessors.[106] The violations faced after the raid by new workers included: dangerous working conditions (such as machines being turned on while people were cleaning them), contracts with undisclosed clauses, unhealthy/unsafe living conditions in factory supplied housing, long hours, and illegally withheld wages. Ludden reports that the Iowa Labor Department found Agriprocessors culpable for numerous safety violations. This report resulted in Agriprocessors hiring a new safety and compliance officer; however, the new workers' testimonies challenge the effectiveness of this new hire.

"At Iowa Meatpacking Plant New Workers Complain" identifies the Agriprocessors employees detained during the immigration raid as "illegal immigrants" a total of five times throughout the short three-minute broadcast. However, the text's word choice changes when Ludden interviews community members about the "unwelcome change" that the "replacement workers [who were] nearly all single men" brought to the community. Postville Lutheran Pastor Steve Brackett explains some reasons why the older community members did not welcome new factory workers:

PASTOR STEVE BRACKETT (POSTVILLE LUTHERAN CHURCH): We had fights [because of the replacement workers]. We had a stabbing. We've had crime go up. There've been other problems and difficulties. And I think it will be several years once again before that stabilizes.[107]

---

105. Ludden.
106. Each of the aforementioned replacement workers had the legal right to be in the United States because they were US citizens, recognized refugees, or lived in a United States-administered UN Territory (Palau).
107. Ludden, "At Iowa Meatpacking Plant, New Workers Complain."

The Postville community did not experience "problems and difficulties" with the transmigrant community members who were detained by ICE. In fact, Ludden reports, "Many of the Latino workers arrested in the immigration raid had settled in the community, having children, buying homes."[108] This is the only time in her coverage of the raid on *Morning Edition* and *All Things Considered* that Ludden, or any NPR reporter for that matter, addresses all of the workers detained in the raid as "Latino." The word choice—from illegal immigrant to Latino—is telling and performs the ideological work of suggesting that contributing to a positive community dynamic, as well as being economically productive members of the community, is not a part of the narrative constructed about "illegal aliens."

On September 25, 2008, *All Things Considered* aired the report titled "After Raid, Iowa Meatpacker Seeks Palau Workers"[109] that confirms Ludden's earlier speculation that Agriprocessors recruiters sought to employ Palauan workers.[110] Again, the whereabouts of the detained transmigrant workers is not discussed. This broadcast is a conversation between Jennifer Ludden and host Melissa Block about Agriprocessors hiring workers from the former US occupied territory of Palau. As US nationals, Palauans have the ability to travel to the US with nonimmigrant visas and can stay indefinitely. The report details that Palauan workers were given a one-way ticket to Iowa and were promised housing, compensation, and an eventual return ticket. Ludden discusses that Palau's government at first remained cautious of Agriprocessors' attempts at labor recruitment:

> LUDDEN: Palau's president held a news conference to warn people [about "allegations of the mistreatment of employees"], but [Palau's Ambassador] Kyota says the government can't prevent anyone from coming. The Palauans began arriving in Postville in mid-September and have told local residents Agriprocessors paid for their plane tickets. The workers have declined to be interviewed. And a spokesman for Agriprocessors declined repeated requests for comment.[111]

---

108. Ludden.
109. This aired twice with two different titles: "Raided Iowa Meatpacking Plant Gets Palau Workers" on September 25, 2008, during the *All Things Considered* program, and "After Raid, Iowa Meatpacker Seeks Palau Workers" on October 2, 2008, also on *All Things Considered*. The first title was deleted in 2009 from NPR's database of stories, which are all available for free in audio and written files on their website www.npr.org. For this reason and to avoid redundancies, I cite this story using the second title, Ludden, "After Raid, Iowa Meatpacker Seeks Palau Workers."
110. Ludden, "After Raid, Iowa Meatpacker Seeks Palau Workers."
111. Ludden.

After visiting Agriprocessors, Ambassador Kyota "came away thanking the company for its job opportunities."[112] At the same time, Ludden also reports that, in the past, there have been "problems" for Micronesians and Marshall Islanders who were brought to the United States to work; for instance, they were not given housing or a plane ticket home. Agriprocessors filed for bankruptcy, and the plant was sold at action on July 20, 2009, for 8.5 million dollars; however, NPR did not report on the fate of these Palauan workers. Agriprocessors now operates at a much smaller scale, which also suggests a need for fewer employees. This is a humanizing story as NPR makes efforts to show that transmigrants do not take jobs that US Americans or documented refugees are willing to work.[113]

Airing on the October 31, 2013, broadcast of *Morning Edition,* Jennifer Ludden's report, "Kosher Slaughterhouse Former Manager Arrested," discusses the charges and arrest of Agriprocessors CEO Sholom Rubaskin who knowingly hired workers without US work permits. In this piece, Ludden again interviews Elver Herrera, now labeled as a "former employee" at Agriprocessors, about the labor abuses that he reported to Rubashkin while employed at his company. Ludden first interviewed Herrera in the September 1, 2008, *All Things Considered* piece titled "Iowa Plant Charged with Hiring Minors." In reaction to Rubashkin's arrest, Herrera explained what the charges against his former employer meant to him:

MR. ELVER HERRERA (FORMER EMPLOYEE, AGRIPROCESSORS): It's a big—a big day. It's a beautiful day, really.

LUDDEN: Elver Herrera worked seven years at Agriprocessors. He says there's no question Sholom Rubashkin knew hundreds of workers were illegal, because Herrera told him.

MR. HERRERA: I talked to him several time. I told him about what's going on in the plant, about the corruption about it, every about it—underage, because the last meeting I had with him, I told him about it.

LUDDEN: By underage, Herrera means he even told Rubashkin there were immigrant workers who were minors. The State of Iowa last month brought 9,000 counts of child labor violations, which could put company officials in jail for many years if they're convicted. Agriprocessors had no comment on these latest charges, but an attorney for the plant owner Aaron Rubashkin, Sholom's father denied them.[114]

---

112. Ludden.

113. For more discussion of how humanizing representations can perpetuate exclusionary logics, see Alsultany, Arabs and Muslims in the Media.

114. Ludden, "After Raid, Iowa Meatpacker Seeks Palau Workers."

Rubashkin was released from court after paying a million-dollar bond and agreeing to wear a monitoring device. This piece is particularly interesting as the plant CEO was arrested, an uncommon incidence during or after immigration raids. This report also represents the second appearances of two people that Ludden interviewed in the September 1 broadcast: Herrera and Jeff Abbas. In this piece Abbas, the news director for the local radio station, only provides the context as to what type of production still occurs at the Meatpacking plant.

In this second exchange, Herrera distinguishes himself from transmigrant workers by reporting to Ludden that he told Rubashkin "hundreds of workers were illegal."[115] Considering that this piece aired almost six months after the immigration raid, Ludden may have not interviewed any apprehended workers simply because they were already undergoing deportation hearings or otherwise no longer in Postville. What is particularly interesting is that, in his second testimony, Herrera makes an effort to differentiate himself from the apprehended workers. There are many reasons why Herrera may do this because, as Chavez points out, accented English-speaking Latinxs in particular experience a type of second-class citizenship where they are presumed to lack US citizenship until proven otherwise. After the immigration raid there was a White supremacist march through the streets of Postville, and, as the letters read on NPR suggest, even NPR's progressive listeners were sometimes unwilling to sympathize with someone branded "illegal." Given these multiple realities, it makes sense that Herrera would take his second chance at an interview to make sure that the NPR audience implicitly knew that he held legal US work papers. Such rhetoric is also indictive of Nakayama and Krizek's (1995) discussion of Whiteness as a strategic rhetoric,[116] or a series of discursive maneuvers used to resecure dominance—in this case claiming privileges of Whiteness through US citizenship—that can be embodied by members of any race or ethnicity.

Conclusions: Framing Inequity

Framing mechanisms have the power to shape how we view a subject, and what we consider as possible solutions to a problem. Throughout NPR's coverage of the Postville raid, "illegal" becomes shorthand for devalued, yet economically essential, subject/worker under racial capitalism. NPR's imagined

---

115. Ludden.
116. Nakayama and Krizek, "Whiteness."

listening community is defined as predominantly a population of White, affluent, English-speaking US citizens. NPR's coverage of the Postville raid discursively casts Latinxs, specifically Spanish-speaking and Mexican Latinxs, as threatening noncitizens who are excluded from the imagined listening community of the US nation. In reality, US citizen and non-US citizen Latinx laborers are exploited—in terms of long working hours with low pay and dangerous working conditions—by global capitalism.

As a White progressive and an avid NPR listener, I began this chapter as a study of the ways in which Latinx transmigrants, mostly of Guatemalans, were represented—or strategically left absent—in the Postville raid coverage. Joe Feagin tells us most of the information, history, media, and institutionalized content we are exposed to is from a White racial frame that gives a preferential treatment toward Whites. This framing is not always overt to other Whites, yet it is painfully obvious to members of historically marginalized groups. Whiteness is also a discursive construction, one that works in ways—like through frames of problem and threat—that posit, sometimes on colorblind terms, that marginalized groups are somehow a problem, threat, or should be feared. In reality, the supremacy of Whiteness frames all parts of our lives, and it is important that White liberals take a step back and question. Whites, liberals and even progressives, too, are invested in *not* seeing. This is the discursive project of Whiteness, to allow those with relative power the ease, peace, and taken-for-granted safety of not seeing. Transmigrants were very rarely represented in the coverage, NPR—except for a story mentioned at length in this chapter—had other groups—citizen coworkers, community officials, and lawyers mostly speak for them. As Eduardo Bonilla-Silva tells us, this is yet another common frame of White liberal thinking: to speak for or to educate marginalized groups about their struggles with our supremacy. White liberals very rarely assume what Rosario Lippi-Green (1998) calls the communicative burden of learning another language;[117] but this also extends to truly studying the discursive manifestations of our own White identity. The epilogue of this book points toward new trajectories of research in critical Whiteness studies through considering what White allyship means in a transmediated age. As I explore, potential answers to this prompt are more complicated than turning off a radio station and involve careful retrospection, listening, learning, and a willingness to forego the privileges of Whiteness.

---

117. Lippi-Green, *English with an Accent*.

EPILOGUE

Performative Allyship and the Future of Critical Whiteness Studies

White deflection is a two-step dialectic that relies on aggrievement and the appropriation of racial justice frameworks in the service of White supremacy. While using critical rhetoric of race to identify, analyze, and deconstruct the ways overt and inferential deflection operate, I complicated Whiteness in my study of gender and class differences among Whites. In so doing, I have found that presentations of overt militant White deflection are similar in tone, address, and sentiment to masculine rhetoric; yet, they are also performed by cisgender women. Through the performance of militant rhetoric by cisgender women orators, the often-codependent relationship between the discourses of dominance—hegemonic masculinity and Whiteness—are frequently obscured. White deflection is in the news we read, the advertisements that inundate us, and in the social media and music we seek out as entertainment. White deflection itself often works as a framing mechanism, shaping the way news is covered, as well as what is covered, for both conservative and liberal echo chambers. Through strategic discursive shifts in stories; the inferential racializing of its national public as well educated, affluent and White; and episodic coverage of events that decontextualizes greater narratives of legal violence against transmigrants, even NPR's coverage of the Postville immigration raid practiced White deflection. Under racial capitalism where a largely Latinx labor force manufactured goods, the notion of ethical consumption is an exercise in White dilution and deflection of the actual organizing efforts of a workforce with a generational history laboring in Los Angeles. White deflection is indeed invested in obscuring White reliance on the physical and creative labor of historically marginalized groups under racial capitalism. For instance, country music may sound White to many, but it has deep Black and Brown roots; a willful forgetting of this history, as well as racist tropes, shape the narratives of bro-country music as well as online discourse communities.

Of the various types of White deflection mapped throughout the constellation of research sites in this book, inferential White deflection—everyday acts of racism—are the most elusive to identify and strategic in their exploitation of historically marginalized groups. Liberal Whiteness, similar to the conservative variety, has a performative and self-serving aspect that scholars of Black radical thought have identified for generations. Charles W. Mills (1997) begins *The Racial Contract,* a book about how "white supremacy is the unnamed political system that has made the modern world what it is today," with a "black American folk aphorism": "When white people say 'Justice,' they mean 'Just us.'"[1] As an overture toward future scholarship and inspired by the work of Mills and others, I would like to briefly position performative allyship as a type of liberal White deflection through a contemporary example.

While kneeling in front of an open JP Morgan Chase bank vault with the company's sapphire blue octagon logo above it, the sixty-three-year-old CEO Jamie Dimon posed for a photograph at a Mt. Kisco, New York, branch in June 2020 (see fig. 4). Dimon was informally dressed in a blue t-shirt, shorts, and black-and-white sneakers. Joining the CEO were eleven bank employees, all but one wearing a mask properly covering their noses and mouths to prevent the spread of the novel coronavirus. Six of the bank employees knelt with Dimon, and six others stood behind them.[2] The image quickly spread across social media and online media outlets.

In the now viral photograph, the White CEO of the largest US bank mimicked NFL player Colin Kaepernick's kneeling gesture—a choice that resulted in the athlete's blacklisting from his profession. Unlike Kaepernick's protest of police brutality that resulted in severe professional and financial sacrifices for the athlete, Dimon's job security was never at risk and the act linked him with a progressive cause. In a memo to Chase bank staff, Dimon clarified his intentions: "Let us be clear—we are watching, listening and want every single one of you to know we are committed to fighting against racism and discrimination wherever and however it exists."[3]

---

1. Mills, *Racial Contract,* 1.
2. McEnery, "Jamie Dimon Drops into Mt. Kisco."
3. McEnery.

FIGURE 4. Chase CEO Jamie Dimon kneeling with workers

With his choreographed kneeling photograph in support of racial justice, Dimon made a brief social media spectacle. But this symbolic action was done in a safe space, he did not lose his career like Kaepernick, and the CEO gained significant free media attention for himself and his company. Some social activists critiqued Dimon's viral post as an opportunistic example of performative allyship.[4] Performative allyship, or as Leandra H. Hernández (2020) terms it "performative white allyship," involves antiracist pronouncements that do not address the systemic and institutionalized nature of racism. The broad gestures of performative allyship—that could include the simple act of sharing an image or post—may not address how exactly an individual or corporation plans to use their relative privilege and power to end the institutionalized oppression of historically marginalized groups. In fact, such actions can actually make systemic racism worse by focusing on elaborate personal gestures, rather than the wide-sweeping systemic influences of White supremacy. Hernández finds that "when performative white allyship is represented by centering one's self or expecting recognition, this can result in the perpetuation of white saviorism and white martyrdom that further recenters whiteness."[5] Individuals and corporations that practice performative allyship seek to build their social capital, or brand identity, as politically and socially

---

4. Jan et al., "As Big Corporations Say 'Black Lives Matter.'"
5. Hernández, "Silence, (In)Action," 150.

aware without inherently investing in the cause of antiracism. Perhaps in an attempt to counter claims of performative allyship, the *Washington Post* reported that JP Morgan Chase spokeswomen Patricia Wexler clarified that the image of Dimon shows his "support for social justice. . . . Our leader (Dimon) and our company (JP Morgan Chase) have done a lot more than kneel, investing hundreds of millions of dollars in combined philanthropic and business resources to address some of the most persistent challenges facing the black community."[6] Wexler's defense of Dixon presumes that capitalism is a moral system, and the ways to address inequality are through charitable donations—that JP Morgan Chase is the corporate benefactor of social justice. This rationale does not consider the ways that racial capitalism demands and maintains the institutionalized exploitation of an underclass made up of largely historically marginalized groups. In other words, the very lifeblood of JP Morgan Chase—capitalism—demands a racial caste system.

Throughout this book I have argued that White racial discourse represents a struggle for racial dominance. In moments where racism and inequality are laid bare, what I termed racial ruptures, Whites and White allies use a variety of rhetorical mechanisms to strategically sustain power and White supremacy; a common rhetorical example of the fragility of Whiteness is deflective rhetoric. This book focused on two patterns of such discourse: White victimhood and the co-optation of the social movement frames made by historically marginalized groups. I mapped a constellation of deflective discourse throughout online discussions, corporate branding agendas, and through soundscapes (radio and music). Performative allyship represents a related discursive pattern, as it uses the social activism of historically marginalized groups for personal gain. When capitalist corporations make overnight commitments to social justice causes yet gloss over the intrinsic inequity inherit under racial capitalism, their symbolic monetary contributions to progressive causes should be questioned. As Hérnandez (2020) tells us, performative allyship in online discourse reinforces Whites supremacy by framing Whites as both saviors and martyrs for the cause of social justice. In such mediated communication, the deeply rooted, institutionalized nature of White supremacy is not adequately addressed. Whites remain safe and are not forced to truly divest in the system of White supremacy, if even momentarily, through taking personal and social risks to challenge the prevailing social order. Yet, social activism does not necessarily end at the keyboard. Research suggests that sharing spreadable content online does increase the likelihood that a human

---

6. Jan et al., "As Big Corporations Say 'Black Lives Matter.'"

will invest in causes in face-to-face environments, or through monetary support.[7] But, what about corporations?

In the summer of 2020, corporations, including JP Morgan Chase, were encouraged by employees to take stances on social-justice-related causes. Rather than being entirely altruistic, these corporations were motivated by a fear of losing customers to make symbolic gestures in support of diversity, equity, and inclusion.[8] The *Washington Post* reported, for example, that

> Jack Dorsey, chief executive of Twitter and Square, declared Juneteenth (June 19) a corporate holiday to commemorate the end of slavery, a move more companies are making. Reddit founder Alexis Ohanian, who is married to tennis star Serena Williams, resigned from the board to make way for the first black director in the company's history. Bank of America promised to spend $1 billion over the next four years to address "economic and racial inequality accelerated by a global pandemic." Walmart, the country's largest retailer, pledged to stop locking up "multicultural" hair and beauty products in display cases, and Sephora committed to devoting at least 15 percent of its shelf space to black-owned beauty brands. Toymaker LEGO suspended marketing for police-themed sets after video emerged showing an officer kneeling on Floyd's neck for more than eight minutes.[9]

While professing solidarity with the cause of antiracism, these corporations made the calculated capitalist decision to support racial justice while simultaneously building their images as equitable, nonracist brands.

Employees of multinational corporations who—for years—encouraged their employers to support social justice causes also questioned the sincerity of US corporate America's overnight commitment to allyship.[10] National Public Radio's (NPR's) research uncovered that many employees at large technology firms like Google and Facebook were skeptical that the gestures would truly change corporate culture. NPR reporter Bobby Allyn (2020) found that Google's workforce, for instance, is just 3 percent Black, and just 9 percent of Apple employees are Black. It is a pattern widely seen in small tech start-ups and in the venture capital world. Just 1 percent of startup founders who received venture capital money are Black, according to one study that examined data from 10,000 founders and 135 of the most active venture capital firms in the world.

---

7. Shresthova, "'Watch 30 Minute Video,'" 69–70.
8. McGregor and Jan, "As Big Corporations Say 'Black Lives Matter.'"
9. McGregor and Jan.
10. Yuan, "Black Employees Say 'Performative Allyship.'"

Corporations were not the only "people" charged with performative allyship.[11] Others also faulted humans for false pronouncements of racial justice under the guise of hashtag activism, or using hashtags to profess a social movement message without necessarily investing in true commitments to racial justice.[12] For example, the hashtags #JusticeforBreonnaTaylor and #JusticeforAhmaudArbery made social media rounds throughout the summer of 2020. These hashtags remembered the March 13, 2020, murder of Breonna Taylor in her own home by law enforcement and the February 25, 2020, murder of Ahmaud Arbery by a former law enforcement agent and his son. Some individuals faced criticism when they used these hashtags at the end of random posts, like selfies or images of food, as a non sequitur reminder that focused more on the poster's persona than how the poster believed justice for Aubrey and Taylor could be achieved. Similarly, some businesses and individuals participated in Black Out Tuesday; a day where people would remain silent on social media for twenty-four hours, listening and learning about racial injustice in unity with Black Americans.[13] But does blacking out one's social media really mean that individuals—corporations and humans—took the time to research, read, and listen? How do we know?

Using social media to spread viral activist messages through sharable hashtags (hashtag activism) or clickable links to viral videos (clicktivism) is nothing new. In 2012, for instance, Kony 2012, a short viral documentary made by the organization Invisible Children (IC), was a viral sensation. Across Facebook, profile pictures changed to images of IC's Kony 2012 video graphic. Although originally deemed a viral hit by liberals, the thirty-minute video was soon exposed as decontextualizing both African history, as well as the greater US-based activist efforts of IC.[14] Sangita Shresthova (2016) argues that the central paradox of IC was that the organization's goal to expose and lead to the end of Joseph Kony and the Lord's Resistance Army's activities did not correspond with the goal of the human rights organization to expand civic activism in the United States.[15] IC's video was widely criticized for its perpetuation of Eurocentric and neocolonial imagery, as well as its framing of the West as the great White savior. The meteoric rise of IC and Kony 2012, as well as its mirrored cataclysmic downfall, shows the perils of both uninformed social movement activism and allowing internet-based activism to stand in for

---

11. I use the term "individuals" here as a tongue-and-cheek way to highlight how, legally in the United States, corporations are considered people.
12. Rudhran, "What Is Performative Allyship?"
13. Rudhran.
14. Shresthova, "'Watch 30 Minute Video,'" 71, 75.
15. Shresthova, 78.

face-to-face action. Although just one example of internet-based social media activism going awry, Kony 2012 and performative allyship suggest the question: How should White investment in undoing White supremacy take form in hybrid mediated and face-to-face settings?

Lamiya Bahrainwala (2020) finds that "white silence and disengagement [are] the very antithesis of allyship, which is necessarily noisy and disruptive."[16] Scholars from historically marginalized groups suggest that a part of displaying genuine White antiracist commitments means a willingness to forgo privilege and to put oneself at risk—to protest, to correct the behavior of other Whites, and maybe even lose connections with White friends and family members because of these beliefs.[17] Hernández (2020) references Shantal Martinex while noting that Whites should "position themselves not as *allies* but as *accomplices*."[18] Hernández continues:

> White allyship means not centering one's self to position one for an award or recognition; rather, white allyship means moving beyond awareness of privilege to take risks, call out inequities, and dismantle systems of exclusion and oppression that marginalize and disadvantage non-white individuals.[19]

A profound example of Whites acting as accomplices after the murder of Floyd was the viral image of White women locking arms and forming a shield to protect Black Lives Matter protesters. This is a noisy and risky commitment for privileged White women. The vehicle for this noise and disruption can take many forms. In a highly mediated society, social media, when used properly, can be a tool of social activism—but sometimes can run the risk of a performance of allyship.[20] In a racist neoliberal capitalist world order positioning the individual as paramount is common sense. Martinex and Hernández's assertions that White accomplices must be willing to take personal risks to end White supremacy seems like a logical first step in divesting from the benefits of institutionalized and systemic White oppression.

With added focus on performative allyship, additional research on the link between online antiracist content sharing and face-to-face White allyship is desperately needed. White supremacy strategically seeks to hide behind altruism, coded rhetoric, dog whistles, and double-speak. It is of crucial importance Whites take seriously their rhetoric, cross-mediated communications,

---

16. Bahrainwala, "Web of White Disengagement," 139.
17. Bahrainwala; Hernández, "Silence, (In)Action"; Taylor, "Dear Nice White Ladies."
18. Hernández, "Silence, (In)Action," 150.
19. Hernández, 150.
20. Shresthova, "'Watch 30 Minute Video.'"

and how they normalize and secure systems of oppression. Whites across the political spectrum use the identity politics and social movements of historically marginalized groups to further White supremacy. Yet this remains understudied, even within critical Whiteness studies. Although knowledge of racist systems is essential, White investment in undoing White supremacy cannot stop at an antiracist reading list or through buying goods linked with progressive politics. The interplay between capitalism, consumption, politics, and convergent media must be further studied if we are to truly understand—and then be able to deconstruct—the ubiquitous nature of White supremacy laced in even the most ostensibly progressive of gestures.

APPENDIX 1

Blue Lives Matter "About Us"

History

Blue Lives Matter was founded based on the need of law enforcement.

On August 9, 2014, Ferguson PD Officer Darren Wilson was doing his job as he stopped Michael Brown, who had just committed a robbery of a local convenience store. Brown attacked Officer Wilson in an aggravated assault.

Officer Wilson was forced to defend his life by shooting Brown. In the months that followed, agitators spread outright lies and distortions of the truth about Officer Wilson and all police officers.

The media catered to movements such as Black Lives Matter, whose goal was the vilification of law enforcement. Criminals who rioted and victimized innocent citizens were further given legitimacy by the media as "protesters."

America watched as criminals destroyed property, and assaulted and murdered innocent people, and they labeled these criminals as victims.

Personal responsibility for one's actions went away, replaced by accusations of racism and an unjust government.

It seemed that almost every media organization was spreading the absurd message that people were being shot by law enforcement simply because of the color of their skin.

Even our political leaders pandered to these criminals and helped to spread this false narrative, with no thought of the consequences.

On December 20, 2014, NYPD Officer Rafael Ramos and Officer Wenjian Liu were ambushed and murdered by a fanatic who believed the lies of Black Lives Matter, the media, and politicians.

While reporting on the murder of these heroes, the media continued to spread the false narrative of Black Lives Matter.

Even the largest law enforcement media companies, who purport to be all for the police, helped spread misinformation through re-posting articles written with an anti-police bias.

At that moment, we realized that the major law enforcement news companies weren't run by law enforcement, and they only cared about saving time and money by copying anti-police biased news sources.

The officers who founded this organization were motivated by the heroic actions of Officer Darren Wilson, and many others, and decided to create this organization in the hopes that we could prevent more officers from being hurt.

Blue Lives Matter formed and gathered supporters of law enforcement on Facebook to distribute information which accurately reflected the realities of law enforcement.

Feeling the limitations of being contained to Facebook, the Blue Lives Matter news website was launched to provide accurate coverage of law enforcement news, from a law enforcement perspective.

In 2016, after an unprecedented number of ambush attacks on law enforcement officers, the founders decided that we could be doing more to help the officers who are getting attacked in the streets. We began to provide law enforcement officers with life-saving equipment, at no cost to them.

Blue Lives Matter will continue to support law enforcement in any way when there is a need that we can fill.[1]

---

1. "About Us—History," Blue Lives Matter.

APPENDIX 2

Letter to Dov Charney

. . . their lives and helped American Apparel grow. For most of us [it] is really hard to leave a company that has giving us so much.

ICE has send [*sic*] us these letters with them our goals and dreams are gone. They don't understand that we are human. That we are fathers, mothers, brothers, sisters, sons, or daughters of American Citizens and that they depend on us. Our only crime is not having a document. All we want is to work and be treated as human beens [*sic*]. But what do we do when all the doors are closed? Or what do we tell our sons, and daughters, when we don't have enough money and time because we have to work 12 hours a day to earn less than the minimum wage. ICE we are good and hard working people. People in search of the American Dream. We will not go back. We will fight. We all pray that one day immigration laws will change. And that we all [will] be treated equally.

Thank you American Apparel for giving us hope, and thank you to all the people who understand us. People like Dov Charney and Marty Baily. Our hopes and goals are gone but our faith is still very strong.[1]

---

1. Transcribed from Letter from Blog (2010), https://www.americanapparel.net/aboutus/political/legalizela/.

BIBLIOGRAPHY

"2000 Years Ago Jesus Ended the Debate on Which Lives Matter. He Died for All: Jesus, Lives Matter, Debate." Pinterest. Accessed December 21, 2021. https://pin.it/fsRrcRX.

"About Blue Lives Matter." Warrior Maven: Military and Defense News. Accessed June 21, 2019. https://defensemaven.io/bluelivesmatter/pages/about-blue-lives-matter-rF54b2VNMUOrl7wfh8vRXQ/.

"About Us #History." Blue Lives Matter. Warrior Maven: Military and Defense News, January 11, 2017. https://archive.bluelivesmatter.blue/organization/#history.

"About Us—History." Blue Lives Matter. Warrior Maven: Military and Defense News, January 11, 2017. https://defensemaven.io/bluelivesmatter/pages/about-blue-lives-matter-rF54b2VNMUOrl7wfh8vRXQ.

Abrajano, Marisa A., Zoltan Hajnal, and Hans J. G. Hassell. "Media Framing and Partisan Identity: The Case of Immigration Coverage and White Macropartisanship." *Journal of Race, Ethnicity and Politics* 2, no. 1 (Spring 2017): 5–32. https://doi.org/10.1017/rep.2016.25.

Absire, Emily. "Lil Nas X Lassos the Record for Longest-Running No. 1 Song in U.S. Chart History." *NPR News*. Last modified July 29, 2019, https://www.npr.org/2019/07/29/746200139/lil-nas-x-lassos-the-record-for-longest-running-no-1-song-in-u-s-chart-history.

Adjei-Kontoh, Hurbert. "Lil Nas' Song was Removed from Billboard for Not Being 'Country' Enough. But Who Gets to Decide Categories?" *Guardian*, April 2, 2019, https://www.theguardian.com/music/2019/apr/02/lil-nas-song-removed-from-billboard-not-country-enough.

Admin. "Trap Music under Lock and Key." DJ, February 28, 2013, https://djmag.com/content/trap-music-under-lock-key.

"Advertising." Blue Lives Matter. Warrior Maven: Military and Defense News. Accessed June 21, 2019. https://defensemaven.io/bluelivesmatter/_advertising/.

Agozio, Biko. "Black Lives Matter Otherwise All Lives Do Not Matter." *African Journal of Criminology and Justice Studies*, 11, no. 1 (2018): i–xi.

Aguirre Jr., Adalberto, and Jennifer K. Simmers. "Mexican Border Crossers: The Mexican Body in Immigration Discourse." *Social Justice* 35, no. 4 (2008–9): 99–106.

Ahmed, Sara. "Affective Economies." *Social Text* 22, no. 2 (2004): 117–39.

Allegro, Linda, and Andrew Grant Wood. *Latin American Migrations to the U.S. Heartland.* Chicago: University of Illinois Press, 2013.

Allen, Greg. "PETA Footage Puts Kosher Slaughterhouse on Defensive." *All Things Considered,* National Public Radio, January 10, 2009, http://www.npr.org/templates/story/story.php?storyId=4236845.

Allmendinger, Blake. *Imagining the African American West.* Lincoln: University of Nebraska Press, 2005.

Alsultany, Evelyn. *Arabs and Muslims in the Media.* New York: New York University Press, 2012.

Althusser, Louis. *Lenin and Philosophy, and Other Essays.* New York: Monthly Review Press, 2001.

Anderson, Luvell. "Hermeneutical Impasses." *Philosophical Topics* 45, no. 2 (2017): 1–19. https://doi.org/10.5840/philtopics201745211.

Andersen, Margaret L. "Whitewashing Race: A Critical Perspective on Whiteness." In *White Out: The Continuing Significance of Racism,* edited by Ashley W. Doane and Eduardo Bonilla-Silva, 21–34. New York: Routledge, 2003.

Báez, Jillian. "Spreadable Citizenship." In *The Routledge Companion to Latina/o Media,* edited by María Elena Cepeda and Dolores Inés Casillas, 419–32. New York: Routledge, 2017.

Bahrainwala, Laminyah. "The Web of White Disengagement." *Women and Language* 43, no.1 (Spring 2020): 135–40.

Balderrama, Francisco, and Raymond Rodríguez. *Decade of Betrayal.* Albuquerque: University of New Mexico Press, 2006.

Barnett, Clive, Paul Cloke, Nick Clarke, and Alice Malpass. "Consuming Ethics." *Antipode* 37, no. 1 (2005): 23–45.

Barry, Ellen, Nicholas Bogel-Burroughs, and Dave Philipps. "Woman Killed in Capitol Embraced Trump and QAnon," *New York Times,* January 8, 2021, https://www.nytimes.com/2021/01/07/us/who-was-ashli-Babbitt.html.

Bebout, Lee. *Whiteness on the Border: Mapping the US Racial Imagination in Brown and White.* New York: New York University Press, 2016.

Behdad, Ali. *A Forgetful Nation.* Durham, NC: Duke University Press, 2005.

Belay, Tim. "Immigration Raid Leaves Mark on Iowa Town." *All Things Considered,* National Public Radio, June 9, 2008, http://www.npr.org/templates/story/story.php?storyId=91327136.

Bell, Derrick. "Racial Realism." *Connecticut Law Review* 21, no. 2 (1992): 363–79.

Beltrán, Cristina. "Opinion | to Understand Trump's Support, We Must Think in Terms of Multiracial Whiteness." The Washington Post. WP Company, January 16, 2021. https://www.washingtonpost.com/opinions/2021/01/15/understand-trumps-support-we-must-think-terms-multiracial-whiteness/.

Belew, Kathleen. *Bring the War Home: The White Power Movement and Paramilitary America.* Cambridge, MA: Harvard University Press, 2018.

Beltrán, Cristina. "Opinion | to Understand Trump's Support, We Must Think in Terms of Multiracial Whiteness." *Washington Post,* January 16, 2021, https://www.washingtonpost.com/opinions/2021/01/15/understand-trumps-support-we-must-think-terms-multiracial-whiteness/.

Bennett et al., Dalton. "Video Shows Fatal Shooting of Ashli Babbitt in the Capitol," The *Washington Post* (WP Company, February 5, 2021), https://www.washingtonpost.com/investigations/2021/01/08/ashli-Babbitt-shooting-video-capitol/.

Biesecker, Barbara A. "From General History to Philosophy: Black Lives Matter, Late Neoliberal Molecular Biopolitics, and Rhetoric." *Philosophy and Rhetoric* 50, no. 4 (2017): 409–30. http://www.jstor.org/stable/10.5325/philrhet.50.4.0409.

———. "Negotiating with Our Tradition: Reflecting Again (without Apologies) on the Feminization of Rhetoric." *Philosophy & Rhetoric* (1993): 236–41.

Bisset, Jennifer J. "Disney Includes Gina Carano in Its Mandalorian Emmy Awards Push." CNET, May 10, 2021, https://www.cnet.com/news/disney-includes-gina-carano-in-its-the-mandalorian-emmy-awards-push/.

Black Lives Matter. "About." Accessed February 10, 2018. https://blacklivesmatter.com/about/.

Black, Sandy. *Eco-Chic*. London: Black Dog Publishing, 2008.

Block, Melissa, and Michele Norris. "Letters: ICE Raid in Iowa; 'Hockey Night' Song." *All Things Considered*, National Public Radio, June 10, 2008, http://www.npr.org/templates/story/story.php?storyId=91360630.

BlueLivesMatter. "About Us." OfficerBlue. Last modified May 14, 2017. https://www.themaven.net/bluelivesmatter/pages/rF54b2VNMUOrl7wfh8vRXQ.

———. "FB Launches More Changes to Stop You from Seeing Blue Lives Matter." OfficerBlue. Last modified February 2, 2018. https://www.themaven.net/bluelivesmatter/news/fb-launches-more-changes-to-stop-you-from-seeing-blue-lives-matter-Skws2jQ2RUWBi3WfhyB_lw.

"Blue Lives Matter." Warrior Maven: Military and Defense News. Accessed June 21, 2019. https://defensemaven.io/bluelivesmatter/.

Bock, Mary Angela, and Ever Josue Figueroa. "Faith and Reason: An Analysis of the Homologies of Black and Blue Lives Facebook Pages." *New Media and Society* 20, no. 9 (2018): 3097–118. https://doi.org/10.1177/1461444817740822.

Bonacich, Edna, and Richard P. Appelbaum. *Behind the Label*. Los Angeles: University of California Press, 2000.

Bonilla-Silva, Eduardo. *Racism without Racists*. 4th ed. Lanham, MD: Rowman and Littlefield Publishers, 2014.

———. *Racism without Racists*. 5th ed. Lanham, MD: Rowman and Littlefield Publishers, 2018.

Bonilla-Silva, Eduardo, Carla Goar, and David G. Embrick. "When Whites Flock Together: The Social Psychology of White Habitus." *Critical Sociology* no. 2–3 (2006): 229–53. https://doi.org/10.1163/156916306777835268.

Bordelon, Suzanne. "Contradicting and Complicating Feminization of Rhetoric Narratives: Mary Yost and Argument from a Sociological Perspective." *Rhetoric Society Quarterly* 35, no. 3 (2005): 101–24.

Bourdieu, Pierre. *Distinction*. Cambridge, MA: Harvard University Press, 1984.

Bramwell, Anna. *Blood and Soil: Walther Darré and Hitler's Green Party*. Ann Arbor: University of Michigan Press, 1985.

Broadway, Michael J., and Donald D. Stull. "Meat Processing and Garden City, KS: Boom and Bust." *Journal of Rural Studies* 22, no. 1 (2006): 55–66.

Brock, Andre. "From the Blackhand Side: Twitter as a Cultural Conversation." *Journal of Broadcasting and Electronic Media* 56, no. 4 (December 2012): 529–49.

Browne, Irene, and Joya Misra. "The Intersection of Gender and Race in the Labor Market." *Annual Review of Sociology* 29 (2003): 487–513.

Burgess, Jean. "All Your Chocolate Rain Are Belong to Us? Viral Video, YouTube and the Dynamics of Participatory Culture." In *Video Vortex Reader,* edited by Geert Lovink and Sabine Niederer, 101–9. Amsterdam: Institute of Network Cultures, 2008.

Burke, Mary C., and Mary Bernstein. "How the Right Usurped the Queer Agenda: Frame Co-Optation in Political Discourse." *Sociological Forum* 4, no. 29 (2014): 830–50. https://doi.org/10.1111/socf.12122.

Burns, Allan. *Maya in Exile: Guatemalans in Florida.* Philadelphia: Temple University Press, 1993.

Cabrera, Nolan L. *White Guys on Campus: Racism, White Immunity, and the Myth of "Post-Racial" Higher Education.* New Brunswick, NJ: Rutgers University Press, 2019.

Cairns, Kate, Josée Johnston, and Norah MacKendrick. "Feeding the 'Organic Child.'" *Journal of Consumer Culture* 13, no. 2 (2013): 97–118.

Calafell, Bernadette Marie. "The Future of Feminist Scholarship: Beyond the Politics of Inclusion." *Women's Studies in Communication* 37 (2014): 266–70.

Camayd-Freixas, Erik. "Interpreting after the Largest ICE Raid in US History: A Personal Account." *Latino Studies* no. 7 (2009): 23–139. https://doi.org/10.1057/lst.2008.54.

Cammarota, Julio. "The Gendered and Racialized Pathways of Latina and Latino Youth." *Anthropology and Education Quarterly* 1, no. 35 (2004): 53–74.

Caramanica, Jon. "A History of Hick-Hop in 29 Songs." *New York Times,* April 21, 2019, 12L.

Carano, Gina. "Beep/Bop/Boop Has Zero to Do with Mocking Trans People ♡ & 💯 to Do with Exposing the Bullying Mentality of the Mob That Has Taken over the Voices of Many Genuine Causes. I Want People to Know You Can Take Hate with a Smile. So BOOP You for Misunderstanding. 😊 #AllLoveNoHate Pic.twitter.com/Qe48AiZyOL." Twitter, September 14, 2020, https://twitter.com/ginacarano/status/1305301756792860674.

Carney, Nikita. "All Lives Matter, but So Does Race: Black Lives Matter and the Evolving Role of Social Media." *Humanity and Society* 40, no. 2 (2016): 180–99. https://doi.org/10.1177/0160597616643868.

Casillas, Dolores Inés. 2011. "Sounds of Surveillance: U.S. Spanish-Language Radio Patrols La Migra." *American Quarterly* 63, no. 3 (2011): 807–29.

Cepeda, María Elena. "Shakira as the Idealized, Transnational Citizen: A Case Study of Colombianidad in Transition." *Latino Studies* 1, no. 2 (2003): 211–32.

Chang, Andrea. "LA Apparel Firm Lays Off Hundreds." *Los Angeles Times,* December 18, 2008, (c)2.

"Changing Face of America: Iowa Immigrants." *All Things Considered,* National Public Radio, March 28, 2001, http://www.npr.org/templates/story/story.php?storyId=1120656.

"Changing Face of America: Postcards from Postville." *All Things Considered,* National Public Radio, November 29, 2004.

"Changing Face of America: Postville, Iowa." *All Things Considered,* National Public Radio, March 29, 2001, http://www.npr.org/templates/story/story.php?storyId=1120752.

Charnas, Dan. *The Big Payback: The History of the Business of Hip-Hop.* New York: Penguin Publishing Group, 2011.

Chavez, Leo R. *Covering Immigration: Popular Images and the Politics of the Nation.* Berkeley: University of California Press, 2001.

———. *The Latino Threat.* Stanford, CA: Stanford University Press, 2008.

Chavez, Leo R., F. Allen Hubbell, Shiraz I. Mishra, and R. Burciaga Valdez. "Undocumented Latina Immigrants in Orange County." *International Migration Review* 31, no. 1 (1997): 88–107.

Ching, Barbara. *Wrong's What I Do Best: Hard Country Music and Contemporary Culture.* Oxford, UK: Oxford University Press, 2001.

Chow, Andrew R. "Lil Nas X Talks 'Old Town Road' and the Billboard Controversy." *Time,* April 5, 2019, https://time.com/5561466/lil-nas-x-old-town-road-billboard.

Cisneros, J. David, and Thomas K. Nakayama. "New Media, Old Racisms: Twitter, Miss America, and Cultural Logics of Race." *Journal of International and Intercultural Communication* 8, no. 2 (2015): 108–27. https://doi.org/10.1080/17513057.2015.1025328.

Clarke, Stuart Alan. "Fear of a Black Planet." *Socialist Review* 21, nos. 3–4 (1991): 37–59.

Coffey, Brian, and Charles Roberts. "Racial Differences in Mortgage Lending in the Southeastern United States." *Southeastern Geographer* 39, no. 1 (1999): 46–60.

Cole, Nicki Lisa. "Ethical Consumption in the Global Age." In *Consumer Culture, Modernity and Identity,* edited by Nita Matur, 213–344. London: Sage Publications, 2014.

———. "On the Cultural Logic of Ethical Capitalism." *Consumers, Commodities & Consumption* 9, no. 2 (2008). https://csrn.camden.rutgers.edu/newsletters/9-2/cole.htm.

Connell, Robert W., and James W. Messerschmidt. "Hegemonic Masculinity: Rethinking the Concept." *Gender & Society* 19, no. 6 (2005): 829–59.

Cooper, Matt. "What TV to Watch: Ewan McGregor, Angelina Jolie, Gina Carano." *Los Angeles Times,* May 9, 2021, https://www.latimes.com/entertainment-arts/tv/story/2021-05-09/what-to-watch-angelina-jolie-ewan-mcgregor-halston-mandalorian-gina-carano-running-wild.

Cornell, Stephen, and Douglas Hartmann. *Ethnicity and Race: Making Identities in a Changing World.* New York: Sage Publications, 2006.

Cusic, Don. "Country Green: The Money in Country Music." In *Reading Country Music: Steel Guitars, Opry Stars, and Honkey-Tonk Bars,* edited by Cecilia Tichi, 200–208. Durham, NC: Duke University Press, 1998.

Dahlgren, Peter. *Television and the Public Sphere: Citizenship, Democracy, and the Media.* London: Sage, 1995.

Dávila, Arlene. *Latinos, Inc.: The Marketing and Making of a People.* Berkeley: University of California Press, 2001.

———. *Latino Spin: Public Image and the Whitewashing of Race.* New York: New York University Press, 2009.

Davison, Patrick. "The Language of Internet Memes." In *The Social Media Reader,* edited by Michael Mandiberg, 120–34. New York: New York University Press, 2012.

Dawkins, Richard. *The Selfish Gene.* New York: Oxford University Press, 1976.

de Certeau, Michel. *The Practice of Everyday Life.* Berkeley: University of California Press, 1984.

De Genova, Nicholas. "The Legal Production of Mexican/Migrant 'Illegality.'" *Latino Studies* no. 4 (2004): 160–85.

Delgado, Richard. "Recasting the American Race Problem." *California Law Review* 79 (1991): 1389–1400.

Delgado, Richard, and Jean Stefancic. *An Introduction to Critical Race Theory.* 3rd ed. New York: New York University Press, 2017.

"Department of Justice Closes Investigation into the Death of Ashli Babbitt." United States Department of Justice. United States Attorney's Office, April 14, 2021, https://www.justice.gov/usao-dc/pr/department-justice-closes-investigation-death-ashli-Babbitt.

DiAngelo, Robin. "My Class Didn't Trump My Race: Using Oppression to Face Privilege." *Multicultural Perspectives* 8, no. 1 (2006): 51–56.

———. "What Does It Mean to Be White in America?" Paper presentation, O'Hara Lecture, Miami University, Oxford, OH, April 5, 2017.

———. "White Fragility." *International Journal of Critical Pedagogy* 3, no. 3, (2011): 54–70.

———. *White Fragility: Why It's So Hard for White People to Talk about Racism*. Boston: Beacon Press, 2018.

Doane, Ashley W. "Shades of Colorblindness." In *The Colorblind Screen*, edited by Sarah Nilsen and Sarah E. Turner, 15–38. New York: New York University Press, 2014.

Doane, Ashley W., and Eduardo Bonilla-Silva, eds. *White Out: The Continuing Significance of Racism*. East Sussex, UK: Psychology Press, 2003.

Douglas, Susan J. *Listening In: Radio and the American Imagination*. Minneapolis: University of Minnesota Press, 2004.

Dowling, Julie A., and Jonathan Xavier Inda. *Governing Immigration through Crime: A Reader*. Stanford, CA: Stanford University Press, 2013.

Dubrofsky, Rachel E. "Monstrous Authenticity: Trump's Whiteness." In *Interrogating the Communicative Power of Whiteness*, edited by Dawn Marie D. McIntosh, Dreama G. Moon, and Thomas K. Nakayama, 155–75. New York: Routledge, 2018.

Duggan, Lisa. *The Twilight of Equality?* Boston: Beacon Press, 2003.

Dunn, Tasha R. "Diggin In: White Trash, Trailer Trash, and the (In)Mobility of Whiteness." In *Interrogating the Communicative Power of Whiteness*, edited by Dawn Marie D. McIntosh, Dreama G. Moon, and Thomas K. Nakayama, 117–32. New York: Routledge, 2018.

Durón, Clementina. "Mexican Women and Labor Conflict in Los Angeles." *Aztlán* 15, no. 1 (1984): 145–61.

Dyer, Richard. *White: Essays on Race and Culture*. New York: Routledge, 1997.

Eguchi, Shinsuke. "Queerness as Strategic Whiteness: A Queer Asian American Critique." In *Interrogating the Communicative Power of Whiteness*, edited by Dawn Marie D. McIntosh, Dreama G. Moon, and Thomas K. Nakayama. New York: Routledge, 2018.

Eldredge, Richard L. "Jason Aldean Sticks Up for Blue Collar America: 'Don't Talk Down about Things You've Never Experienced.'" *Billboard*, October 25, 2016, https://www.billboard.com/articles/news/magazine-feature/7502841/jason-aldean-blue-collar-america.

Esposito, Luigi, and Victor Romano. "Benevolent Racism and the Co-Optation of the Black Lives Matter Movement." *Western Journal of Black Studies* 40, no. 3 (2016): 161–73.

Eustachewich, Lia. "Ashli Babbitt, Killed in Capitol, Criticized Politicians for 'Refusing to Choose America,'" *New York Post*, January 7, 2021, https://nypost.com/2021/01/07/ashli-Babbitt-shot-dead-in-us-capitol-posted-tirades-against-politicians/.

Fairclough, Norman. *Language and Power*. New York: Routledge, 2015.

"Faith Matters: Kosher Slaughterhouse Raises Ethical Dilemma." *Tell Me More*, National Public Radio, August 8, 2008, http://www.npr.org/templates/story/story.php?storyId=93411669.

"Faith Matters: Religion a Big Story in 2008." *Tell Me More*, January 2, 2009, National Public Radio, http://www.npr.org/templates/story/story.php?storyId=98946854.

Feagin, Joe. *The White Racial Frame*. 2nd ed. New York: Routledge, 2013.

Feagin, Joe, and José A. Cobas. "Latinos/as and White Racial Frame: The Procrustean Bed of Assimilation." *Sociological Inquiry* 78, no. 1 (2008): 39–53.

Feagin, Joe, and Sean Elias. "Rethinking Racial Formation Theory: A Systemic Racism Critique." *Ethnic and Racial Studies* 36, no. 6 (2013): 931–60.

Fernández-Kelly, M. Patricia, and Anna M. García. "Informalization at the Core." In *The Informal Economy*, edited by Alejandro Portes, Manuel Castells, and Lauren Benton, 247–67. Baltimore: John Hopkins University Press, 1989.

———. "Power Surrendered, Power Restored." In *Women, Politics, and Social Change*, edited by Louise A. Tilly and Patricia Gurin, 130–49. New York: Russell Sage Foundation, 1991.

Ferrence, Matthew J. *All-American Redneck: Variations on an Icon, from James Fenimore Cooper to the Dixie Chicks*. Knoxville: University of Tennessee Press, 2014.

Fillingim, David. *Redneck Liberation: Country Music as Theology*. Macon, GA: Mercer University Press, 2003.

Fink, Leon. *The Maya of Morganton: Work and Community in the Nuevo New South*. Chapel Hill: University of North Carolina Press, 2003.

Flores, Lisa A. "Between Abundance and Marginalization: The Imperative of Racial Rhetorical Criticism." *Review of Communication* 16, no. 1 (2016): 4–24.

Florini, Sarah. "Tweets, Tweeps, and Signifyin' Communication and Cultural Performance on 'Black Twitter.'" *Television & New Media* 15, no. 3 (2014): 223–37.

Fondas, Nanette. "Feminization Unveiled: Management Qualities in Contemporary Writings." *Academy of Management Review* 22, no. 1 (1997): 257–82.

Ford, Tiffany, Sarah Reber, and Richard V. Reeves. "Up Front: Race Gaps in COVID-19 Deaths Are Even Bigger Than They Appear." Brookings Institute. Last modified June 16, 2020. https://www.brookings.edu/blog/up-front/2020/06/16/race-gaps-in-covid-19-deaths-are-even-bigger-than-they-appear/.

Fox, Aaron A. "'Alternative' to What? O Brother, September 11, and the Politics of Country Music." In *Country Music Goes to War*, edited by Charles K. Wolfe and James E. Akenson, 164–91. Lexington: University of Kentucky Press, 2005.

———. *Real Country: Music and Language in Working-Class Culture*. Durham, NC: Duke University Press, 2004.

———. "White Trash Alchemies of the Abject Sublime: Country as 'Bad' Music." In *Bad Music: The Music We Love to Hate*, edited by Christopher J. Washburne and Maiken Derno, 39–61. New York: Routledge, 2004.

Frankenberg, Ruth. "The Mirage of an Unmarked Whiteness." In *The Making and Unmaking of Whiteness*, edited by Birgit Brander Rasmussen, Eric Klinenberg, Irene J. Nexica, and Matt Wray, 72–96. Durham, NC: Duke University Press, 2001.

———. *White Women, Race Matters: The Social Construction of Whiteness*. New York: Routledge, 1993.

Gallagher, Ryan J., Andrew J. Reagan, Christopher M. Danforth, and Peter Sheridan Dodds. "Divergent Discourse between Protest and Counter-Protests: #BlackLivesMatter and #AllLivesMatter." *PLoS ONE* 13, no. 4 (2018). https://doi.org/10.1371/journal.pone.0195644.

Gates, Henry Louis, Jr. "The 'Blackness of Blackness': A Critique of the Sign and the Signifying Monkey." *Critical Inquiry* 9, no. 4 (1983): 685–723.

Gereffi, Gary, David Spencer, and Jennifer Bair. *Free Trade and Uneven Development*. Philadelphia: Temple University Press, 2002.

Gilbert, Calvin. "Muzik Mafia Make Vegas an Offer It Couldn't Refuse." *CMT News*, May 27, 2004, http://www.cmt.com/news/1487969/muzik-mafia-make-vegas-an-offer-it-couldnt-refuse/.

Gladstone, Brooke. "The Listeners of National Public Radio." *On the Media*, National Public Radio, September 1, 2006, http://www.onthemedia.org/story/128613-the-listeners-of-national-public-radio/transcript/.

———. "The Listeners of National Public Radio: On the Media." *On the Media*, National Public Radio, September 1, 2006, https://www.wqxr.org/story/128613-the-listeners-of-national-public-radio/?tab=summary.

Goad, Jim. *The Redneck Manifesto: How Hillbillies, Hicks, and White Trash Became America's Scapegoats.* New York: Simon and Schuster, 1998.

Gobé, Marc. *Citizen Brand: 10 Commandments for Transforming Brand Culture in a Consumer Democracy.* New York: Watson-Guptill, 2002.

Goffman, Erving. *Frame Analysis: An Essay on the Organization of Experience.* Cambridge, MA: Harvard University Press, 1974.

Gonzalez, Alfonso. *Reform without Justice: Latino Migrant Politics and the Homeland Security State.* Oxford: Oxford University Press, 2013.

Gramlich, John. "Black Imprisonment in the US Has Fallen by a Third Since 2006." Pew Research. Last modified May 6, 2020. https://www.pewresearch.org/fact-tank/2020/05/06/share-of-black-white-hispanic-americans-in-prison-2018-vs-2006/.

Gresson, Aaron David, III. *America's Atonement: Racial Pain, Recovery Rhetoric, and the Pedagogy of Healing.* Bern: Peter Lang, 2004.

Griffin, Rachel Alicia. "Black Women's Intellectualism and Deconstructing Donald Trump's Toxic White Masculinity." In *Interrogating the Communicative Power of Whiteness,* 67–93. New York: Routledge, 2018.

Grissim, John. *Country Music: White Man's Blues.* New York: Paperback Library, 1970.

Gussow, Aaron. "Playing Chicken with the Train: Cowboy Troy's Hick-Hop and the Transracial Country West." *Southern Cultures* 16, no. 4 (Winter 2010): 41–70.

Guthman, Julie. "Fast Food/Organic Food." *Social and Cultural Geography* 4, no. 1 (2003): 45–58.

———. "'If They Only Knew': Color Blindness and Universalism in California Alternative Food Institutions." *Professional Geographer* 60, no. 3 (2008): 387–97.

Hobson, Kathryn, and Sophia B. Margulies. "A Forgotten History of Eugenics: Reimagining Whiteness and Disability in the Case of Carrie Buck." In *Interrogating the Communicative Power of Whiteness,* edited by Dawn Marie D. McIntosh, Dreama G. Moon, and Thomas K. Nakayama. New York: Routledge, 2018.

Halberstam, Jack. *Female Masculinity.* Durham, NC: Duke University Press, 2018.

Hall, Stuart. "Encoding, Decoding." In *The Cultural Studies Reader,* edited by Simon During, 507–17. London: Routledge, 1993.

———. "Some 'Politically Incorrect' Pathways through PC." In *The War of the Words: The Political Correctness Debate,* edited by Sarah Dunant, 167–84. London: Virago Press, 1994.

———. "The Spectacle of the 'Other.'" In *Discourse Theory and Practice,* edited by Margaret Wetherell, Stephanie Joyce Ann Taylor, and Simeon J. Yates, 324–44. London: Sage Publications, 2001.

———. "The Whites of Their Eyes: Racist Ideologies in the Media." In *Silver Lining: Some Strategies for the Eighties,* edited by George Bridges and Rosalind Brunt, 28–52. London: Lawrence and Wishart, 1981.

Hamilton, Nora, and Norma Stoltz Chinchilla. *Seeking Community in a Global City.* Philadelphia: Temple University Press, 2001.

Haney-López, Ian. *Dog Whistle Politics: How Coded Racial Appeals Have Reinvented Racism and Wrecked the Middle Class.* Oxford: Oxford University Press, 2014.

———. "Social Construction of Race." *Harvard Civil Rights–Civil Liberties Law Review* 29, no. 1 (1994): 1–62.

———. *White by Law.* New York: New York University Press, 1996.

"Hardy–Rednecker (Official Video)." Released June 13, 2019. Video, 3:21. https://www.youtube.com/watch?v=Sn2RBKPMpUo&feature=youtu.be.

Hartigan, John, Jr. "Who Are These White People?: 'Rednecks,' 'Hillbillies,' and 'White Trash' As Marked Racial Subjects." In *White Out: The Continuing Significance of Racism,* edited by Ashley W. Doane and Eduardo Bonilla-Silva, 95–112. New York: Routledge, 2003.

Hartmann, David, and Joyce M. Bell. "Race-Based Critical Theory and the 'Happy Talk' of Diversity in America." In *Illuminating Social Life,* edited by Peter Kivisto, 229–48. Los Angeles: Sage Publications, 2013.

Harvey, David. *A Brief History of Neoliberalism.* Oxford: Oxford University Press, 2007.

Hass, Kristin Ann. *Carried to the Wall.* Berkeley: University of California Press, 1998.

Herman, Eduard S., and Noam Chomsky. *Manufacturing Consent: The Political Economy of the Mass Media.* New York: Pantheon Books, 1998.

Hernández, David Manuel. "Pursuant to Deportation: Latinos and Immigrant Detention." *Latino Studies* 6, no. 1 (2008): 35–63.

Hernández, Leandra H. "Silence, (In)Action, and the Downfalls of White Allyship." *Women and Language* 43, no. 1 (Spring 2020): 147–52.

Hill, Jane H. *The Everyday Language of White Racism.* Hoboken, NJ: Wiley-Blackwell, 2008.

———. "Language, Race, and White Public Space." *American Anthropologist* 100, no. 3 (1998): 680–89.

Holling, Michelle A. "5. Patrolling National Identity, Masking White Supremacy." In *Critical Rhetorics of Race,* 98–116. New York: New York University Press, 2011.

———. "Rhetorical Contours of Violent Frames and the Production of Discursive Violence." *Critical Studies in Media Communication* 36, no. 3 (2019): 249–71.

Holling, Michelle A., Dreama G. Moon, and Alexandra Jackson Nevis. "Racist Violations and Racializing Apologia in a Post-Racism Era." *Journal of International and Intercultural Communication* 7, no. 4 (2014): 260–86. https://doi.org/10.1080/17513057.2014.964144.

Honig, Bonnie. "Immigrant America? How Foreignness "Solves" Democracy's Problems." *Social Text* 56 (1998): 1–27.

Housloher, Abigail. "ICE Agents Raid Miss. Work Sites, Arrest 680 People in Largest Single-State Immigration Enforcement Action in U.S. History." *Washington Post,* August 7, 2019, https://www.washingtonpost.com/immigration/ice-agents-raid-miss-work-sites-arrest-680-people-in-largest-single-state-immigration-enforcement-action-in-us-history/2019/08/07/801d5cfe-b94e-11e9-b3b4-2bb69e8c4e39_story.html.

Hsu, Spencer S. "Immigration Raid Jars a Small Town." *Washington Post,* May 18, 2013, http://www.washingtonpost.com/wp-dyn/content/article/2008/05/17/AR2008051702474.html.

Hubbs, Nadine. *Rednecks, Queers, and Country Music.* Berkeley: University of California Press, 2014.

Inda, Jonathan Xavier. "The Value of Immigrant Life." In *Women and Migration in the U.S.-Mexican Borderlands,* edited by Denise A. Segura and Patricia Zavella, 134–60. Durham, NC: Duke University Press, 2007.

Ioanide, Paula. *The Emotional Politics of Racism: How Feelings Trump Facts in an Era of Colorblindness.* Stanford, CA: Stanford University Press, 2015.

Isenburg, Nancy. *White Trash: The 400-Year Untold History of Class in America.* New York: Viking, 2016.

Jackson, Sarah J., and Brooke Foucault Welles. "Hijacking #myNYPD: Social Media Dissent and Networked Counterpublics." *Journal of Communication* 65, no. 6 (2015): 1–21. https://doi.org/10.1111/jcom.12185.

Jägel, Thomas, Kathy Keeling, Alexander Rappel, and Thorsten Gruber. "Individual Values and Motivational Complexities in Ethical Clothing Consumption." *Journal of Marketing Management* 23, nos. 3–4 (2012): 373–96.

Jameson, Frederic. "Postmodernism and Consumer Society." 1984. Accessed December 20, 2014. www.sok.bz/web/media/video/JamesonPostmoderism.pdf.

Jan, Tracy, Jena McGregor, Renae Merle, and Nitasha Tiku. "As Big Corporations Say 'Black Lives Matter,' Their Track Records Raise Skepticism." *Washington Post,* June 13, 2020. https://www.washingtonpost.com/business/2020/06/13/after-years-marginalizing-black-employees-customers-corporate-america-says-black-lives-matter/.

Jardina, Ashley. *White Identity Politics.* Cambridge, UK: Cambridge University Press, 2019.

Jenkins, Henry, Joshua Green, and Sam Ford. *Spreadable Media: Creating Value and Meaning in a Networked Culture.* New York: New York University Press, 2013.

Johnson, Josée. "The Citizen-Consumer Hybrid." *Theoretical Sociology* 37 (2008): 229–70.

Johnson, Josée, Michelle Szabo, and Alexandra Rodney. "Good Food, Good People." *Journal of Consumer Culture* 11, no. 3 (2011): 293–318.

Johnson, Victoria E. "Monday Night Football: Brand Identity." In *How to Watch Television,* edited by Ethan Thompson and Jason Mittell, 262–70. New York: New York University Press, 2013.

Jones, Dustin. "Officer Cleared in the Shooting Death of Ashli Babbitt During Capitol Riot," National Public Radio, April 14, 2021, https://www.npr.org/2021/04/14/987425312/officer-cleared-in-the-shooting-of-ashli-Babbitt-during-capitol-riot.

Kandel, William, and Emilio A. Parrado. "Restructuring of the US Meat Processing Industry and New Hispanic Migrant Destinations." *Population and Development Review* 31, no. 3 (Sept. 2005): 447–71.

Kanter, Deborah. "Faith and Family for Early Mexican Immigrants to Chicago: The Diary of Elidia Barroso." *Diálogo* 16, no. 1 (Spring 2013): 21–34.

Kazyak, Emily. "Midwest or Lesbian?" *Gender & Society* 26, no. 6 (2012): 825–48.

Kelly, Casey Ryan. *Apocalypse Man.* Columbus: Ohio State University Press, 2020.

———. "Détournement, Decolonization, and the American Indian Occupation of Alcatraz Island (1969–1971)." *Rhetoric Society Quarterly* 44, no. 2 (2014): 168–90.

———. "Donald J. Trump and the Rhetoric of Resentment." *Quarterly Journal of Speech* 106, no. 1 (2020): 2–24.

———. "The Man-Apocalypse." *Text and Performance Quarterly* 36, no. 2–3 (2016): 95–114.

———. "The Wounded Man." *Communication and Critical/Cultural Studies* 15, no. 2 (2018): 161–78.

Kelly, Mary Louise, and Heidi Glenn, "Say Her Name: How the Fight for Racial Justice Can Be More Inclusive of Black Women." National Public Radio, July 7, 2020, https://www.npr.org/sections/live-updates-protests-for-racial-justice/2020/07/07/888498009/say-her-name-how-the-fight-for-racial-justice-can-be-more-inclusive-of-black-wom.

Kessler, Judy A. "The Impact of North American Economic Integration on the Los Angeles Apparel Industry." In *Free Trade and Uneven Development,* edited by Gary Gereffi, David Spenser, and Jennifer Bair, 74–99. Philadelphia: Temple University Press, 2002.

Kieran, Michael. "Objectivity, Impartiality and Good Journalism." In *Media Ethics,* edited by Michael Kieran, 23–26. London: Routledge, 1998.

Kimmel, Michael. *Angry White Men.* New York: Hachette, 2017.

Kindlon, Dan, and Michael Thompson. *Raising Cain: Protecting the Emotional Life of Boys.* New York: Ballantine Books, 2000.

Kingkade, Tyler, Brandy Zadrozny, and Ben Collins. "Critical Race Theory Battle Invades School Boards—with Help from Conservative Groups." NBCNews.com, June 16, 2021, https://www.nbcnews.com/news/us-news/critical-race-theory-invades-school-boards-help-conservative-groups-n1270794.

Kirby, James B., and Toshiko Kaneda. "Unhealthy and Uninsured: Exploring Racial Differences in Health and Health Insurance Coverage Using a Life Table Approach." *Demography* 47, no. 4 (2010): 1035–51.

Klein, Naomi. *No Logo*. New York: Picador Press, 2009.

Krupers, T. A. "Toxic Masculinity as a Barrier to Mental Health Treatment in Prisons." *Journal of Clinical Psychology* 61, no. 6 (2005): 713–24.

Kun, Josh. *Audiotopia: Music, Race, and America*. Berkeley: University of California Press, 2005.

Lakoff, George, and Sam Ferguson, "Crucial Issues Not Addressed in the Immigration Debate: Why Deep Framing Matters." Rockridge Institute, May 28, 2006, https://georgelakoff.files.wordpress.com/2011/03/2006-crucial-issues-not-addressed-in-the-immigration-debate.doc.

Langmann, Brady. "Gina Carano's 'The Mandalorian' Controversy Isn't Going Anywhere." *Esquire*, February 22, 2021, https://www.esquire.com/entertainment/tv/a35478544/gina-carano-the-mandalorian-social-media-posts-lucasfilm-controversy-fired-explained/.

Laslett, John, and Mary Tyler. *The ILGWU in Los Angeles 1907–1988*. Inglewood, IN: Ten Star Press, 1989.

Lauer, Janice M. "The Feminization of Rhetoric and Composition Studies?." *Rhetoric Review* 13, no. 2 (1995): 276–86.

Lebron, Christopher J. *The Making of Black Lives Matter: A Brief History of an Idea*. Oxford, UK: Oxford University Press, 2017.

Lennard, Natasha. "How the Government Is Turning Protestors into Felons." *Esquire*, April 14, 2017, http://www.esquire.com/news-politics/a54391/how-the-government-is-turning-protesters-into-felons/?src=socialflowTW.

Leonardo, Zeus. "The Color of Supremacy: Beyond the Discourse of 'White Privilege.'" *Educational Philosophy and Theory* 36, no. 2 (2004): 137–52.

Lewis, Lynn C. "The Participatory Meme Chronotope: Fixity of Space/Rapture of Time." In *New Media Literacies and Participatory Popular Culture across Borders*, edited by Bronwyn Williams and Amy A. Zenger, 106–21. New York: Routledge, 2012.

Lippi-Green, Rosina. *English with an Accent: Language, Ideology, and Discrimination in the United States*. New York: Routledge, 1997.

Lipsitz, George. "Forward." In *My Music: Explorations of Music in Daily Life*, edited by Susan D. Crafts, Daniel Cavicchi, and Charles Keil, ix–xx. Middletown, CT: Wesleyan University Press, 1993.

———. *The Possessive Investment in Whiteness*. Philadelphia: Temple University Press, 1998.

Littler, Jo. "Celebrity CEOs and the Cultural Economy of Tabloid Intimacy." In *Stardom and Celebrity: A Reader*, edited by Sean Redmond and Su Holmes, 230–43. London: Sage Publications, 2007.

Lopenzina, Drew. *Red Ink: Native Americans Picking Up the Pen in the Colonial Period*. Albany: State University of New York Press, 2012.

Lopez, Mark Hugo, Ana Gonzalez-Berrera, and Seth Motel. "As Deportations Rise to Record Levels, Most Latinos Oppose Obama's Policy: President's Approval Rating Drops." Pew Hispanic Center. Last modified December 21, 2011. http://www.pewhispanic.org/files/2011/12/Deportations-and-Latinos.pdf.

López-Garza, Marta. "A Study of the Informal Economy and Latinx Immigrants in Greater Los Angeles." In *Asian and Latino Immigrants in a Restructuring Economy,* edited by Marta López-Garza and David R. Dias, 141–68. Stanford, CA: Stanford University Press, 2002.

Loucky, James, and Marilyn M. Moors, eds. *The Maya Diaspora: Guatemalan Roots, New American Lives.* Philadelphia: Temple University Press, 2000.

Ludden, Jennifer. "After Raid, Iowa Meatpacker Seeks Palau Workers." *All Things Considered,* National Public Radio, October 2, 2008, http://www.npr.org/templates/story/story.php?storyId=95306524.

———. "At Iowa Meatpacking Plant, New Workers Complain." *All Things Considered,* National Public Radio, September 2, 2008, http://www.npr.org/templates/story/story.php?storyId=95306524.

———. Email interview by author, May 21, 2012.

———. "Immigrant Rights Groups Challenge ID Theft Arrests." *Morning Edition,* National Public Radio, July 24, 2008, https://www.npr.org/templates/story/story.php?storyId=92830188.

———. "Iowa Plant Charged with Hiring Minors." *All Things Considered,* National Public Radio, September 1, 2008, https://www.npr.org/templates/story/story.php?storyId=94176233.

———. "Kosher Slaughterhouse Former Manager Arrested." *Morning Edition,* National Public Radio, October 31, 2008, https://www.npr.org/templates/story/story.php?storyId=96369300.

Macklem, Katherine. "Doing the Rag Trade Right." *Maclean's Magazine,* April 14, 2003, 40.

Makkula, Annu. "Meanings of Ethical Consumption in Fashion and Clothing Markets." *Latin American Advances in Consumer Research* 2 (2008): 193–94.

Mamdani, Mahmood. *Good Muslim, Bad Muslim: American, the Cold War, and the Roots of Terror.* New York: Harmony Press, 2005.

"Mandalorian Star Gina Carano Was Just Fired." *Esquire,* February 11, 2021, https://www.esquireme.com/content/50674-mandalorian-star-gina-carano-was-just-fired.

Mann, Geoff. "Why Does Country Music Sound White? Race and the Voice of Nostalgia." *Ethnic and Racial Studies* 31, no. 1 (2008): 73–100.

Marchevsky, Alejandra, and Jeanne Theoharis. *Not Working.* New York: New York University Press, 2006.

Martinot, Steve. *The Machinery of Whiteness: Studies in the Structure of Racialization.* Philadelphia: Temple University Press, 2010.

McEnery, Thornton. "Jamie Dimon Drops into Mt. Kisco Chase Branch, Takes a Knee with Staff." *New York Post,* June 5, 2020, https://nypost.com/2020/06/05/mending-jpm-chief-drops-into-mt-kisco-chase-branch/.

McGreal, Chris. "Federal Agents Show Stronger Force at Portland Protests Despite Order to Withdraw." *Guardian,* July 30, 2020, https://www.theguardian.com/us-news/2020/jul/30/federal-agents-portland-oregon-trump-troops.

McIntosh, Dawn Marie D., Dreama G. Moon, and Thomas K. Nakayama, eds. *Interrogating the Communicative Power of Whiteness.* New York: Routledge, 2018.

McIntosh, Peggy. "White Privilege, Color, and Crime." In *Images of Color, Images of Crime,* edited by Coramae Richey Mann and Marjorie S. Zatz, 207–16. Los Angeles: Roxbury, 1998.

McKinney, Karyn D. *Being White: Stories of Race and Racism.* New York: Routledge, 2005.

Melamed, Jodi. *Represent and Destroy: Racializing Violence in the New Racial Capitalism.* Minneapolis: University of Minnesota Press, 2011.

Menjívar, Cecilia, and Leisy J. Abrego. "Legal Violence: Immigration Law and the Lives of Central American Immigrants." *American Journal of Sociology* 117, no. 5 (March 2012): 1380–421. doi:10.1086/663575.

Meyler, Deana, and Milagros Peña. "Walking with Latinas in the Struggle for Justice." *Journal of Feminist Studies in Religion* 24, vol. 2 (2008): 97–113.

"Military Expert Kris Osborn Brings Warrior to Maven's Network of Diverse Voices." Business Wire, January 30, 2018, https://www.businesswire.com/news/home/20180130005570/en/.

"Military Expert Kris Osborn Brings Warrior to Maven's Network of Diverse Voices." Bloomberg.com, January 30, 2018, https://www.bloomberg.com/press-releases/2018-01-30/military-expert-kris-osborn-brings-warrior-to-maven-s-network-of-diverse-voices.

Millard, Ann V., Jorge Chapa, and Catalina Burillo. *Apple Pie and Enchiladas: Latino Newcomers in the Rural Midwest*. Austin: University of Texas Press, 2004.

Mills, Charles W. *The Racial Contract*. Ithaca: Cornell University Press, 1997.

Milner, David. "'By Right of Discovery': The Media and the Native American Occupation of Alcatraz, 1969–1971." *Australasian Journal of American Studies* (2014): 73–86.

Mohanty, Chadra Talpade. *Feminism without Borders*. Durham, NC: Duke University Press, 2003.

Molina, Natalia. *How Race Is Made in America*. Berkeley: University of California Press, 2014.

———. "The Power of Racial Scripts: What the History of Mexican Immigration to the United States Teaches Us about Relational Notions of Race." *Latino Studies* vol. 8, no. 2 (2010): 156–75.

Mondragón, Delfi. "No More 'Let Them Eat Admonitions': The Clinton Administration's Emerging Approach to Minority Health." *Journal of Health Care for the Poor and Underserved* 4, no. 2 (1993): 77–82.

Moon, Dreama. G. "White Enculturation and Bourgeois Ideology: The Discursive Production of 'Good' (White) Girls." In *Whiteness: The Communication of Social Identity*, edited by T. K. Nakayama and J. N. Martin, 77–97. New York: Sage Publications, 1999.

Moon, Dreama G., and Michelle A. Holling. "'White Supremacy in Heels': (White) Feminism, White Supremacy, and Discursive Violence." *Communication and Critical/Cultural Studies* 17, no. 2 (2020): 253–60.

Moor, Liz, and Jo Littler. "Fourth Worlds and Neo-Fordism." *Cultural Studies* 5, no. 22 (2008): 700–723.

Morales, Rebecca. "Undocumented Workers in the Los Angeles Automobile Industry." *International Migration Review* 17, no. 4 (Winter 1983–84): 570–96.

Morales, Rebecca, and Paul M. Ong. "The Illusion of Progress." In *Latinos in a Changing US Economy*, edited by Rebecca Morales and Frank Bonilla, 55–84. Newbury Park, CA: Sage Publications, 1993.

Moreau, Jordan. "'Mandalorian' Star Gina Carano under Fire for Controversial Social Media Posts." *Variety*, February 11, 2021, https://variety.com/2021/tv/news/gina-carano-mandalorian-controversy-twitter-1234905140/.

Morris, David. "Hick-Hop Hooray? 'Honky Tonk Badonkadonk,' Musical Genre, and the Misrecognition of Hybridity." *Critical Studies in Media Communication* 28, no. 5 (2001): 466–88.

Mukherjee, Roopali, and Sarah Banet-Weiser. "Introduction." In *Commodity Activism*, edited by Roopali Mukherjee and Sarah Banet-Weiser, 1–22. New York: New York University Press, 2012.

Murphy, Clifford R. *Yankee Twang: Country and Western Music in New England*. Urbana: University of Illinois Press, 2014.

Myers, Kristen. "White Fright: Reproducing White Supremacy through Casual Discourse." In *White Out: The Continuing Significance of Racism*, edited by Ashley W. Doane and Eduardo Bonilla-Silva, 129–44. New York: Routledge, 2003.

Nakayama, Thomas K. "What's Next for Whiteness and the Internet." *Critical Studies in Media Communication* 34, no. 1 (2017): 68–72. https://doi.org/10.1080/15295036.2016.1266684.

Nakayama, Thomas K., and Robert L. Krizek. "Whiteness: A Strategic Rhetoric." *Quarterly Journal of Speech* 81, no. 3 (1995): 291–309. https://doi.org/10.1080/00335639509384117.

Nelson, Joshua Q. "America to Ban Funding for Critical Race Theory in Schools." *Fox News*. Accessed July 13, 2021. https://www.foxnews.com/politics/nikki-haley-calls-for-every-governor-in-america-to-ban-funding-for-critical-race-theory-in-schools.

Newholm, Terry, and Deirdre Shaw. "Studying the Ethical Consumer: A Review of Research." *Journal of Consumer Behaviour* 6, no. 5 (2007): 253–70. https://www.doi.org/10.1002/cb.225.

Ngai, Mae. *Impossible Subjects*. Princeton: Princeton University Press, 2004.

Nicholls, Alex, and Charlotte Opal. *Fair Trade*. London: Sage Publications, 2005.

Nielsen, Rasmus Kleis, and Lucas Graves. "'News You Don't Believe': Audience Perspectives on Fake News." Reuters Institute for the Study of Journalism. Last modified October 2017. https://reutersinstitute.politics.ox.ac.uk/our-research/news-you-dont-believe-audience-perspectives-fake-news.

No Sweat. Directed by Amie Williams. Los Angeles, CA: Bal Maiden Films, 2006. DVD.

Noel, Hannah, "Branding Guilt: American Apparel Inc. and Latina Labor in Los Angeles," *Diálogo* 18, no. 2 (2015): 37–52.

———. "Deflective Whiteness." *Kalfou* 5, no. 2 (2018): 322.

———. "White Female Pain: Cis White Women and Digital Masculine Rhetoric." In *White Supremacy and the American Media*, edited by Sarah D. Nilsen and Sarah E. Turner. New York: Routledge, 2022.

Norris, Micelle. "Deportation Hearings Follow Iowa Raid." *All Things Considered*, National Public Radio, May 19, 2008, https://www.npr.org/templates/story/story.php?storyId=90603031.

Omi, Michael, and Howard Winant. *Racial Formation in the United States*. 3rd ed. New York: Routledge, 2015.

Ono, Kent, and Alison Yeh Cheung. "Asian American Performance in White Supremacist Representation." In *Interrogating the Communicative Power of Whiteness*, edited by Dawn Marie D. McIntosh, Dreama G. Moon, and Thomas K. Nakayama, 15–28. New York: Routledge, 2018.

Ono, Kent A., and Michael G. Lacy. *Critical Rhetorics of Race*. New York: New York University Press, 2011.

"Orthodox Jews in Rural Iowa." *Morning Edition*, National Public Radio, December 7, 1988, http://www.npr.org/templates/story/story.php?storyId=1023695.

Oullette, Laurie. "Citizen Brand." In *Commodity Activism: Cultural Resistance in Neoliberal Times*, edited by Laurie Oullette, 57–75. New York: New York University Press, 2012.

Paoletta, M. "Adkins' Booty Romp Bumps Album Sales." *Billboard* 118, no. 10 (2006): 10.

Parks, Miles. "Outrage as a Business Model: How Ben Shapiro Is Using Facebook to Build an Empire." National Public Radio, July 19, 2021, https://www.npr.org/2021/07/19/1013793067/outrage-as-a-business-model-how-ben-shapiro-is-using-facebook-to-build-an-empire.

Pascoe, Cheri Jo. *Dude, You're a Fag: Masculinity and Sexuality in High School*. Berkeley: University of California Press, 2007.

Pearce, Tim. "Gina Carano to Produce and Star in Upcoming Film for the *Daily Wire*," *Daily Wire*, February 12, 2021, https://www.dailywire.com/news/gina-carano-to-produce-and-star-in-upcoming-film-for-the-daily-wire.

Phillips, Anne, and Barbara Taylor. "Sex And Skill: Notes Towards a Feminist Economics." *Feminist Review* 6, no. 1 (1980): 79–88. https://www.doi.org/10.1057/fr.1980.20.

Phillips, Holiday. "Performative Allyship Is Deadly (Here's What to Do Instead)." *Forge*, May 9, 2020, https://forge.medium.com/performative-allyship-is-deadly-c900645d9f1f.

Pilgeram, Ryann. "'Ass-Kicking' Women." *Gender, Work & Organization* 14, no. 6 (2007): 572–95.

Preston, Julia. "Immigration Crackdown with Firings, Not Raids." *New York Times*, September 29, 2009, http://www.nytimes.com/2009/09/30/us/30factory.html?pagewanted=all&_r=0.

Rasmussen, Eric E., and Rebecca L. Densley. "Girl in a Country Song: Gender Roles and Objectification of Women in Popular Country Music across 1990 to 2014." *Sex Roles* 76 (2017): 188–201. https://www.doi.org/10.1007/s11199-016-0670-6.

Ratcliff, Krista. *Rhetorical Listening: Identification, Gender, Whiteness*. Carbondale: Southern Illinois University Press, 2005.

Reese, Ashley. "What Everyone Is Getting Wrong about the 'Yee Haw Agenda,' According to Bri Malandro, the Woman Who Coined the Term." *Jezebel*, March 27, 2019, https://jezebel.com/what-everyone-is-getting-wrong-about-the-yee-haw-agenda-1833558033.

Reynolds, Jennifer F., and Caitlin Didier. "Contesting Diversity and Community within Postville, Iowa 'Hometown to the World.'" In *Latin American Migrations to the US Heartland: Changing Social Landscapes in Middle America*, edited by Linda Allegro and Andrew Grant Wood. 169–97. Champaign: University of Illinois Press, 2013.

Robinson, Cedric J. "Oliver Cromwell and the History of the West." In *Cedric J. Robinson: On Racial Capitalism, Black Internationalism, and Cultures of Resistance*, editor H. L. T. Quan, 75–86. London: Pluto Press, 2019.

Roediger, David. *The Wages of Whiteness: Race and the Making of the American Working Class*. New York: Verso, 1999.

Rosaldo, Renato. *Culture & Truth: The Remaking of Social Analysis*. Beacon Press, 1993.

Rose, Tricia. *Black Noise: Rap Music and Black Culture in Contemporary America*. Middletown, CT: Wesleyan University Press, 1994.

Rudhran, Monisha. "What Is Performative Allyship?: Making Sure Anti-Racism Efforts Are Helpful." *Elle Australia*, June 3, 2020. https://www.elle.com.au/news/performative-allyship-23586.

Sample, Tex. *White Soul: Country Music, the Church, and Working Americans*. Nashville: Abingdon Press, 1996.

Sanjek, David. "Blue Moon of Kentucky Rising over the Mystery Train: The Complex Construction of Country Music." In *Reading Country Music: Steel Guitars, Opry Stars, and Honkey-Tonk Bar*, edited by Cecilia Tichi, 22–44. Durham, NC: Duke University Press, 1998.

Santa Ana, Otto. *Brown Tide Rising: Metaphors of Latinos in Contemporary American Public Discourse*. Austin: University of Texas Press, 2002.

"SAY HER NAME." African American Policy Forum. Accessed April 29, 2021, https://www.aapf.org/sayhername.

Schaeffer-Gabriel, Felicia. "Flexible Technologies of Subjectivity." *American Quarterly* 58, no. 3 (2006): 891–914.

Schippers, Mimi. "Recovering the Feminine Other: Masculinity, Femininity, and Gender Hegemony." *Theory and Society* 36, no.1 (March 2007): 85–102.

Shabazz, Rashad. *Specializing Blackness: Architectures of Confinement and Black Masculinity in Chicago*. Urbana: University of Illinois Press, 2015.

Shifman, Limor. "An Anatomy of a YouTube Meme." *New Media Society* 14, no. 2 (2011): 187–203.

Shohat, Ella, and Robert Stam. *Unthinking Eurocentrism: Multiculturalism and the Media*. New York: Routledge, 1994.

Shrestova, Sagita. "'Watch 30 Minute Video on Internet, Become Social Activist'?: Koney 2012, Invisible Children, and the Paradoxes of Participatory Politics." In *By Any Media Necessary: The New Youth Activism,* edited by Henry Jenkins, Sangita Shresthova, Liana Gamber-Thompson, Neta Kligler-Vilenchik, and Arely Zimmerman, 61–101. New York: New York University Press, 2016.

Siek, Stephanie, and Joe Sterling. "Census: Fewer White Babies Being Born." CNN.com. May 17, 2012.

Soldatenko, María Angelina. "Organizing Latina Garment Workers in Los Angeles." *Aztlán* 20, nos. 1–2 (1991): 73–96.

Story, Louise. "Politics Wrapped in a Clothing Ad." *New York Times,* January 18, 2008, https://www.nytimes.com/2008/01/18/business/media/18adco.html.

Stumpf, Juliet. "The Crimmigration Crisis: Immigrants, Crime, and Sovereign Power." *American University Law Review* 56 (2006): 367.

Suhr, Stephanie, and Sally Johnson. "Re-visiting 'PC.'" *Discourse and Society* 4, no. 1 (2003): 5–16.

Sullivan, Shannon. *Good White People: The Problem with Middle-Class White Anti-Racism.* Albany: State University of New York Press, 2014.

Suro, Roberto. "Introduction." In *Writing Immigration: Scholars and Journalists in Dialogue,* edited by Marcelo Suarez-Orozco, Vivian Louie, and Roberto Suro, 1–22. Berkeley: University of California Press, 2011.

Swaine, Jon, Dalton Bennett, Joyce Sohyun Lee, and Meg Kelly. "Video Shows Fatal Shooting of Ashli Babbitt in the Capitol," *Washington Post,* January 8, 2021, https://www.washingtonpost.com/investigations/2021/01/08/ashli-Babbitt-shooting-video-capitol/.

Tatum, Beverly Daniel. *Can We Talk about Race?* Boston: Beacon Press, 2007.

Taylor, Toniesha L. "Dear Nice White Ladies: A Womanist Response to Intersectional Feminism and Sexual Violence." *Women and Language* 42, no. 1 (Spring 2019): 187–90.

Twine, France Winddance, and Charles Gallagher. "Introduction: The Future of Whiteness: A Map of the 'Third Wave.'" *Ethnic and Racial Studies* 31, no. 1 (2008): 2–24.

Uzzell, David, Enric Pol, and David Badenas. "Place Identification, Social Cohesion, and Environmental Sustainability." *Environment and Behavior* 34, no. 1 (2002): 26–53.

Valerio-Jiménez, Omar Santiago, and Carmen Teresa Whalen, eds. *Major Problems in Latina/o History: Documents and Essays.* Boston: Cengage Learning, 2015.

Van Dijk, Teun A. "Critical Discourse Analysis." In *The Handbook of Discourse Analysis,* edited by Heidi E. Hamilton, Deborah Tannen, and Deborah Schiffrin, 352–71. Hoboken, NJ: Wiley-Blackwell, 2003.

Vargas, Theresa. "Here's What We Know about Trump Inauguration Day Protests." *Washington Post,* January 19, 2017. http://washingtonpost.com/local/hers-what-we-know-about-trump-inauguration-day-protests/2017/01/18/9cc44f6c-ddd6-11e6-ad42-f3375f271c9c_story.html?utm_term=.80f40af054ca.

Vega, Sujey. *Latino Heartland.* New York University Press, 2015.

Warren, Craig A. *The Rebel Yell: A Cultural History.* Tuscaloosa: University of Alabama Press, 2014.

Weiner, Douglas. R. "Demythologizing Environmentalism." *Journal of the History of Biology* 25, no. 3 (Autumn 1992): 385–411.

Weiner, Rachel. "Protest Group Declares Victory, Says Police Are 'Brutal.'" *Washington Post,* January 20, 2017, http://www.washingtonpost.com/local/2017/live-updates/politics/live-coverage-of-trumps-inauguration/protest-group-declares-victory-say-police-brutal/?utm_term=.3528cc9b010f.

Whalen, Carmen T. "Sweatshops Here and There." *International Labor and Working-Class History* 61 (Spring 2002): 45–68.

Williams, Alex. "Check the Label." *New York Times,* September 6, 2007, g1.

Williams, L. Susan, Sandra Alvarez, and Kevin Andrade Hauck. "My Name is Not María." *Social Problems* 49 no. 4 (2002): 563–84.

Williams, Raymond. *The Country and The City.* Edinburgh: T&A Constable Ltd., 1973.

Willmott, Michael. "Citizen Brands: Corporate Citizenship, Trust, and Branding." *Brand Management* 10, nos. 4–5 (2003): 362–69.

Winant, Howard. *The New Politics of Race.* Minneapolis: University of Minnesota Press, 2004.

Wray, Matt, and Annalee Newitz. *White Trash: Race and Class in America.* New York: Routledge, 1997.

Wright, Melissa W. *Disposable Women and Other Myths of Global Capitalism.* New York: Routledge, 2006.

Yuan, Karen. "Black Employees Say 'Performative Allyship' Is an Unchecked Problem in the Office." *Fortune,* June 19, 2020, https://fortune.com/2020/06/19/performative-allyship-working-while-black-white-allies-corporate-diversity-racism/.

Zavella, Patricia. "Mujeres in Factories." In *Gender at the Crossroads of Knowledge,* edited by Micaela di Leonardo, 312–36. Berkeley: University of California Press, 1991.

Zentgraf, Kristin M. "Through Economic Restructuring, Recession, and Rebound." In *Asian and Latino Immigrants in a Restructuring Economy,* edited by Marta López-Garza and David R. Dias, 46–74. Stanford, CA: Stanford University Press, 2002.

INDEX

abjection, 91, 93, 97n45, 104, 107, 108, 120

Abrajano, Marisa A., 32

Abrego, Leisy J., 159. *See also* legal violence

abstract liberalism, 145; definition, 161, 164, 173, 176. *See also* Bonilla-Silva, Eduardo

Adkins, Trace, 92, 109–10

affective economics, 7

Agozio, Biko, 56–57

Agriprocessors, Inc, 23–24, 150–86, 187

Ahmed, Sara, 7

Aldean, Jason, 94, 105–7

Allen, Jimmie, 92

All Lives Matter, 9, 28, 32–34, 56–57, 70

Allmendinger, Blake, 102

Alsultany, Evelyn, 184n113

American Apparel, 123–49, 160–93

Amos, Deborah, 171

Andersen, Margaret L., 12, 70

Anderson, Luvell, 57–58

Babbitt, Ashli, 67–75, 89

Bahrainwala, Lamiya, 193

Barnet, Clive, 129

Barnet-Weiser, Sarah, 129

Bebout, Lee, 12n61; and country music and race, 112; and Mexican Other, 20, 158

Belay, Tim, 164–70, 180

Bell, Derek, 12, 82

Beltrán, Cristina, 6, 67

benevolent racism, 28, 58–60, 107

Biesecker, Barbara A., 56

Big and Rich, 93, 99, 101; artistic collaborations of, 101n68. *See also* Muzik Mafia

Big Smo, 92

Black Lives Matter, 2, 9–10; and Blue Lives History, 195–96; and J20, 4, 45, 51, 53, 55–61; origin, 27–28; representations, 32–37; and White accomplices, 193; and White female pain, 70–71, 75, 85

Black radicalism, 12

Block, Melissa, 169–70, 183

Blue Lives Matter, 9, 21–22, 28, 32–33, 36, 46–47, 52, 56–58, 61, 70, 80; website history, 37n41, 195–96

Bock, Mary Angela, 37, 59

Bone Thugs, 102

Bonilla-Silva, Eduardo: and abstract liberalism, 23, 145, 176, 186; and colorblindness, 161; and covert racism, 59; and systemic racism, 4, 10; and White habitus, 30

Bonner, Petrella Ann, 92

Boone, Danny, 93–94

Bourdieu, Pierre, 30

Brock, Andre, 27

Brown, Kane, 92

Brown, Michael, 46, 50, 55, 195

Bryan, Luke, 94, 106

Bubba Sparxxx, 94

Burke, Mary C., 32, 70. *See also* frame co-optation

Burnstein, Mary, 32, 70. *See also* frame co-optation

Cabrera, Nolan L., 10; on capitalization of White, 1n1; and male emotional illiteracy, 35

California Proposition 187, 163

Camayd-Frexias, Erik, 172, 174–75

Carano, Gina, 67–69, 75–79

Carney, Nikita, 60

celebrity CEO, 127, 130, 136, 147–48

Cepeda, María Elena, 166n59

Charlottesville, Virginia, 1–19, 21, 63

Charney, Dov, 123–49; letter to, 197–88

Chauvin, Derek, 27, 74–75

Chavez, Leo R.: and accented English, 185; and Latino threat, 20, 157–58, 168

Ching, Barbara, 95, 97n45, 120

Chomsky, Noam, 61

citizen brand, 54–55, 61, 126n7

Cole, Nicki Lisa, 126, 130. *See also* ethical consumption

Coleman, Troy, 99–103

colorblind: consumption, 133, 141; frame, 80, 142, 149, 161, 164, 186; ideology, 13, 40, 53, 59, 82, 86; music, 109, 114, 124; rhetoric, 3, 33–34, 43, 49, 56, 60, 83, 158; social media, 34, 58; Whiteness, 1n1

Combs, Luke, 111–12

Connell, Robert W., 64n5. *See also* hegemonic masculinity

country: racialized geography of, 2, 91, 95–96

country music, 18, 22, 90–120, 131, 149

covert race discourse, 3, 10–11, 14, 17, 21, 23–24, 33, 49, 59, 69, 93, 114

Cowboy Troy. *See* Coleman, Troy

Crenshaw, Kimberlé, 12, 71, 82

crimmigration and crimmigrant frame, 156–60

critical discourse analysis, 21, 30, 36, 43–44, 80–81, 140, 162

critical race theory, 3, 5n20, 22, 67, 79; conservative attacks against, 82–89

critical rhetorics of race, 20–22, 93, 125

Cyrus, Billy Ray, 92–93, 94n21, 98–100, 103

Daily Wire, 74, 78, 83–85, 88–89

Darré, Richard, 2, 8

Dawkins, Richard, 38–39. *See also* meme

de Certeau, Michel, 65–66, 160

De Genova, Nicholas, 156

Delgado, Richard, 82

Densley, Rebecca L., 99–100. *See also* country music

DiAngelo, Robin, 15; and social class, 96, 104, 105, 105n87. *See also* White fragility

Didier, Caitlin, 123n1, 177

Dimon, Jamie, 188–90

discourse: definition, 2

discursive violence, 65–69, 80, 88. *See also* Holling, Michelle

Disrupt J20, 39–41

Doane, Ashley W., 67n20

dog whistle politics, 17, 34, 114

Douglas, Susan J., 103–4, 166n56

Dowling, Julie A., 158, 180

Dubrofsky, Rachel E., 117–18

Durón, Clementina, 137–38

Dyer, Richard, 34

Elias, Sean, 13

Esposito, Luigi, 58–59. *See also* benevolent racism

Esquire, 41

ethical advertising, 124–26; history of, 126–32

ethical consumption, 126n7, 136, 147–48, 187. *See also* ethical advertising

Farr, Tyler, 94
Feagin, Joe: and systemic racism theory, 13–14; and White racial frame, 20, 71, 156, 161, 186
Figueroa, Ever Josue, 37, 59
Flores, Lisa A., 21, 83
Flores-Figueroa v. US, 176
Florida Georgia Line, 94, 106
Florini, Sarah, 27
folk theory of race and racism, 4. *See also* Hill, Jane H.
Ford, Colt, 93–94
Foucault Welles, Brooke, 37
Fox, Aaron A., 95, 97, 104, 108, 114
frame co-optation, 32, 51, 56, 58, 70

Gallagher, Charles, 60, 66. *See also* Third-Wave Whiteness
Gallagher, Ryan J., Andrew J. Reagan, Christopher M. Danforth, and Peter Sheridan Dodds, 60
Gates, Henry Louis, Jr., 27
Gilbert, Brantley, 112
Gladstone, Brook, 153–54
Glover, Henry, 92
Gobé, Marc, 54. *See also* citizen brand
Goffman, Erving, 155–56
Gonzales, Alfonso, 159–60
Gresson, Aaron David, III, 16, 51. *See also* White pain
Gussow, Adam, 101–2
Guthman, Julie, 141

Halberstam, Jack, 63–64, 68n24, 68n25, 80
Hall, Stuart: and colonizing race discourse, 6; and inferential racism, 11; and naturalization, 15; and political correctness, 43; and racial binaries, 158; and racialized regime of representation, 32, 65
Haggard, Merle, 109, 115
Hajnal, Zolton, 32
Haley, Nikki, 67, 83–89

Haney-López, Ian: and dog whistle politics, 17, 34, 36, 42, 114, 118n146, 164; and racial fabrication, 4, 7, 15, 39
HARDY, 92, 116–19
Hartigan, John, Jr., 104
Harvey, David, 128
Hassel, Hans J. G., 32
Haynes, Joshua, 118n146
hegemonic femininity, 31, 63–65
hegemonic masculinity, 22, 63–64, 65, 79, 117, 187
Herman, Edward S., 61
Hernández, Leandra H., 189, 193
hijacking hashtags, 37
Hill, Jane H.: on capitalization of White, 1n1; and country music, 102; and folk theory of race and racism, 4–5, 10; and mock Spanish, 17
hillbilly, 18, 104
Holling, Michelle: and discursive violence, 65–69, 80, 88; and racializing apologia, 106; and White pain, 51–52
Hubbs, Nadine, 97, 106
Hunt, Sam, 94, 111–12

Ice Cube, 102
Illegal Immigration Reform and Immigrant Responsibility and Control Act (IIRICA), 159
Immigration Customs and Enforcement (ICE), 139, 143, 147: and corporate labor violations, 145; and immigration raid, 150–51; representing officers, 44, 47, 59, 75, 80
Immigration Reform and Control Act (IRCA), 145
Inda, Jonathan Xavier, 158–59, 169, 180
inferential racism: definition, 11, 21, 23, 125, 149, 151, 154, 157, 188. *See also* covert race discourse
International Ladies Garment Workers Union (ILGWU), 132, 134, 136
interpellation, 36, 69, 95–97, 120, 129
Ioanide, Paula: and emotional politics of racism, 35

220 · INDEX

J20 (Donald J. Trump's Presidential Inauguration on January 20, 2017), 39–40
Jackson, Sarah J., 37
Jameson, Frederic, 130
Jardina, Ashley E.: and White political identity, 44–45
Johnson, Josée, 128, 130
journalism ethics, 44

Kaepernick, Colin, 188–89
Kazyak, Emily, 68n24
Keith, Toby, 94
Kelly, Casey Ryan: and hegemonic masculinity and White men, 31, 63; and Occupation of Alcatraz, 8n36; and rhetoric of Donald J. Trump, 68
Kid Rock, 92, 104
Kieran, Mathew, 44
Klein, Naomi, 129
Krizek, Robert L., 66, 154, 160, 185
Kun, Josh, 115
Kupers, Terry, 117. See also toxic masculinity

Lacy, Michael G., 20, 125
Lakoff, George, 156
Latino Threat Frame, 156–58
Latinx labor: in food processing industry, 150–86; in garment industry, 123–49
Legalize LA. See American Apparel
legal violence, 159–62
Leonardo, Zeus: and White privilege, 12
Lewis, Lynn C., 39
Lil Nas X, 22, 90–103, 112, 120
Lippi-Green, Rosaria, 186
Lipsitz, George: and possessive investment in Whiteness, 5, 14
Littler, Jo, 127, 131–32, 131n33
Lopenzina, Drew, 3. See also unwitnessing
Los Angeles Times, 139, 143, 145
Ludden, Jenifer, 151, 151n7, 166n57, 170n72, 171–85, 171n77

machinery of Whiteness, 114
Mann, Geoff, 96–97, 117

masculinity. See hegemonic masculinity
Marchevsky, Alejandra, 138
Martinex, Shantal, 193
Martinot, Steve, 13–14. See also machinery of Whiteness
McKinney, Karyn, 4–5
militant victimhood, 43–62; feminized, 79–81
Mills, Charles W., 3, 9, 12, 125, 188. See also racial contract
Mississippi Band of Choctaw Indians, 188
meme, 38–39
Menjívar, Cecilia, 159. See also legal violence
Messerschmidt, James W., 64n5. See also hegemonic masculinity
Molina, Natalia, 8, 8n41
Monday Night Football, 91–92
Moon, Dreama G., 64n5, 68, 69, 106; and whitespeak, 114
Morales, Rebecca, 131, 134, 139
Morris, David, 110–11
Mowitt, John, 96. See also musical interpellation
Mukherjee, Roopali, 129
multicultural Whiteness, 6, 87
Murphy, Clifford R., 98
musical interpellation, 96
Muzik Mafia, 101, 101n68, 110
Myers, Julie, 173–74

Nakayama, Thomas K., 66, 154, 160–61, 185
Nashville music, 93, 95–96, 98, 100, 100n65, 101, 103, 110, 112n123
National Public Radio (NPR), 150–86
neofordism, 127, 131; definition, 127n11
neoliberal values, 4
Neville, Aaron, 92
Nevis, Alexandra Jackson, 106
New York Times, 33, 48, 53, 84, 139, 143, 145, 147–48, 154
Norris, Michele, 150–52, 163–64, 167, 169–70
No Sweat, 123n2, 133, 136–48

Old Dominion, 94

Olivio, Antonio, 150–52, 151n7, 163–64
Omi, Michael, 13. *See also* racial formation
Ono, Kent A., 20, 125
Ong, Paul M., 131, 139
Operation Streamline, 175
Owens, Candace, 67, 83–86, 87, 89

Paisley, Brad, 94
parasitic rhetoric, 9, 32
participatory internet meme. *See* meme
Pascoe, Cheri Jo, 64n5, 68n24
performative allyship, 188–94
Pesotta, Rose, 134
Phillips, Anne, 138
police brutality, 27–29, 34, 56, 61, 120, 188
Postville, Iowa, 150–86
Presley, Elvis, 93
Preston, Julia, 147
Pride, Charley, 92

race liberals, 14
racial capitalism, 9, 23, 28, 33, 36, 57, 83, 123–25, 155n16, 185–87, 188–89. *See also* Robinson, Cedric J.
racial contract, 3, 7, 9, 29, 125, 188. *See also* Mills, Charles W.
racial formation, 13, 19
racial script, 8; Whiteness as, 8n41
racialized: apologia, 106–7; environmentalism, 1
Rasmussen, Eric E., 99–100. *See also* country music
Ratcliff, Krista, 17
redneck, 18, 91, 93, 95–96, 104
REDNECKER, 116–19. *See also* HARDY
representational politics of race, 21. *See also* Flores, Lisa A.
Reynolds, Jennifer F., 123n1, 177
rhetoric: definition, 2
Rhett, Thomas, 94, 104
Rice, Chase, 94
Robinson, Cedric J., 9, 12, 125
Roediger, David, 3, 5

Romano, Victor, 58–59. *See also* benevolent racism
Rubashkin, Sholom, 177, 184–85
Rucker, Darius, 92

Santa Ana, Otto, 163
SAY HER NAME, 71. *See also* Crenshaw, Kimberlé
Schippers, Mimi, 64n5, 68n25
Shelton, Blake, 91–92
Shohat, Ella, 6
Shresthova, Sangita, 192
signifyin', 34. *See also* Gates, Henry Louis, Jr.
Soldatenko, María Angelina, 134
spreadability, 39n53
Stam, Robert, 6
strategic rhetoric. *See* Nakayama, Thomas K.
Stumph, Juliet. *See* crimmigration and crimmigrant frame
Sullivan, Shannon, 18, 104–5, 108
Suro, Roberto, 151, 155, 161
systemic racism theory, 10, 13, 129

Taylor, Barbara, 138
Telecommunications Act of 1996, 54n87
Theoharis, Jeanne, 138
Third-Wave Whiteness, 19, 22; and musical interpellation, 95–98
Tik-Tok, 90
toxic masculinity, 22, 31, 35, 44–45, 52, 117–18
transmigrant: as term, 123n1
Turner, Tina, 92
Twine, France Winddance, 66
Twitter: Black, 27; methods, 36–38

United Food and Commercial Workers International Union (UFCW), 179, 180
Union of Needletrades, Industrial, and Textile Employees (UNITE!), 137
Unite the Right Rally, 1, 2, 8
unwitnessing, 3, 8, 104, 109, 118

Vásquez, Christina, 137

vertical integration, 141–42

Warren, Craig A., 112–13
Washington Post, 148, 167, 190–91
Welch, Gillian, 95
White, capitalization of, 1n1
White-allied individuals, 3n7. *See also* multicultural Whiteness
White deflection: definition, 2; intellectual history, 2–11
White fragility, 69. *See also* DiAngelo, Robin
White fright, 5, 14
White identity politics, 11–18
White masculine victimhood, 14, 31
White male pain: definition, 31
White female pain: definition, 64
White pain, 14, 16, 51

White racial frame, 8, 20, 30, 34, 42, 71, 106, 158, 160–62, 186
White trash, 18–19, 95–96, 104. *See also* Sullivan, Shannon
Williams, Hank, 97n45, 113
Williams, Hank, Jr., 91, 113, 115–16
Williams, Raymond, 95
Willmott, Michael, 54
Winant, Howard, 13. *See also* racial formation
Wright, Melissa, 138

Young, Chris, 115
YouTube, 116–19

Zac Brown Band, 111–12
Zavella, Patricia, 134

www.ingramcontent.com/pod-product-compliance
Lightning Source LLC
Chambersburg PA
CBHW021214240426
43672CB00026B/146